291.44 Gri

2610

Grimbol, W.
Life's big questions.

PRICE: $19.95 (3559/br)

Life's

Q BIG uestions

*Pastor William R. Grimbol
and Rabbi Jeffrey Astrachan*

ALPHA
A Pearson Education Company

APR 3 0 2002

From Pastor William R. Grimbol:

I dedicate this book to the two Jeans, and the wonderful folks of Bay Shore Lutheran Church in Whitefish Bay, Wisconsin.

To Jean Leslie, who got smart—and sick of writing my schedules—and decided she was capable of bigger and better things. (She was and is.) She was also my secretary, confidant, and friend during my first years of ministry. She shaped that ministry with her compassion, wisdom, humor, and belief in me—I won't ever forget it.

To Dr. Jean Lang, who traded in what would have been a thriving medical practice to bring joy and hope to hundreds of Sunday School children. I have never known a person of greater warmth and grace, nor one who healed more souls with laughter. No matter what she says, she is solely responsible for The Great Goldfish Massacre of 1977.

To the congregation of Bay Shore Lutheran Church. Together we addressed all of the questions contained in this book. We did so with courage, creativity, and abundant love. I am so grateful that my first ministerial position was in a true community. It was an amazing celebration of diversity—a miracle of a kind. I found my faith with all of you.

Not all the answers, but all the right questions.

From Rabbi Jeffrey R. Astrachan:

I dedicate this book to my family:

To my wife, Shelley, and our magnificently amazing and always entertaining twins, Abby and Steven: Nothing could possibly make my life more complete or give it greater meaning than the three of you. You give me the spirit to do what I do.

To my parents, Rabbi George and Rita: You have always been and continue to be my greatest fans.

To my brother, Bruce: No one in this world makes me more proud, laugh harder, or feel better about myself than you. Thanks.

To Andrea, Max, Paul, Gina, Paige, Mia, Howard, Nana, Poppy, Rose, and Zaydeeee: I love you all.

CONTENTS

INTRODUCTION
(BY PASTOR GRIMBOL)

11:45 P.M., Tuesday, September 11, 2001. The phone rings. Late, but no surprise. The phone had been ringing all night.

As always, I had watched the 11 P.M. news. For the hundredth time that day I watched the footage of two terrorist-flown planes devouring the twin towers of the World Trade Center. Each viewing was equally horrifying but progressively numbing. Terror freezes the mind and scalds the heart. I welcomed the phone call.

"Pastor Bill?" the young voice spoke.

"Yes," I replied, trying to sort out the voice.

"It's Greg," he replied in a tremor.

"Greg? Greg. Oh my God, Greg, I forgot!" What I had forgotten was that Greg worked at the World Trade Center.

"I needed to hear your voice," he said softly.

"Thank you." My reply felt oddly appropriate. Greg had been part of my youth group seven years earlier, and I remained his pastor.

Though we infrequently talked these days, our relationship had been forged during the furnace of Greg's adolescence, and so was quite intimate.

Greg then told me his story of being met at the elevator doors by the grimaced faces of co-workers. Of hearing the chants of "Run, get out!" Of how he memorized the faces of the young firefighters going up as he and thousands of others raced down.

Of how he ran through a sleet of debris and bodies—the bodies only recognizable because they failed to shine, and when they hit "looked like tomatoes." Of how he ran and ran and kept on running.

Of the numerous failed efforts to reach his parents and girlfriend by cell phone. Of his panic in knowing that they would have watched as the second plane hit in the vicinity of his Morgan Stanley office. Of the swarming relief of reaching them by phone. Of the exhilaration of a shower to remove the ash. Of the settling in of a shroud of fog—a new reality.

"Will I ever feel the same? I mean, be normal?" Greg asked in a whisper.

That question opened a gaping wound in my heart. I knew the answer. Greg knew the answer. The whole world had grown strangely silent that day, because everyone knew the answer. Terror had been unleashed on the American mainland. Thousands of innocent human beings were swept away by an explosion of evil. The American public now walked on shifting soil. The vulnerability in the air was so thick it had a taste—bitter.

I am a Presbyterian minister and my co-author is a Reform Rabbi. Since that dreadful day, we have had to preach, teach, and hold discussions with children, youth groups, and worried-sick parents. We have been invited to speak to gatherings of teachers and students at several area schools, and we cannot create enough slots for pastoral care appointments. It has been a dizzying time. Hard to grasp. Impossible to focus. Still, we have been struck hard by the following trio of observations.

First, all of America was shocked by these terrorist attacks. Ironically, most Americans were just as stunned to witness the outpouring of graciousness and generosity in New York City. "It is like this great big city became a little village," Greg said in a subsequent call. Even Mayor Guiliani, often the stirrer of the pot, became the essence of dignified calm. In the aftermath of experiencing some of the most vile behavior we had ever known, the whole nation was on its best behavior.

Observation #1 — We should never be stunned by good behavior. We should never be bowled over by folks choosing to be good neighbors. Kindness and decency and civility must once again be the norm.

Second, the world is rife with radical religious fundamentalism. Islamic. Christian. Jewish. Scores of small sects. Fundamentalism is a call to return to the basics of a particular religion. This sounds innocent enough, just religious conservatism. However, it is human beings who will decide what these basics will be and what will be the consequences for those who fail to obey.

The real dangers of fundamentalism are these:

- ✦ The belief that God is solely on their side.
- ✦ The belief that God is against their opponents or enemies.
- ✦ The belief that they not only have the right answers, but also the *only* answers.
- ✦ A genuine lack of respect for diversity.
- ✦ A fervent passion for uniformity of belief.
- ✦ A call for blind faith.
- ✦ A call to not only be willing to die for your faith, but to kill for it, too.
- ✦ A call to a faith in a God who espouses war.
- ✦ The belief that the *end* is the *hope*.
- ✦ The belief that only believers will gain entrance to heaven.
- ✦ The removal of power and choice from women.
- ✦ A rigid, black-and-white exposition of sacred scripture.
- ✦ The providing of simplistic legalistic answers to life's most complex questions.

Reverend Jerry Falwell said "I really believe that the pagans, and the abortionists, and the feminists, and the gays and lesbians who are actively trying to make that an alternative lifestyle; the ACLU; People for the American Way—all of them who have tried to secularize America—I point the finger in their face and say, 'You helped this happen.'" This is an excellent example of the potential evil of fundamentalism. Mr. Falwell's claims, for which he later apologized, are blatantly judgmental and self-righteous in the extreme. Ironically, his fundamentalist fervor is akin to that which motivated the terrorists. No matter how you slice it, hate is never spiritual.

Fundamentalism is rampant in today's religious world. It poses an enormous threat to our religious freedom. Fundamentalism simply lacks the flexibility, tolerance, imagination, and compassion necessary to create a civil world. Fundamentalism demands the building of walls at the very time we need bridges. Fundamentalism too often fuels the conflict, when what is needed are strategies for dousing the flames.

Observation #2—Whenever someone claims to have God on his side; to have God in his hip pocket; to know exactly what God wants, danger lurks and physical, emotional, or spiritual damage is on the horizon.

September 11, 2001, marked an explosion of questioning. Who is my neighbor? What is the point? When will it end? Where do I find hope? Why is there evil? How can I live life to the fullest?

With Greg's initial inquiry, "Will I ever feel the same? I mean, be normal?" came a flood of questions. The questions came from everywhere and without ceasing. The questions were no longer avoidable. The questions seemed to be the literal remains of the day.

In the darkness of these days, I have found these questions to be the fire in my hearth. They offer light and warmth. They are a place of gathering. They continue to flicker with magic and mystery and miracle. They are inextinguishable. I experience them as a pathway to faith, hope, and love.

Never before have I been more sure that there is no rule book of answers. There are no human beings in possession of all the answers. The claim of certainty is an illusion. Answers fail to grasp the bottom line—we are not in control. Only questions lift up the magnificent notion that God must be in charge.

Observation #3—Living the questions is the answer. Celebrating the questions themselves is what gives life its fullness and meaning. The questions give vision and voice to our deepest longings that call us to holy lives.

This little book is framed and focused by the enormous events of September 11, 2001. As is the function of frames, these terrorist attacks on our nation will serve only to give depth and meaning to our questioning and wisdom to how we live our answers. These acts of barbaric cruelty will only focus our need to mature, to become a nation whose greatness is grounded in our goodness. The good life must once again have something to do with goodness.

It is our questions that can lead us home to the America we love: a true melting pot; a land of mercy and justice; a beacon of hope; a champion of the poor and outcast; a people of tolerance, creativity, courage, and the will to celebrate our greatest strength— the diversity of our answers.

Life's big questions have never been bigger. They are critical to be asked. They are vital to be shared. As we live our answers, we will refine our will not merely to survive, or endure, but to flourish on this good Earth. But first, it all begins with lifting up the questions. The healing. The hope. The whole health of our nation and our world. We must start by embracing life's biggest and boldest questions.

This is our attempt to do just that!

ACKNOWLEDGMENTS FOR PASTOR GRIMBOL

First and foremost, I wish to thank Randy Ladenheim-Gil for having the wisdom to suggest that this book be shared with a rabbi. Rabbi Jeffrey Astrachan is a man of great faith, intellect, grace, and humor. It has been an honor to work with him on this manuscript and to count him as a friend. This has been a writing adventure that has made me think hard, feel deeply, and spiritually stretch and grow in all directions. I could not have asked for more from the experience.

I am once again indebted to Christy Wagner and Nancy Warner for shaping and forming this book into a working whole. Their talent is only exceeded by their humility and kindness in doing their job with such skill.

ACKNOWLEDGMENTS FOR RABBI ASTRACHAN

So many are to be thanked for their part in making the publication of this book—and my participation in it—possible. Included among them are:

Pastor William Grimbol, whose vision gave this project life and whose calming presence enhanced mine. Together we have journeyed through a difficult time in our lives, learned much from each other, and forged a relationship which will withstand time and trial. It has been a privilege to work with you, Bill. You have awakened within me a passion for expressing myself through words.

Randy Ladenheim-Gil, for having the courage and the vision to pursue this project.

Nancy Warner, for understanding that I have never done anything like this before. Your patience and guidance were tremendous.

Laurie Rozakis, for inviting me to write the Foreword to her book, *The Complete Idiot's Guide to Interfaith Relationships*. She opened the door to wonderful possibilities.

Robyn Smith, for thinking of me.

The members of Temple Beth Elohim, my congregation in Old Bethpage, New York, for allowing me the opportunity to pursue the challenges of this time-consuming effort. May we continue to go from strength to strength.

Last, my wife, Shelley, for patiently allowing me the time to work on this project during moments when—after the kids were asleep—she would have much preferred that I was with her.

NOTE ON THE SCRIPTURE PASSAGES

The scripture passages used by Pastor Grimbol are from the *Holy Bible New Living Translation* (Tyndale House Publishers, Inc.), copyright © 1996. Used by permission of Tyndale House Publishers, Inc., Wheaton, IL 60189.

The scriptural references used by Rabbi Astrachan were taken from a variety of study sources on the Internet as well as from *TANAKH, The Holy Scriptures* (Jewish Publication Society, Inc.).

Part 1

The Who Questions

Our book begins with questions of identity. Who we are and in what way we establish ourselves within the world around us are among the most important aspects of our very existence. Descartes, the wise seventeenth-century philosopher, is perhaps most famous for his statement, "Cogito, ergo sum," "I think, therefore I am." What we are left to discover for ourselves, however, is, "Who am I in the first place?"

In Genesis 18, Isaac calls out to Abraham, his father, as they journey toward the fateful mountain that God will show them. Abraham answers, "Hineini, b'ni," "Here I am, my son." Later, atop the mountain, just as Abraham is to slay his favored son, an angel of God calls out a halting order and Abraham replies, "Hineini," "Here I am." In this moment Abraham is fully present and fully aware of God's call. He is unquestionably ready to undertake whatever it is that God wants of him. His faith demands nothing less.

So it is with each of us. We must identify who we are, what our role is on this earth, and what, ultimately, God wants of us. We know that Abraham passed God's test and found himself to be worthy of greatness. His identity, his family, his life—all were changed by this singular momentous event. As stentorian as Abraham's testing or perhaps more subdued, each of us must discover for ourselves, "Who am I?" "Who are my neighbors?" and "Who are my enemies?"

WHO AM I?

Rabbi Jeffrey R. Astrachan

Each of us is born into this world as the embodiment of our parents' vision of perfection. As a result of their love for each other, we were created to both give and receive love and to eventually make our mark on this world. As we grow and mature, we gain greater understanding of what it means to be alive: We experience the world around us and begin to see where and how we fit in.

From the very earliest recorded accounts of religious history, we learn that on the sixth day of the world's existence, Adam was created by the will of God. (Genesis 1:27ff) As with every newborn, Adam—in his *own* infancy of existence—found himself in a world unfamiliar to him; strange sounds, objects, and smells flooded his senses. Among Adam's primary tasks were learning how to adjust to his surroundings and adapting to the world around him (a world that had been created entirely over the preceding five days). In essence, Adam had to discover who he was and why he was there in a very short time. Unlike a newborn infant who is given the opportunity to grow slowly and grasp everything in moderation, Adam was thrust into the world with the expectation that he would hit the ground running.

Fortunately for us, in our infancy, the world seems to come to us. At the very least, our parents come to us, our food comes to us, and our entertainment comes to us. Over time we realize that we actually have to fend for ourselves. We eventually learn that our *actions* are followed by *consequences*.

As we continue to grow, we find that more important actions are accompanied by more formidable consequences. As I have discovered through the help of my own two children, throughout our early years, we find ourselves continually asking "*Why?*" in search of answers to what the world around us is doing.

Although adulthood brings new challenges, including the vocations and obligations that fill our days, we find ourselves still needing to know *why*, albeit on a more esoteric level. Many of us find ourselves questioning the purpose of our existence, the role we are to play, and the goals we are to fulfill while we are alive. In this chapter we will begin to explore—through a spiritual eye—*who, what,* and *why* we are.

I Am Body and Soul

Perhaps the most often-asked question to a member of the clergy is "What will happen to me when I die?" Difficult enough as it is to ask the question and, therefore, face the fact of our own mortality, the question is no less difficult to answer. Most religious doctrines provide one or more theories to help make some sense of death, the afterlife, and the purpose of our existence. Depending on whom you ask, possibilities exist which may provide some comfort to those pursuing such elusive knowledge. Quite frankly, the fact is that no one really knows the answer to the question. No one, that is, can answer the question with any degree of certainty—at least not from a religious perspective.

Of course, we understand the *science* of death: The heart stops beating, blood stops pumping, oxygen stops flowing, and the body ceases to function. Science also neatly explains how the cycle of life begins—though, not surprisingly, few congregants ever ask for a religious explanation of this process. We generally accept the scientific approach to procreation. That's all well and good for the scientists and the pure-rationalists, but what about those of us who want more?

Certainly we all have at least a very rudimentary understanding of the process of creating a new life. But truly, how many of us could explain the irrationality of the process of a new human being being formed out of the tiniest mass of cells with no distinguishable human characteristics? This is where the "birds and the bees" falls far short of an acceptable, never mind complete, answer.

This being the case, why, then, don't more religious leaders find themselves posed with the question of the beginnings of life itself? For the curious among you, read on ....

According to Jewish thought, life begins at birth. While I understand that this alone may be a difficult stumbling block for those who consider the moment of conception to be the beginning of life, this is not a book that argues when life begins. Therefore, allow me to assert that Judaism maintains that when a child is born, both the physical and metaphysical come together to form complementary pieces of the puzzle that becomes the individual.

How does this happen? Simply put, we don't have an answer for this. It is an action by God that is carried out in a manner unexplainable and imperceptible by us mere humans. Nonetheless, it is a fundamental Jewish belief that at that glorious moment of birth—as we exit the womb—the soul that God breathes into us is pure. (Judaism does not maintain a concept of *original sin*.)

In coming to understand the connection between the science of the body and the faith of the soul, we begin to understand the elements that make us who we are. Judaism teaches that the body is merely a temporary housing for the soul—which, at the moment of death, is reclaimed by God, again, pure. It is a fundamental Jewish belief that all souls are the "property" of God. Therefore, regardless of what the individual did with the soul while in its temporary possession, God receives all souls, cleansed of any earthly burdens, pure.

In understanding that there is a combining of both scientific and spiritual processes taking place in this act of procreation, we must then come to terms with what responsibilities each of us has to ourselves and to the world around us. We must accept that in our creation we are also given purpose. What we are not given, however, is a complete understanding of what that purpose is. None of us knows for sure what specific goals we have been placed on this earth to fulfill. None of us has been so privileged as to speak directly with God in order to fully appreciate why we are here.

That being the case, each of us should feel the greatest responsibility to continually strive for the perfection of our world. In Judaism, this concept is called "*Tikkun Olam*" and gives us a sense of helping God put the finishing touches on what was started in those first six days. God has given us bodies to be put to work for noble tasks. It is up to each of us to accomplish the very best work that our bodies can manage. To put this another way, I recall a huge banner that hung at the front of my high school band room that read "Leave this place better than you found it." I learned a great lesson in high school!

I Am Heart and Mind

Gaining insight into what processes brought us to this place is only part of the challenge of understanding who we are. Within each individual are component parts that work together—in a scientifically explainable symbiosis—keeping us healthy, warning us when we are not, alerting us to dangers, and keeping us steadfast on a task.

We take so much of what our bodies do for granted as simply being expected functions. We are caught by great surprise when something goes wrong. Perhaps something as insignificant as a paper cut that stings for a few hours is all some need to be reminded that there are unknown events that can break up the casual and routine flow of our day. Perhaps for some it is a horrifying and unanticipated cancer, which, we know, stings forever.

Regardless of who we are or what we do to occupy our days, each of us is both *effected* and *affected* by the events we witness or in which we participate every day. With our heart and our mind, we are able to feel and interpret all that goes on in our world. It is this ability that makes us unique and allows us to relate to one another. How many of us have used or heard any of the following:

"My heart aches for your loss."

"In my heart, I know what you mean."

"My heart says one thing, but my mind knows better."

The fact is, each of us is completely reliant on both our heart and our mind—not only for their medically proven functions, but for their irrational functioning as well, which allows us to conduct ourselves in more spiritually aware ways. When we love our children or care for a wounded animal, when we see a rainbow or marvel at how clear the sky appears, these show us the spiritual value of our component parts.

A traditional Jewish prayer, recited as part of a regimented morning worship ritual, praises God for allowing each of our necessary life-sustaining organs to function at its peak. As a prayer of thanksgiving for health, it says ...

"Blessed is the Eternal God, Creator of the universe, who has made our bodies with wisdom, combining veins, arteries, and vital organs into a finely balanced network ..."

What we must come to understand and appreciate is that the continuous operation of each of our internal systems does not just happen because of a particularly explainable and rational health-science. Consideration must be given to the faith that allows each one of us the luxury of approaching life from a multitude of angles, both psychologically and emotionally—that is, one that is God-centered and one that is more rationally explainable. The miracle of life—and what keeps our bodies doing what they're supposed to do—must be further attributable to something outside the realm of explainable rationalism.

Each of us, throughout our lives, will inevitably face challenges to our health and constitution that seem to defy reason. We will ask God why we have been chosen to suffer such a disease or sustain such an injury. Some of us will find our pain in concert with that of Job 10:1 in the stories of our ancestors. We read ...

> "I am disgusted with life;
> I will give rein to my complaint,
> speak in the bitterness of my soul."

Or perhaps we look to Psalm 6:7 to find understanding:

> "I am worn out with my groaning;
> every night I flood my bed with tears;
> I melt my couch with weeping."

We wonder if we are alone in our grief and our pain. We scream out feeling helpless—can our hearts and our minds handle this intensity?—and we again find a connection in Psalm 22:2–3:

> "My God, my God, why have You abandoned me;
> why so far from delivering me
> and from my anguished roaring?
> My God, I cry by day—You answer not;
> by night, and have no respite."

There is so much more to us than what we can plainly see. Genesis teaches us that we have been created in the image of God but that we are not gods ourselves. Therefore, our pain is real and our suffering, too, is real—regardless of whether that pain is physical or emotional or whether it is felt in our hearts or in our minds.

Many of us are so quick to condemn God when we are ill, but far fewer of us praise God when we are well. We damn our commitment to our faith when someone we love is taken from us, but we fail to solidify our faith while they are in our lives.

We read in Psalm 34:19, "God is near to those that are of a broken heart." We must also remember that God is with us at all times: morning, noon, and night, as well as in health and in sickness. As we care for our physical being, we must also care for our spiritual being. Together they combine to form the essence of who we are.

I AM COMMON AND UNIQUE

Each of us struggles to understand our personal identity and the reason behind every challenge we face. The fact is, each of us faces *some* challenge every day of our lives. The problem is, when the challenge is our own, it often seems like the world has come down harder on us than on everyone else. What coping mechanisms do our faith traditions provide for us to help realize that we are really not alone in our daily challenges?

One aspect of faith maintains that God challenges those capable of sustaining the challenge. But when it is our turn to be challenged, how many of us have crumbled in on ourselves, begging the question "Why me, God?" And we ask ourselves what we might have done to bring about such pain or stress in our lives.

Perhaps our problem is that instead of looking at the problem from the outside—that is, how everyone else sees it—we manage only to see the relevance of the thing from our own perspective. We fail to recognize that even though the challenge may seem very great—be it the death of a loved one, the loss of a job, a debilitating illness—someone else has already faced this challenge and survived!

Certainly we grieve. Of course we mourn. Without question, we cry aloud as we pass through the fiery trial. We languish in the thought that we have been burdened with an overwhelming and life-changing event. But in our faith, we learn that eventually we *are* able to cope. We *are* given the strength to pick up the pieces of our lives. In Isaiah 40:31 we find:

> "But those who trust in God shall renew their strength
> As eagles grow new plumes.
> They shall run and not grow weary.
> They shall march and not grow faint."

We are never left alone to face God's challenges in our lives. We are provided with family and friends; we are given tools and resources; and we are granted wisdom and strength.

Another of Judaism's many words of thanksgiving includes one morning prayer, which begins with the following words:

> "My God, the breath that you have given me is pure."

Here, the "breath" this prayer speaks of is often referred to as the "soul" within each of us. What the Jewish tradition is teaching us here is that in every moment, continually throughout our lives, God is renewing within us that very breath that gives us life. This prayer, remember, is not recited once and then forgotten. Rather, it is recited every morning (by traditionally observant Jews) as a part of a ritual upon waking.

How many times have we been faced with challenges—great or small—and had someone say to us "Calm down. Take a breath." The Torah tells us, in Genesis, that God breathed life into Adam. There are actually three distinct words in Hebrew which relate to this concept: *neshamah* (the breath of life), *ruach* (spirit), and *nefesh* (soul). Each of these three words gives us insight into the life given to us by God.

In Psalm 121 the psalmist asks, "I lift my eyes to the mountains; what is the source of my help?" And the answer follows, "My help comes from God, maker of heaven and earth." Our goal is to recognize the grandeur of those elements in our lives that provide us with comfort and remind us that we are part of something much more expansive than ourselves.

After creating the world and nearly everything in it, on it, and over it, God makes the following important declaration, "It is not good for a human being to be alone." (Genesis 2:18) The fact is, we all need somebody to help us cope with the stresses that encroach upon our otherwise mundane day-to-day life. We all need someone to care for us, and we all need to have the opportunity to care for others. We are encouraged by the words of our faith to seek the company of friends. In the power of relationships we are able to see that the problems and challenges we face throughout our lives are not so unique. Rather, drawing strength from others who have faced similar stresses in their lives, we are able to better cope with our own.

I Am Ordinary and Extraordinary

Each one of us is, in so many ways, just like everyone else. After all, most Judeo-Christian faith groups teach that we are all created in God's image. The assumption, based on a system of well-grounded Biblical beliefs, therefore, must assume that God's mold for human beings was a paradigm to which every individual must conform in at least some small measure. However, we are each individuals, which makes us unique in comparison to all others.

We are each a part of something much larger than ourselves. How we come to understand what that larger part is may be a unique process in itself. Each of us must recognize that we have been chosen for a purpose outside the mundane mediocrity with which so many of us feel we must contend each wakeful moment of our lives.

As I was studying to become a rabbi, I had the wonderful opportunity to sit at a local walk-in clinic with people who were contemplating their own future. On a good number of occasions I talked with a variety of men and women at various stages in their lives who—for whatever reason—needed help in sorting out what job they might be best suited to do. I found it curious that more often than not these warm, caring, sensitive souls felt they were so *normal* in every way that they were unable to find anything at which they could truly excel. This usually brought me to use that ever-popular bumper-sticker phrase "Why be normal?"

Thank God we were each created in God's image! That is, each of us looks reasonably similar with, of course, certain identifiable characteristics that allow us to assume that either God had a wonderful sense of humor at the time we were created or that God doled out the responsibility of putting on the finishing touches of humanity to one-too-many assistants.

The fact that we awake each day must demand our respect for the miraculous and amazing fact of what it means to simply be alive. In that fact is our God, who gave us life, continually gives us life, and with ongoing patience allows generation after generation to come and go.

Judaism provides a wonderful prayer of thanksgiving to God for each moment we remember that life is, truly, a gift. In the blessing called "Shehechiyanu," we thank God for giving us life, for sustaining us, and for allowing us to reach whatever that extraordinary moment might be.

And so, in speaking with these men and women at the walk-in clinic, I would always ask them to share with me five extraordinary qualities, characteristics, or skills they possessed which made them so completely different than anyone else they had ever met. What a liberating exercise! In fact, I challenge each of you reading this book to pause here and try it for yourselves.

Did you do it? I would be curious to know how long it took you to find five. I suspect the first few were more difficult to mete out than the last. You see, the challenge that so many of us face in our lives is coming to grips with the fact that it's okay to be different. In fact, it would be great if each of us took the time to make a bigger deal about the wonderful differences that make us *abnormal*. Who needs to be just like everyone else? (Don't ask a teenager that question—"normal" is the only way to be for them!)

In Psalm 36:10 we read, "For with You is the source of life; in Your light do we see light." As we travel our unique paths through life, may we be open to the light that shines within us.

Chapter Response by Pastor Grimbol

Let me begin by saying that in my conversations with Rabbi Astrachan, I was repeatedly struck by how much we spiritually held in common. At times I thought of our faiths as conjoined twins, connected at the heart but with different minds. I seldom found myself at odds with Jeff, and that was even more true in reviewing his written sections of the manuscript. I found many of our differences to be subtle, more issues of focus and interpretation and even history than glaring points of conflict.

Obviously, the divinity of Jesus remains the single greatest point of demarcation. I understand Jesus as the Messiah. Jeff does not. As for the ministry and message of Jesus, however, both are dominated by Jesus' Jewish roots. For me personally and professionally, I have no need to prove the divinity of Jesus. I cannot. That is strictly a leap of faith. What I care about is the ministry and message. In that regard, Jeff and I were often on very familiar turf.

In this first chapter I found myself agreeing with Jeff on some major points. I must admit that there are a good many Christian clergy who do not share my views. My beliefs are shaped and formed by my own spiritual relationship with God—Holy Spirit communicating with human spirit.

I, too, see life as beginning at birth. It is at birth that I see life being infused with all of those realities—physical, emotional, relational, and spiritual—that make life *life*. Life, for me, has always been more than just breathing in and out. Life is what takes place outside the womb.

I, also, have never accepted or understood the concept of original sin. I believe in original blessing. I believe we are born as God's own beloved children. I believe we are surrounded by grace from the moment of birth. This grace is ours to accept or reject, but it is always present and available. Our sin is rooted in rejecting this grace, which is not the act of a child, nor the mark born by humanity. For me, to reject grace is the risk of being human and the price of being free.

I loved Jeff's explanation of the Jewish concept of "Tikkun Olam," in which he states, "gives us a sense of helping God put the finishing touches on what was started in those first six days."

In Christianity, this concept would be called either sanctification (the process of becoming holy) or discipleship (the idea of patterning one's life after that of Jesus).

In the Christian faith, we are first justified by our faith in Christ. It is Jesus who illumines for us that we are God's beloved children. In faith we are led to respond to the love we have come to know in Christ. This response is a desire to become holy or to sanctify our lives. To become holy is not about pursuing perfection or sainthood. Holiness is found in the celebration of our humanness. Holiness is simply to become the person God has created us to be.

Sanctification and discipleship are pretty much one and the same. Both answer the question "Who am I?" with the assertion that we belong to God and that we are called to conform our will to God's. Discipleship does offer clarity on what holiness might look like. Who are disciples? We are a people of faith called by Jesus to preach good news to the poor, to bind broken hearts, to be extravagant in thanks and mercy, to minister to the outcast, to believe in the power of prayer and the possibility of miracles, and to receive the gifts of grace as well as the promise of eternal life.

For the Christian, who we are is shaped by our relationship to Jesus. Jesus is our mentor and our role model. In following Jesus, we find our way to happy and healthy and hope-filled lives. The great irony of faith is that we become free to be our true selves to the degree we surrender our egos to the desires of God.

I heartily concur with Jeff's admonitions to define who we are in relationship to others, in the practice of thanksgiving, and in recognizing that we were created in the image of God. Here, too, our faiths blend as easily as a marble cake. We may be able to see the differences, but we are not quite sure how they took shape. The cake itself tastes delicious—both flavors.

WHO IS MY NEIGHBOR?

Rabbi Jeffrey R. Astrachan

In the first chapter we learned that our bodies are infinitely complex structures composed of interwoven organs and connective tissue. How our bodies work and how we are given the opportunity to perform our daily tasks are questions with both rational and irrational answers. That is, we can rely on the sciences to explain how we function or we can look to our faith in the miraculous nature of God's all-encompassing works to fulfill our curiosities.

In this chapter we will begin to look outside ourselves to the world around us. Too many of us focus too much attention on the world of the "self" and neglect or forsake any responsibility to the world of the "selfless." When we begin to recognize that we exist for a purpose, when we see that our lives operate in concert with the lives of others, when we truly act as though our existence makes a difference in someone else's life, then and only then can we begin to realize our fullest potential.

Whether we look within our own homes, across the street, in the next town, or across the oceans, we can easily find others who are, in many ways, just like each one of us—people in need of other people, of companionship, of connection to something outside themselves. What many of these people are seeking, like us, is God and a connection with God, which is particularly comforting to know that we are not alone on our journey through life. Together we now explore ways in which we can seek comfort in ourselves and in others while we all seek a relationship with God.

I Am My Neighbor

Not so many years ago, in the midst of terrifying race-riots in Los Angeles, Rodney King, a man who was videotaped being beaten by police officers, not only made headlines following his ordeal but also entered the fabric of American culture with his still-famous question, "Can't we all just get along?"

It was a wonderful question that gave each of us pause to consider the fact that we, as individuals, *are* responsible for our actions and our thoughts. Unfortunately, too many of us neglect such responsibility, believing that we act independently of others and, therefore, impact only ourselves *unless we willfully choose to do otherwise.* We forget that most everything we do actually makes an impact on everything else in our world.

One of Judaism's most revered ancient scholars, Hillel (70 B.C.E.–11 C.E.) (because Judaism does not recognize a messiah who has already come, the notations "B.C." and "A.D." are inappropriate; "B.C.E." for Before the Common Era and "C.E." for Common Era are used instead—the dating to which the terms refer is the same), was quoted with one of the most poignant series of thought-provoking questions:

> "If I am not for myself, who will be for me? If I am only for myself, what am I? If not now, when?"

What Hillel is reminding us through these questions is that we have certain obligations in our lives—obligations to ourselves and to those around us. It is a rejoinder which pleads that we not be so self-centered as to forget that others actually depend on us—that we have a purpose to our lives. But before we can reach out to help others, we must reach inward to help ourselves.

I remember back to my days in school when teachers' expectations seemed to exceed my abilities. There were many days when I almost chose to turn back, throw it all away, and forsake my goals. I was lucky to have terrific people to encourage me along that part of my life's journey, but despite their greatest efforts, only I could make the ultimate choice to reconsider the challenges facing me. As Hillel said, "If I am not for myself ..." In the end, I had to look inward. I had to begin to answer some very tough questions. I had to accept the responsibilities put upon me, knowing that the merit of my struggle was to exceed the struggle itself.

Now, as a rabbi with my own synagogue, I find the tables are turned. Boys and girls who are approaching their thirteenth birthday—who have been enrolled in formal religious training classes since many of them were in kindergarten—find themselves only months shy of the date of their bar or bat mitzvah, struggling between knowing that they have so much yet to prepare for and the natural tendency to avoid such obligations. As I stand with such students, I firmly remind them that "I know this stuff. You are the ones who have to realize the importance of learning it for yourself." Although I know that each child who comes before me is fully capable of mastering the challenge set before them, they need to be reminded that while such mastery is possible, it only comes when the one struggling is dedicated to the task and to himself.

So, too, for each of us. The tasks set before us are very great. Life is not always easy, as we have come to discover. But that doesn't mean we can deny the need to fulfill a certain destiny. Another great sage of the Jewish people, Rabbi Tarfon (who lived in Israel, late first century) has been credited with the statement "You are not required to complete the work, but neither are you at liberty to abstain from it."

What we learn from this statement is an understanding that the tasks each of us face can certainly be overwhelming. There are times when we feel the weight of the world is pressing on us. There are days when nothing seems to go right for us. Nevertheless, we learn from Rabbi Tarfon the importance of finding it within ourselves to take on the challenge, relying on ourselves and our God-given talents of body, mind, and spirit. When we realize that we can count on ourselves to accept the challenges that lie ahead, we can begin to love ourselves with all our heart, all our soul, and all our might.

My Friends and Family Are My Neighbors

We know that we exist. This is a fact without argument. What we often question, however, is *why* we exist. Do we live for ourselves, or do we live for something outside ourselves? Ultimately, this is something each of us must answer in our own way with fine degrees of variance. Of course we must recognize, continually, the importance of our own existence for our own sake. After all, I'm me, you're you, and the rest of the people in our world are who they are. We do, act, say, believe, and function according to a set of rules that are engrained in the genes that make us who we are. Nothing readily known to modern science can change that with any notable degree of success.

But looking back at Hillel's wonderful statement of relationships, we find that we have an obligation to accept our role in the greater scheme of living. That is, we do not exist solely for ourselves and our own satisfaction. The people with whom we come into contact most often are the ones we effect and who effect us most directly. Our friends (with varying degrees of relationship) and our family (be they immediate or more distant) each impact upon our lives as much as we impact upon theirs. These people give us strength, and we, in turn, give strength to them. We share love and affection. We offer each other support and consolation. We help the other to achieve goals and to process the challenges of life.

"If I am only for myself, what am I?" wrote Hillel. If we do not recognize the value of human relationships, we darken our world by shutting out the light of personal contact and the warmth of the spirit that can be shared. We exist, then, by filling space with loneliness and filling time with emptiness.

Living in an Emotional Neighborhood

"Human being in search of meaningful relationship with any-body!" Not the most common personal ad, to be sure. But how many of us have had moments in our lives when we felt so desperate to be appreciated that resorting to such an advertisement of our vacuous soul seemed the only remaining measure available to us? So what can we do to change the way we feel?

That's a difficult question. And the fact that I am a rabbi, not a psychologist, probably does not permit me to adequately answer it here. I will, however, offer some personal thoughts on this issue. We begin to change the way we feel when we recognize that we are not alone. We begin to change the way we feel when we look outside ourselves and find that there are people around us who may very well be feeling the same way we feel. We begin to change the way we feel when we lead by example—when we take the hand of a friend and declare, "We have each other!"

I do not need to write a book to tell you that not everybody has a loving, warm, touchy-feely family. This is something which is, unfortunately, so common that I would bet that every person reading this book knows someone who resides in a household— or came from one—where *love* was nothing more than a tennis score. I have counseled countless people who told me of family dynamics that have left me so saddened. Brothers who don't speak. Sisters who can't be in the same room. Parents who hate the person their child married. And on and on.

These are stories about the people who should be our first line of defense. Our families are the people who are supposed to care the very best for us and our needs. They are the ones who are supposed to support our goals and nurture our emotions. Yet we find such dynamics to be more idealistic than realistic. Often, however, such dynamics are more a matter of perception. It behooves us to step back and evaluate the relationships for what they truly are rather than what we perceive them to be. We might be surprised.

Jewish tradition provides its adherents with an annual cycle of opportunity to renew relationships. At Rosh HaShanah and Yom Kippur (referred to as the High Holy Days), we take time to be especially introspective. Looking inside ourselves to seek inner-wisdom and guidance, we evaluate shortcomings and failings throughout the past year. We give ourselves the chance to wipe the slate clean and refresh our lives. As a part of this, we are encouraged to rekindle connections with siblings, parents, children, friends, and others with whom we may have fallen out of touch or favor. Of course, this process of renewal is one that we encourage throughout the year, as well, but at the time of the High Holy Days, we make certain to confront the task, regardless of previous attempts.

This is a great first step. Let us acknowledge the importance of family and friends; let us come to realize the important role they play in our lives; and let us understand the role we can play in theirs.

A Stranger or Enemy Is Still My Neighbor

We are currently a country in crisis. Understanding that our way of life has been altered, our freedoms have been compromised, and our security is no longer certain has been distressing to all of us. In my role as clergy I have not yet met an individual unaffected by recent events. I have spoken with many individuals who have shared with me greatly disturbing stories and concerns regarding groups of people they do not personally know but who they would like to see annihilated for acts of terrorism within our borders.

The concern I share with them—and that I share with you now—is that when we have such feelings for people, we reduce ourselves to the same playing field that they, themselves, occupy. That is, our feelings of vengeance and the attempt to mete out justice through hatred leads us to become perpetrators of terror just the same.

"But Rabbi, how can they think that resorting to terrorism and killing innocent people could possibly be in keeping with religious thought?" The number of times clergy have heard similar questions is mind-numbing. The fact is, what terrorists accomplish "in the name of God" is nothing but a sham. Throughout history, people have been declaring holy wars on offending peoples simply because of an inability to recognize the legitimacy of a multitude of belief systems, religious or otherwise. Many wars have been fought in God's name that have had nothing whatsoever to do with God. What they have to do with is distaste for a particular political agenda, which is believed to be in conflict with another political agenda. Call this an affront to God, and we suddenly have a holy war. There is nothing at all *holy* about *war*.

But what of those who happen to share views unlike our own? Quite simply, avoid them. That's your choice insofar as you have the choice to make. We do not always like our neighbors—maybe the kids make a mess of your lawn, or their dog wanders the streets, or they play their music too loud on Saturday night—but, nonetheless, they are our neighbors. The difference here, though, is that if our home life is made too uncomfortable by our neighbors, we have the option to move elsewhere. When we are confronted with acts of aggression from another country or from a particular group of like-minded militants who choose to attack our very way of life—loading our belongings into a truck is not a viable option.

We all have family histories that trace our ancestry back through multiple generations. Nearly all of us find that our families came to the United States sometime during the past 225 years from other countries and other ways of life. They settled here with the promise of a brilliant future filled with opportunity to thrive, succeed, and provide a better life for their family and their future generations.

The goals were noble, the desires were strong, and the journey was difficult. In the end, they made it to these shores, and they left for us a legacy we can be infinitely proud of.

In Exodus 22:20, we find the text, "You shall not wrong a stranger, nor oppress him; for you were strangers in the land of Egypt." Each one of us has found our lot in life through the grace of others. Let us always be mindful of our task to improve this world by doing our part to fix what is broken. We are obligated to mend relationships and to begin to understand that differences should be a unifying factor, not a divisive one.

THE WORLD IS MY NEIGHBOR

The words of the prophet Isaiah further our mission to eradicate hatred and again instill goodness and understanding. In Isaiah 42:6, Isaiah's words from God ring out in favor of an acceptance of God's expectations of those who inhabit this world. The message is a universal one:

> "I the Lord have called you in righteousness and will hold your hand and will keep you and give you for a covenant of the people, for a light to the nations."

God's declaration that those who are gladdened by God's goodness shall serve as a "light to the nations" can be rendered as a call to justice of the heart. As we shine the light of our own goodness, as we serve as an example to those countries of the world that do not hold dear the values of compassion, kindness, and peace, we then begin to fulfill our mission. We stand resolute in our God-guided efforts to teach goodness over evil, to stand for justice over vengeance, and to entreat understanding over ignorance.

We hear people telling us that we must learn to *tolerate* in order to understand others. I remember learning as a child the concept of "tolerance" in regard to accepting other children who might be different. As I grew, I found that the way in which we used the word *tolerance* changed the intended meaning of the word from something that was seemingly very positive and warm to something very unsatisfying and empty. To tolerate something is to simply "put up with it." When we go to the doctor, we tolerate the pain of an injection. When we work with our employees, we tolerate an infraction or two. Parents often tolerate the annoying habits of their own children more than they would someone else's child. In the end, tolerance is not the answer. Tolerance is something we accept when we are not really ready to see others for who they are and for what they believe or practice.

What we should be striving for, instead, is *acceptance*. Our world is inhabited by a tremendous number of peoples with an unfathomable number of differences. What makes us all the same, however, is that we each occupy the same earth and, therefore, are confronted with the same challenges of understanding and *accepting* those who are different from us.

Let us truly examine the meaning of the words of Isaiah, and let us strive wholeheartedly to be a light to the nations. Let us each do our part—not to *tolerate,* but to *accept* the differences that have the potential to make all people great.

God Lives Right Next Door

We are faced with a great many challenges and stresses in life. Daily we question what we might find as we leave our homes and make our way to work. We might hear unsettling news or witness an accident. Perhaps we have the opportunity to speak with a friend who is feeling depressed or another who just lost his job.

Each of us has been confronted with challenges and trials. Maybe we have something upcoming, like a doctor appointment, which we dread for fear of what we might learn. Countless examples of tensions fill our lives. What does religion offer us to help cope with these unavoidable stumbling blocks?

Judaism teaches that when we are faced with anxiety or fear, when life is burdensome, or when the pressures of daily tasks become too difficult, we are to examine the lessons in the Psalms.

Following is a lengthy, though not comprehensive, list of challenges or conditions that we all face from time to time and appropriate Psalms we might use to seek solace or comfort (original editor of the following list unknown). I encourage you to begin with these as a guide, but then explore other Psalms and other Biblical readings that may also provide you with some relief in what is often a disordered world.

When you are anxious for dear ones: Psalm 121

When business is poor: Psalms 37 and 92

When sorrow overtakes you: Psalm 46

When you find yourself tempted to do wrong: Psalms 15 and 19

When you are having difficulty going to sleep: Psalms 4 and 56

When you are tired: Psalm 95:1–7

When you are jealous: Psalm 49

When you are impatient: Psalms 40 and 90

When you are bereaved: Psalms 23 and 90

When you are bored: Psalms 103–104

When all is going well: Psalms 100 and 118

When you are starting a new job: Psalm 1

When you are making a new home: Psalm 127

When you are in need of forgiveness: Psalm 51

When you are ill or in pain: Psalms 6, 39, and 41

When your faith has weakened: Psalms 113 and 126

When you think God seems far away: Psalms 25 and 125

When you are lonely or fearful: Psalms 27 and 91

When you fear death: Psalms 71 and 103

When you want a prayerful mood: Psalm 24, 84, and 116

CHAPTER RESPONSE BY PASTOR GRIMBOL

I would have to say that I envied Rabbi Astrachan in this chapter. Judaism has a rich history of focusing on the importance of human relationships. The centrality of community is obvious within Jeff's writing and faith. Judaism has a rich and deep heritage of understanding relationships in a global context.

As an example, the High Holy Days of Rosh HaShanah and Yom Kippur are truly seen as times of relational healing. Forgiveness is one of the featured activities of the High Holy Days. The season of Lent, which would be the Christian equivalent of a sacred time of introspection and healing, tends to be far more personal in focus and tone. Though Christians take the matter of forgiveness seriously, as a crucial task of faith, I suspect that we think of it in a more limited setting—in terms of family and friends.

I found Jeff's words on tolerance and acceptance to be inspiring. True tolerance is indeed genuine acceptance. Acceptance is the celebration of diversity. Acceptance is to show respect for those differences we experience in others. Acceptance is to acknowledge that God knew what he was doing in creating a world of difference.

I believe that Jesus Christ was a true champion of acceptance. His message and ministry were jammed with examples and calls to love the outcast and to embrace the rejected. Jesus lived in such a way that all people were to be treated as equal in value.

The prostitute, the tax collector, the Samaritan, the leper, the mentally ill, the wretched of the earth—all were elevated by Jesus. Jesus commanded his followers to symbolically invite these folks to the banquet table. Jesus asks us to open our hearts—and minds and doors—to those rejected by the world.

Here I must be honest and candid. I am greatly disturbed by how increasingly un-Christ-like I experience much of the Christian Church. Christianity appears to be growing less and less accepting of difference, and more and more hard-line in attitude and belief. I am saddened by how much energy I see being expended in my own Presbyterian denomination on whether gay and lesbian folks can be ordained. A much healthier debate would be whether or not we should ordain bigots. I fear the growing rigidity and judgmentalness I witness within much of American Christianity.

Still, the Christian faith is grounded in the life and death of Jesus. If we follow his example, then acceptance will be our calling card. Jesus answers the question "Who is my neighbor?" by simply telling us that we know who our neighbor is and that we know that we are called to love that neighbor. Jesus goes so far as to demand an extravagant love and mercy for those neighbors we find offensive or who the world might paint in ugly colors.

Jesus challenges us to love even the enemy. Love begins with acceptance. Have you ever felt loved by someone who did not accept you? No! Acceptance is the guarantee and warranty of love. Acceptance is the force of grace, and as Christians, we believe Jesus to be the very event of grace. As Christians, I believe we must come home to the core of our faith, a Jesus whose ministry oozed unconditional love. If we love only on the condition that we share the same beliefs or the same interpretation of Scripture, we have lost the graciousness that was to be the emblem of our faith.

I often think of Jesus standing before us and being asked this age-old question, "Who is my neighbor?" I think of him smiling and nodding and quietly saying, "Please open your eyes." We know our neighbor. We know the difficulty of loving our neighbor. We know that acceptance gets us past the first great hurdle, the need to judge, or the desire to find the flaw. Acceptance releases the power of love.

Who Is My Enemy?

Rabbi Jeffrey R. Astrachan

In the previous chapter we approached the issue of neighbors and the world community as our enemies in relation to how we perceive others, interact with them, and resolve to accept differences as a common bond which should hold us together rather than alienate us. In this chapter we will look at a different kind of enemy: our friends, our parents, and ourselves.

As stated earlier, our perception of reality is often nothing like reality itself. Whether we view ourselves more harshly than others view us, or we fail to recognize positive or negative qualities in our friends, or we forsake the wisdom of those who might actually know better than us, it may very well be that the enemy we should fear most is ourselves.

In this chapter we will focus on four problems: the misconception of self-perception, falling *in* with the *out*-crowd, patronizing the wisdom of our parents, and finally, accountability for our actions. In addressing each of these problems, we will see the value of assessing our role in our own life's happiness and accepting responsibility for the choices we make.

Being My Own Worst Enemy

Not so long ago, seeing a therapist to help work through life's challenges was viewed as a weakness or even as a failure to cope with the onslaught of daily challenges. From time management to personal appearance to relationship problems—if we could not handle these on our own, we were seen as weak, emotionally deficient, or, even worse, mentally unstable. Today, who doesn't see a therapist? *Everybody* sees *somebody*, it seems.

What is the difference between our current generation and the ones that preceded us? I haven't the slightest idea, to be honest— at least not in terms of our willingness to more openly admit or accept that we need help from an outside qualified "emotional technician." It seems, though, that everything we do today is so technical. If something is broken, we can find a tool to fix it. So why not try that with our own emotions? If we need some help mending our spirits, we seek the counsel of one able to advise us in such matters of the heart or mind.

I am certain that with some very specific and individual challenges, many of us are faced with quite similar issues. Again looking back on the problem of *perception,* each of us has the daily renewing challenge to "face our face." Each morning we rise from our slumber, trod our path to the bathroom, and engage in our daily ritual, which inevitably includes a necessary gaze into a mirror. We stare at ourselves and wonder, "Does everyone else see me the same way *I* see me?" And for most of us, the answer is "Yes, of course they do." But that can be an unfortunate response, because for most of us, what we see and what others see are two different things—again, an issue of perception.

Remember that our traditions teach us from the early verses of Genesis that God chose to mold us in his image. In understanding this text we must, therefore, assume that each of us is shaped with a certain amount of God's perfection. The problem, though, is that although God gave us all what the Heavenly Hosts would call a "10," what we often see is a "3." No one is more critical of our own bodies and our own physical appearance than we are to ourselves. We spend precious time—often, hours—primping and styling, setting and conditioning, toning and shaping, all to feel good enough about ourselves to go to the grocery store.

Of course, we all should take time to show the world (and ourselves) that we, in fact, care enough about ourselves that we choose to appropriately groom ourselves as to not appear unkempt, emit some unpleasant aroma, or dress in a manner that would present an obvious violation of some expected societal norm. But for so many the childhood taunt, "You're fat, you're ugly, and your mother dresses you funny," hits too close to home and cuts painfully into our very being. Let's face it. We live in a world filled with cruel people who do cruel things and say utterly cruel statements that, frankly, hurt our feelings. But we also, affected by the human condition, can be remarkably cruel to ourselves. We love a good pity-party. We do a great job of cutting ourselves down the rungs of the self-esteem ladder.

What we need to do—but what is so difficult to accomplish—is stop giving in to the pressures of the society that surrounds us, stop pretending we have to look or act just like a few selectively air-brushed models on the pages of magazines, stop feeling like we're the only ones who feel so down about ourselves, and accept that we are very handsomely packaged just the way we are.

Consider the average clothing store—not a specialty boutique, but something more like your run-of-the-mill mall shop. Most of us already know that the most popular sizes for women's clothing lie between 12 and 16. Unfortunately, when we see stores advertising the styles we will eventually buy, the models wearing those clothes on television and in the Sunday circulars are between sizes 2 and 6 at best!

We know these things, but we don't think about the logic and the reality of the marketing strategies that shape so much of our society's perceptions and values.

Most of us could use the opportunity to talk with somebody at some time about something in our life that is eating us from the inside out. But I would feel safe saying that in a good many situations, the problems and challenges we are facing are a result of our own inability to come to terms with who we are and what our lot in life has become.

Remember, there are some things in life over which we have great control and some things over which we have absolutely no control. Many of us are familiar with the words of the Serenity Prayer:

> Grant me the serenity to accept the things I cannot change; courage to change the things I can; and the wisdom to know the difference.

When we recognize the truths contained in these statements, we can begin to make changes in our lives that help us see the real beauty that makes up who we are both internally and externally. Don't let anyone tell you this is an easy task. It's quite the opposite. But the journey of our lives is not always easy. We grow from our experiences in both the world around us and the world that *is* us.

WITH FRIENDS LIKE THESE ...

Peer pressure can be amazingly difficult to overcome. How we fit in to a friendship circle or relate to members of a group we would like to be a part of ranks high on the chart of socially important accomplishments in life. None of us wants to be an *out*cast or an *out*sider. We have a natural tendency to desire *in*clusion and *in*volvement. These prefixes have pre-fixed our hardwired systems to react to the need for others to see us as we see them.

As teens, we need to be part of a certain school clique. We buy the "right" jeans and wear the "right" sneakers. We say the "right" things and date the "right" people. Oftentimes forsaking our own true feelings, we sacrifice our sense of self in order to feel we belong. As adults, we have similar needs (although usually expressed in different ways) to form associations, and we, too, often sacrifice a piece of our own integrity to that end.

Teens smoke and drink. Adults smoke and drink. Teens abuse drugs. Adults abuse drugs. Teens lie and cheat. Adults lie and cheat. Teens know what they're doing is wrong. Adults know, too. So what's the difference? Good question; however, there's no good answer. What's the implication? Teens can often get away with such behavior and chalk it up to naiveté and "sowing their wild oats." Adults are just supposed to know better because they're adults.

Each of us has faced a time (or two) in our lives when we were asked by someone who claimed to be a friend to do something we had no doubt was illegal, dangerous, offensive, or just plain stupid. And after giving the request some thought, we dove right in to undertake some ridiculous task that might still haunt us to this day. It was usually at those times that a parent would get hold of us, express some nonsensical verbiage that only a parent can express (now that I'm a parent, I understand the jargon perfectly!), and scream out something like, "If all your friends jumped off a bridge, would you do it, too?" My father, a man wise beyond his years, has a favorite expression, which he used to share with me when I was younger: "Better to be a live chicken than a dead duck."

Corny though it might be, I know that throughout my college years—and until this very day—that maxim of my father's rang true on countless occasions. There are times in life when we have to evaluate the friendships or so-called friendships we maintain. Do our friends share the same moral character we expect in ourselves? Do our friends always express themselves in ways we are comfortable with? Do our friends ask us to do things for which we have to stop—even for a second—and consider the possibility that the task might be less than noble? I pose these questions to all the readers of this book, young and not so young. We all must ask ourselves whether our friends look out for us as much as we look out for ourselves.

Comedian Jeff Foxworthy has a rather funny routine in which he talks about some of his best friends and the crazy things they did together when they were younger. He relates the time they engaged in some absurd stunt that resulted in him and one other friend spending the night in jail. Foxworthy goes on to talk about what great friends he had—but then qualifies the statement saying that if they were really *good* friends, they would have been in jail with him. It's funny but also telling. When we look at the relationships we cherish most, we have to be willing to put them to the test and not just settle on a connection with someone because it allows us to feel included.

It is difficult, sure, but wise as well, to excuse oneself from an unfaithful or unsatisfying relationship with friends because our values have grown apart from the group. When we settle, we stagnate. We fail to grow and mature. We stop progressing emotionally. We cease to be true to ourselves. Life is too short to worry about what one group of people might say or think about us. Remember bringing home a bad grade in school and trying to explain it away based on the pitiful performance of the rest of the class? I can't wait for my kids to do that so I can share with them the same wisdom of all parents, "I don't care if the rest of the class failed. I only care that *you* failed." It isn't always so great to be included in a group. Sometimes we just have to do our own thing, our own way, in our own time. Maybe if we did that, we wouldn't need all the therapists!

They Only Want What Is Best for You

I don't actually remember the first time my parents told me that they used to be teenagers, but I'm certain it was a time that I had done something particularly disturbing for which they chose to teach me a lesson rather than just punish me. I think it was an attempt to connect with me on a new level. I was a teenager, I guess, so they felt the best way to handle the situation was to tell me that they understood what I was feeling or thinking or doing because they must have felt or thought or done that in their own day, too. Hokey as it is, probably every parent has told their teenager that they, too, used to be in their shoes.

The Bible teaches us that without exception we are to honor the people who gave us life. "Honor your mother and your father," we read in the Book of Exodus. What is the penalty for disobeying this commandment? Death by stoning—a horribly painful way to be executed. Although the exact process of how stoning was carried out is questioned by leading scholars, few would argue that it was a cruel and inhumane punishment.

The funny thing is, though, that while we never actually learn of anyone in history facing a death by stoning, especially for the case of dishonoring a parent, I question how many of us would still be around today if the practice was enforced in our generation. I should point out that the great rabbis of our past concluded that even questioning a decision, disobeying a request, raising our voices, and expressing other common modern improprieties would be considered dishonoring our parents.

So many of us grew up thinking that our parents were from another planet—that we could not have possibly been born to them. They don't act like us; they don't talk like us; they don't dress like us; they don't like our music. We must have been hatched! Or maybe switched at birth—and our *real* parents are fighting with the kid they got, who all along is wondering the same thing we are. It isn't until we grow and mature to an indefinable point that we begin to realize that our parents might actually have had our best interests in mind all along. Crazy as it may sound, mother and father might really have known best.

Our parents are certainly not our enemies, although so many people treat them as though they are. I recently officiated at a funeral for a woman whose personality made relationships with her very difficult, even with members of her family. Her son, now a grandfather himself, had very few nice things to share with me about his mother. In fact, he told me that he had no real relationship with his mother at all, despite his best efforts, and that he had actually given up trying a long time ago. Speaking with other members of the family, I heard some rather beautiful stories about relationships with her grandchildren and great-grandchildren. In the end I prepared a very lovely eulogy that spoke highly of the woman's affection for her youngest admirers. During the funeral I noticed her son crying several times when I spoke of the relationships his mother shared with others. I believe there was goodness within this woman that the son never had the privilege to know for himself. I believe there is goodness inside all our parents. Some of us are lucky to know it fully, while others see only rare glimpses.

There is an old story of a father and son who speak often but see each other rarely. The son is very busy with his career, and the father is busy doing his own thing. The father continually asks his son to take some time off to come visit, but to no avail. Finally the father says to his son, "When the day comes that I should die, will you take time off to come to my funeral?" The son, expectedly replies, "What nonsense, Dad. Of course I would come to your funeral." The father then replies, "I don't want you to wait until my funeral. I want you to come now."

How many of us forsake our duty to honor our parents? How many of us go through our lives believing with such certainty that what our parents tried to tell us when we were younger was absolute nonsense—that we were always smarter and better and more savvy than they were? How many of us failed to take advantage of the wisdom and the love of the ones who gave us life, who provided for our needs, and who helped us find our way?

Those of us who are fortunate to still have our parents in our lives ought to strive to make the time remaining the very best possible. Death is inevitable. What we do with the time we have left is up to us. Make every phone call and visit count.

THE DEVIL MADE ME DO IT!

Bad things happen. This should not come as a huge surprise to any of us. And when bad things happen—when a loved one is diagnosed with a terminal illness, when a child is born with complications, when groups of people are the targets of hatred and marked for destruction—one of the first things some of us do is question God's role in the event. We cry out to God in search of answers. The problem we face in raising our voices to God is that we all too often are unable to bring ourselves to hear God's response.

Years ago I preached a sermon on the benefits of building a relationship with God at an early age and continually restructuring our relationship with God throughout our lives. Too many of us go through life with only a cursory perception of God—we only call upon God as we would a genie in a bottle—when we need a miracle, when we need a scapegoat, when we need to point a finger, when we need to place blame. The difficulty in this, though, is that in only calling upon God when our needs are dire, the stress of the moment clouds our minds and disquiets our visions. Rather, when we go through life *practicing* how to relate to God, we have the benefit of a certain familiarity such that when we call upon God we, perhaps, have a better idea of what kind of responses God is capable of providing.

When we were very young, perhaps in grade school, friendships came and went like the wind. In an instant another child went from being our *best friend in the whole wide world* to just another "meanie" who wouldn't play with us. As we got older, we came to understand that relationships were tenuous and had to be nurtured. So, too, with God. If we forsake our role in the relationship, simply expecting God to be there when we call upon him, we risk distancing ourselves from our ability to perceive God.

Many have referred to an understanding of God as our *conscience.* That is, when we consider the kind of person we ought to be and the ways in which we ought to conduct ourselves, we realize that the kind of person we are supposed to be is one that was created in God's image. We should consider ourselves capable of justice, kindness, compassion, goodness, love, and all sorts of other positive characteristics and qualities. We are, in essence, supposed to be *do-gooders*. In Hebrew there is a unique term called the *Yetzer Tov,* which, loosely translated, refers to what we might call the *inclination to do goodness.* The ancient sages considered this model to teach us the importance of allowing our conscience to direct our behavior.

Of course, what would a *Yetzer Tov* be without a negative counterpart—the *Yetzer Ra*—the inclination to do evil; the evil inclination within each one of us. This duality stems from a verse in Genesis 2:7, which states that God formed (*vayyitzer*) man. The spelling of this word is unusual in that it uses a doubling of letters (the double "y" in the English spelling) instead of one that we would expect. The rabbis inferred that these two letters stand for the word *Yetzer*, which, by itself means "impulse" or "inclination." The existence of two Yetzers, therefore, must infer that humanity was created with two impulses: a good impulse and an evil impulse.

Since both impulses were given to us by God, neither should be considered bad, because all things created by God are, inherently good. In the Talmud (a great corpus of rabbinic commentary dating from approximately 300 B.C.E.–500 C.E.), we learn that without the Yetzer Ra (which they call the desire to satisfy personal needs) we would not build a house, marry, have children, or do business. However, the Ra can lead to wrongdoing when it is not kept in check by the Tov. There is nothing inherently wrong with hunger, but it can lead you to steal food. There is nothing inherently wrong with sexual desire, but it can lead to rape, adultery, incest, or other sexual perversions.

The Yetzer Ra is generally seen as something internal, not an external force acting on a person. The idea that "the devil made me do it" is not in line with a majority of thought in Judaism. There are those who equate Ra with Satan, another often misunderstood concept within Judaism. In Jewish philosophy, Satan is best understood as a personification of our own selfish desires, rather than the idea that our selfish desires are caused by some external force.

In the end, we must come to understand and accept that responsibility to act according to the Ra or the Tov rests plainly within each one of us. That is at the heart of what we call free will. We all have the ability to make our own choice, and we will all be held responsible for the choices we make.

Chapter Response by Pastor Grimbol

In this chapter I found myself concurring with most of what Rabbi Astrachan had to say, but I felt that my Christian faith offers a sharply different focus. Christianity and Judaism both do agree that we tend to waste an enormous amount of time, energy, and money on worrying about appearances. I suspect that both faith traditions encourage us to overcome our tendency to beat up on ourselves or to measure ourselves by impossible cultural standards. Both faiths recognize that God tells us we are enough, while the world shouts that we are not.

So where is the difference? I suspect that it is in the use of the word *perfection*. I think that Jesus offers an understanding of perfection as achieving wholeness. Paul was quite clear that it was his religious perfectionism that became his chief sin. He spent so much time trying to follow the Law that he had little spirit left to offer the mercy and love that was supposedly the essence of that Law. The Law seeks perfection. Grace seeks wholeness.

The Christian faith would hold it as crucial that we learn to accept our true selves. Just as we are called to accept others, we are asked to be merciful in our dealings with our own souls. We must accept our flaws and failings, claim our grudges and greed, and know the truth of our own doubts and fears. A whole person is not one who has eliminated all imperfections, but one who has embraced them with grace. It is the grace that will do the erasing. Jesus Christ, as the mediator of that grace, heals our sinful ways.

I think of perfect in terms of being pure. Perfection requires the removal of the stain of sin. To pursue perfection is to work at rubbing out that stain. Wholeness is not about pursuit, it is about reception. Wholeness receives grace, and grace alone creates the clean heart. Perfectionism sets up a religious paradigm that we are never enough. Wholeness affirms that it is only in faith that we come to know we are more than enough.

God created everything. This includes mosquitoes, malignant cells, volcanoes, and phlegm. Remember, it was God who put the snake in the Garden of Eden. We may view many aspects of Creation as imperfect, but in God's eyes the perfection is found only in the wholeness.

God created the whole package, zits and hemorrhoids included. Wholeness declares that the mystery remains secure and supreme. Perfectionism whispers that we may some day unravel all the answers.

Jeff speaks eloquently of the need for honoring parents. Christianity is paradoxical on this matter. Certainly, as Christians we are taught to respect our parents, even honor them, but we are also warned that a break from parents is a spiritual requirement of following Jesus. This is a truly offensive assertion of Christianity. Why would Jesus go so far as to tell us that we will need to hate our families in order to follow him?

Jesus understood the huge risk of following. Parents want their children to be safe, secure, and successful. Jesus knew that a life of faith would often be dangerous, offensive to others, and bring more persecution than praise. Jesus knew full well that he was asking his followers to go in a direction opposite to the one advocated by the culture. Jesus accepts that following him will not yield power, position, popularity, or possessions. Following him will most likely lead only to ridicule and rejection. The offensiveness of this commentary remains difficult for most Christians to swallow.

Where I found greatest agreement with Rabbi Astrachan was in his explanation of the Hebrew concepts of Yetzer Tov, the inclination to do goodness, and Yetzer Ra, the inclination to do evil. Here I see an excellent model for wholeness, as Jeff affirms that we contain both impulses. I also fully agree that these impulses are the result of our choices and actions, and not the promptings of Satan. It would be easy to pawn the Holocaust off on the actions of Satan, but to do so gets us off a hook on which we need to hang. The hook makes us bleed, and the bleeding remembers. The remembering restores our soul, and the soul reclaims the faith that will make sure it never happens again.

For my Christian faith, Satan has power only in symbolic terms. I, too, have wrestled with Satan in the desert. I, too, know the inclination to do evil. Satan may help me flesh out the meaning of my inclination to turn my back on God, but I have never thought of Satan as being a presence of the power or reality of Jesus. Satan, for me, is an effective symbol for the lust or wrongdoings that can tempt us on a daily basis. As a symbol, Satan helps me know the gospel truth of who I am and who others may choose to be. As an entity who makes me do things, Satan is no more than an effective spiritual scapegoat.

I would add that I am confident that Rabbi Astrachan and I would probably share many of the same convictions about the uses of words *wholeness* and *perfection*. My point was simply to stress the focus I believe is central to the Christian faith.

PART 2

THE WHAT QUESTIONS

What questions root us in time. They ground us in reality. They are the foundation upon which we build our daily lives. What questions are ghosts from our past that haunt us. What happened? What was I thinking? What was the point of that? What have I learned from this experience? What impact has my family had on my life? What have been my greatest failures? My greatest achievements? What questions examine the past. They offer an effective means of evaluation. They offer us closure. They free us to move on. They enable us to let go.

What questions inform the future. What will I be like? What will the world be like? What is my calling? What do I hope to accomplish? What will be my legacy? What questions wrestle with the Goliath of tomorrow. What questions fell the giant by slinging the question at a vulnerable spot—right between the eyes. What questions honestly and courageously confront the future. What questions give faith to the future. They bring tomorrow down to manageable size. Most of all, what questions locate us in the present. What now?

What is the point? What is the truth? What is my purpose? These are questions that can only be answered with our lives. These are the questions that serve up the day on a plate. What questions invite us to life's banquet. They are its menu. They take our order. They serve our selection. What questions ask only that we eat, devour, chew, taste, savor, swallow, and digest the day.

WHAT IS THE POINT?

Pastor William R. Grimbol

"What is the point?" is an old, old, old question. It is a question born from feeling that life itself has grown old. This inquiry emanates from a spiritually parched throat. It is the result of a soul on empty. It sounds as if it is half yawn and half scream.

I believe we all hit a bottom where this question echoes. Every human at some point puzzles over the point and purpose of existence, the rhyme or reason, the meaning or value. The question is unavoidable. It does not beg to be asked—it demands. We seldom choose to ask it. We are consumed by the question itself. This is a question that can drive us crazy, and we are not even the driver. The question is our chauffeur. Only with this driver, we go where it wants.

A wide range of life experiences or events can force us to confront this question. The most common are ...

+ Being physically exhausted.

+ Being emotionally spent.

+ Being spiritually burned-out.

+ The loss of a dream.

+ The loss of a loved one.

+ The loss of one's health.

+ The loss of one's youth.

+ A major crisis, disappointment, or failure.

+ A major shock or trauma.

+ Facing addiction.

+ Facing chronic stress or pain.

- ✦ Facing illness.
- ✦ Facing mortality.

"What is the point?" is a question that rides piggyback on one or more of these experiences or events. Once the question is asked, there is no turning back. Because there is no clear, simple answer, we must patiently wait until the experience or event has run its course. While we're waiting, we also may locate a partial or temporary answer.

One thing is certain. This question wrestles us to the mat and pins us there. We need to accept our position graciously. The question has already claimed victory. That is what this chapter is about, asking ourselves about the point of our lives. We will look at both the experience of despair, life without a point, and life lived to the fullest, which is a life with myriad points.

Finding Meaning

"'Everything is meaningless,' says the teacher, 'utterly meaningless!'

"What do people get for all their hard work? Generations come and go, but nothing really changes. The sun rises and sets and hurries around to rise again. The wind blows south and north, here and there, twisting back and forth, getting nowhere. The rivers run into the sea, but the sea is never full. Then the water returns again to the rivers and flows again to the sea.

"Everything is so weary and tiresome! No matter how much we see, we are never satisfied. No matter how much we hear, we are not content.

"History merely repeats itself. It has all been done before.

"Nothing under the sun is truly new. What can you point to that is new? How do you know it didn't already exist long ago? We don't remember what happened in those former times. And in future generations, no one will remember what we are doing now."

—Ecclesiastes 1:1–11

Ecclesiastes is a preacher. This sermon would not make him a popular preacher. It is a sermon that is remarkably candid. Ecclesiastes is addressing his spiritual pain. He questions the point and purpose of life. He claims his frustration with life's predictability and routine. He gives voice to his despair. Ecclesiastes rips out his heart and offers it to us. He does not hold back. Even as a man of faith, he acknowledges the struggle to find meaning in his existence.

This is the kind of sermon that is rarely preached. It is a risky topic. It is hard for a preacher to affirm his or her own doubts. It is even harder to be so brutally honest—so vulnerable and human. Ironically, it is also the kind of sermon that we need to hear. It is one with which we can easily identify. The message resonates with us all. We all have known those days when he have dreaded the dawn and cursed the dusk. I give thanks for the gift of Ecclesiastes spiritual candor.

POINTLESS

The past year and a half of my life has been a demolition derby. On April 1, 2000, my father died after a long, bleak bout with Alzheimer's. On April 18, 2000, my wife, Christine, died tragically following complications from surgery. In August, my mother's wet macular degeneration left her legally blind. In October, my sister had a hip replacement, followed by a heart attack in early 2001. I began dating a lovely woman in the spring of 2001; she suffered a heart attack in July.

I began to feel like Job. Even a member of my youth group asked, "Geez, Pastor Bill, maybe you need to rethink this God and faith stuff." I knew what he meant. "What is the point?" is the spiritual equivalent of rethinking your whole belief system—especially your trust in God.

My life had been happily going one direction. I was confident of my path and step. I knew and enjoyed the scenery. I had memorized the potholes. I was traveling at a pace I could handle and with folks I enjoyed. "Merrily we roll along" was a suitable mantra for my life.

Then, suddenly, boom. My life is moving in a whole new direction. I don't know the road. I have no map. There is nobody I truly trust to ask for directions. The road is not only bumpy but dangerous. Most of the time I just pull off to the side and weep. I pound my fists and yell. I am lost. Hopelessly lost.

For the past 18 months, each and every day has been haunted by the question "What is the point?" I cannot escape it. I have learned to live with it, like tinnitus or a remembered melody. I can hear it each time I see my son's far-off stare as he recalls a magical moment with his mother. Every day there is a sound, smell, taste, or view that yanks the question back to center stage.

My son recently said to me that he felt as though he had been working on a jigsaw puzzle his whole life, and then some stranger came in and threw it up in the air. He now looks at all the little pieces scattered all over the floor but just doesn't have the energy to put it back together. He just stares at the pieces. Some days he feels like trying, but then a thick fog settles in. He cannot see a thing. He can't move. So he just sits there and waits. What is the point?

THE POINT IS LIFE

On April 18, 2001, I picked up my son, Justin, and his girlfriend, Dani, from the Buxton School in Williamstown, Massachusetts. We were to drive to Grafton, Vermont, to place my wife's ashes on the land where we had hoped to build a home for our retirement. Justin suddenly asked, "How far is it to Burtonsville?"

I told him it was about the same distance as to Vermont. Then I asked, "Is that where you really want to go?" Justin's moist eyes said a resounding "Yes."

Burtonsville was a vacation spot for Christine's family and our own. It is a miniscule village on the Schoharie Creek, just 30 miles west of Albany, New York. The three of us have trekked to Burtonsville every summer for almost a decade. We stayed in a TV-less, phone-less, air-conditioning–less cottage that Justin called the "Little House on the Prairie." We spent our days at the creek, swimming in the pools, tubing in the gentle rapids, or sitting under mini-waterfall formed by ledges of rock, and filled our evenings with board games, popcorn, stargazing, and listening to my wife reading Agatha Christie mysteries. The only time we ventured up the mile-long path to the road was to head to Gibby's Diner for some home cooking.

So once again, we were headed for Burtonsville. The memories were soon flickering before our eyes, the emotions raw and anxious. The silence of the car ride was deafening until Dani asked, "What is the place like?" Justin explored aloud for her every nook and cranny of his memory of this sacred spot.

We easily found the path to the little house, then bumped and wound our way down the dirt road, noting how the cathedral of trees overhead made the late-afternoon light shimmer. The stone wall marked the opening to the clearing, and there stood the small white house and the freshly painted red barn. We got out of the car and stopped to listen for the creek. The water was rushing. The creek could be savage in spring.

Christine was everywhere. Justin was ecstatic. All year he had complained of not remembering things clearly. Here everything was crystal clear. We could hear her laugh. Her voice still filled the bedrooms with mystery. We could see her at her rock, reading in the sun for an hour, swimming for 15 minutes, sitting under the falls for 10 more, then back to the book. We could smell the popcorn. We could taste the ears of sweet corn. It was all so strangely crisp and fresh.

We walked the perimeters of the property and peeked inside the house and barn. We took the trail to the shore. Her rock was almost submerged, but Justin and I went out as far as we could. I handed him the plastic bag that held his mother's ashes. We hugged. He emptied the contents into the swirling water. We watched it slither away. We wept. Dani graciously gave us space.

As we watched the ashes move downstream, we noticed the roar of Buttermilk Falls, a spot Christine often mentioned when recalling her childhood. Justina, the aunt who raised Christine, would pack her a hobo lunch—a lunch held by a kerchief at the end of a stick—for her journey to the falls.

The falls were roaring. The sun was setting, and the lighting made the falls look like poured gold. The whole scene was momentarily gilded by this liquid light. We were breathless from the beauty of the moment. Neither Justin nor I saw it as a miracle or even a sign. We saw it, simply, as life. Even in the midst of such gaping pain and grief, life defied us not to notice its magnificence. The three of us, speechless, took in the scene and found an answer: "*Life* is the point!"

Life. Nothing more. Nothing less. Just that simple. Just that eternally complex. It was life that called us back to life that day. One year to the day after Christine's death, life called. The message was both gentle and piercing. We could not get enough. We wanted more. We wanted more magical moments that would take our breath away.

I'm not sure who delivered the message—God, angelic Christine, or nature—but I do know that we moved on from that place. We left transformed. We were just a bit more alive.

THE POINT IS LIVING FULLY

Everyone wants a full life. In fact, I suspect that the first answer a majority of folks might give to the question "What is the point?" would be "to live life to the fullest." But what does that mean? Full of what? What will fill life with meaning? With value? With hope?

Well, if we are honest, we know what leaves us empty:

- ✦ A life spent collecting more and more *stuff.*

- ✦ A life spent worshipping money.

- ✦ A life spent trying to be perfect.

- ✦ A life spent trying to please other people.

- ✦ A life spent stressed out by doing too much.

- ✦ A life without a soul.

The rat race is still won by rats. The ladder of success has no rungs in the eyes of God. And no, you cannot take it with you.

As a minister I have sat by a good many deathbeds. Not once have I heard anyone nearing the end of their time on Earth utter the words, "I wish I had more time to work ... to buy more stuff ... to make more money." Always, the regrets are not having spent enough time with loved ones, or the failure to pursue a dream or live out a calling. The final longing is most often about wishing one had paid greater and earlier attention to one's deepest yearnings. Somehow, folks at the end of their days recognize that what they were dying to do or be—they were literally dying to do or be.

A full life has little to do with *doing*. We live in a culture addicted to doing. We are what we do. The busier we are, the more important we are (or we think we are). If you ask a person how they are, they don't tell you. Instead, they tell you *what* they are doing. TV commercials tell us that if we have an acidic stomach, it is a sign of our success. Although people complain about stress, they feel guilty about relaxing. The person who calls himself a workaholic does so with pride.

A man in my congregation in Milwaukee came in for an appointment in a highly agitated state. I asked him what was wrong. He hesitated, and then muttered "Nothing." I told him it was obvious that something was bothering him. Finally, he told me that he had gone for a walk that morning and had sat on a pier off Lake Michigan for over an hour. I told him I couldn't understand why this caused him such anxiety. He then said with clarity, "But what if somebody saw me?" Sadly, it dawned on me. He was the president of a company. Why would a CEO be sitting on a pier?

We discussed his anxiety. He admitted his fear of being seen doing nothing. He was worried that someone might even think he was readying himself for a suicidal jump. How sad. How demanding.

What happens to the human spirit if it is not allowed to relax?

What a hidden stress to feel that one cannot stop and stare at the sea. How tragic that doing so would be thought of as wasting time. Though he was not doing anything of importance to the culture, he was being exactly who God created him to be.

A full life is about *being*. In the days following the World Trade Center and Pentagon attacks, people have wanted to do something in response. Most of us could find little to do, but we could be a presence and a pocketbook filled with mercy. We could be good neighbors to one another. Kinder. Gentler. More positive. We could be good parents and offer our children hugs and tender words of hope. We could be faithful people, giving greater discipline to our worship and prayer life. We could be good citizens, prayerfully supportive of our leaders and troops.

Being is what fills a day. Being is what gives a day radiance and remembrance. Being is what carves our initials in life's holy hide. Here are some ways of being that I believe lead to a full life:

- ✦ Be present in the present, and to the present—life.
- ✦ Be aware of the kingdom in your midst.
- ✦ Be attentive to all that is beautiful.
- ✦ Be genuine and true to your self.
- ✦ Be honest—mean what you say, and say what you mean.
- ✦ Be kind—it matters so very much.
- ✦ Be positive—it makes a world of difference.
- ✦ Be compassionate—it is critical that we feel, and feel deeply.
- ✦ Be creative—it is vital that we think.
- ✦ Be courageous—to pray for strength, not for an easy life.

- Be forgiving—the key to all intimacy; the path that leads out of isolation.

- Be holy—not holier than thou, not a holy roller, but however you define holy living. Live as though life were indeed sacred.

Being, far more than doing, is what is remembered. It is our being that leaves our legacy or makes our mark on the world. It is our being that is eternal. All that is done will fade away, but the spirit with which it is done lasts forever.

I have noted in more than 25 years of ministry that whenever someone tells me they have been *doing* nothing, that they have often *been* everything God would hope them to be. Doing nothing usually means taking walks or naps, reading or painting or puttering in the garden, cooking or cleaning or listening to music, writing a letter, soaking in a tub, or chatting with friends. Doing nothing often frees us to receive the gift of the day. Doing nothing enables us to rejoice, to know that we are not in charge, to wave the white flag of surrender to what God has planned.

THE POINT IS LEARNING

If life is the point, being alive is the purpose. Being alive is more than breathing in and out. It is more than just showing up. Being alive is about being aware, conscious of what you feel and think and believe, noticing the world outside and the intricate world within ourselves, and paying attention to the lessons life is teaching. Life is our tutor. The key to being alive is to be good students.

It is impossible not to feel alive when we learn. Learning activates every aspect of our being. Learning sparks the heart, ignites the mind, and sets the soul aflame. Learning focuses our attention. There can be no learning without open eyes, ears, heart, and mind. To learn is to actively receive. What we receive is the wisdom of the universe—the word of God.

There are few experiences more deadly than stagnation. To stop learning is to cease to grow and mature. I suspect that maturation and spirituality are one and the same, so, in effect, to refuse to learn is to turn one's back on God. Isn't that life's most basic choice? To learn and grow or to stagnate and die?

Is there anything more boring than talking to someone who thinks they have all the answers? Why? Because the assumption is that they have nothing left to learn. The mind that is eager to learn is exciting and enthusiastic. Conversation with such a soul is playful and often exhilarating.

Equally dull is to talk with someone who refuses to grow, whose stories remain the same, whose conversation is full of idle gossip. The onslaught of TV talk shows would make one think that we Americans love witty banter, when in fact the opposite is true. These shows are anesthetizing. At best, they make one feel better only because the lives we hear about are so much worse than our own. These shows are, for the most part, stocked with guests who seldom share an original, insightful, or inspirational thought. The talk is dull because no thoughts are exchanged: Each talking head hears only its own talk. *No one is learning anything!*

Learning is not about earning degrees. Common sense speaks with eloquence and authority, rooted in the basic elements of daily life. The learning of which I speak is the acquisition of wisdom. Wisdom requires openness and attentiveness. Wisdom is the result of receptivity, of being a sponge, of being a magnet, of being a vessel into which God can pour. Learning is knowing that we were all created to be poets, philosophers, artists, and mystics.

Truly, that is the mark of God—the imprint of the divine spirit on the human spirit.

THE POINT IS LOVING

1 Corinthians states that "There are three things that will endure—faith, hope, love—and the greatest of these is love."

What the world needs now is love, sweet love. Love is all we need. Love, love, love, love. Christians, this is your calling. Songs endlessly sing of the virtues of love. Poems speak of love's rewards and ravages. Plays, books, ballets, symphonies, and paintings all extol the centrality of love to our lives. Jesus himself is referred to as the Author of Love, and the gospels summarized are as a radical call to loving.

The fact that love is the point of life is best evidenced by those who do not find it. Without love, the soul withers and the spirit fades. Bitterness sets in, as does the potential for violence or abuse, the disdain for life, and the disregard for others. The first domino of evil is often the denial of love. Without love, life goes flat—like a flat line on a heart monitor.

As adults, most of us know that love is the key. Love provides us with the understanding that grants security, the passion that provides inspiration, the tenderness that heals, the forgiveness that restores, the joy that frees us to live with zest, the intimacy that enables us to stop running from both life and death, and the peace that creates the calm we need to go on. The older we get, the more we know of love's importance and intricacies. Love is hard work, yet love is also delicate work that requires a surgeon's touch.

Erich Fromm wrote a magnificent book titled *The Art of Loving*. I still consider it to be the wisest book on loving that I have read.

The premise of Fromm's book is simple: Loving is an art. We are artists. God equips us with everything we need—the canvas, the paints, and the brushes. Our parents may have been excellent or horrid art teachers, but our assignment remains the same: Paint.

What I found so valuable in Fromm's masterpiece was his focus on the disciplines required to become a great artist. With Fromm as my inspiration, here are the disciplines I have found to be most crucial to the art of loving:

- Endless hours of practice
- Gaining insight as to the immense value of perspective
- Finding the right teachers and subjects
- The willingness to embrace one's mistakes
- The importance of knowing one's natural talents and limitations
- The willingness to keep at it, even when all hope seems lost
- Knowing the importance of matting with covenant and framing with forgiveness
- Thinking of yourself as an artist and being willing to put your signature on all you create

Marc Chagall once said, "In our life there is a single color, as on an artist's palette, which provokes the meaning of life and art. It is the color of love." The point is life. What gives life its color is love.

THE POINT IS LEARNING HOW TO DIE

I showed my confirmation class a watercolor painting I had done. It was a simple piece of sailboats on a silvery sea. The kids liked it. Then I added a bright white mat to the painting. The kids admitted it made a lovely difference. Then I added a second mat of Prussian blue and a silver frame. I got a few "oohs" and "aahs" and one "wow." I asked the kids what had changed. They told me that the painting seemed deeper, that perspective had been added. They commented that the painting appeared brighter, especially the white sails. One youth said, "It just seems more alive now."

I think of death as life's mat and frame. It grants life a richness and depth. It adds vitality to all of life's colors. It gives life perspective. Death is what borders our days. Each day we are living, we are at the same time dying. To live well is intimately connected with not only facing death, but embracing it. A full life cannot be had if we are running from dying. A life filled with learning requires an acceptance of the limits of the human mind and of time itself. A life full of loving is impossible for the person who cannot risk the reality of loss.

As simple, even stupid, as it may sound, death will not go away. It is a permanent fixture on the human landscape. We must claim the truth that death is an expression of God's creation, a movement of the pulse of the Holy Spirit. Coming to terms with death is critical to maturation, at the core of wisdom, and at the heart of true faith.

For Christians, it is required that we know death, even death on a cross. We are mandated to understand why Good Friday is good. Although we don't have to be excited by the prospect, neither should we approach it with dread. I suppose it is fair to say that my Christian faith asks me to go gently into that good night. My faith professes a God who was with me before I was born, is intertwined with my life, and waits to welcome me home in the beyond. Although the conditions of that beyond are never established, I trust that it is a peace that exceeds my ability to understand it.

I am told by scripture that death has no sting. There is nothing to fear. If my faith is full, death poses no threat. Yes, there will be sadness and loss; even Jesus wept at the loss of his friend Lazarus. Yes, there is the trauma of transition. Yes, death at times comes as a brutal swipe, shocking us with its ruthless indifference. But no, there is nothing in death that can vanquish life, not one thing that diminishes the promise of eternal life. Eternity—not endless time, but the absence of time—is the promise of the Christian faith, the defining hope, the eastering offered by Easter.

How do we learn how to die? We do so by not avoiding the topic or the reality. We get to know the subject. We talk about it. We study it. We frequent its presence. We let ourselves think about it, reflect upon it, and feel its touch. We acquire insight. We gain understanding. We receive wisdom. Like all areas of learning, openness and receptivity remain paramount.

So What Is the Point?

This a fun question. It is enjoyable to ask, and exciting to answer. It is also demanding. It makes us think and feel and entertain the mystery. It is a good question. It is important that it be asked on a regular basis. Our answers will change as we change, as life changes, or maybe as God changes the answers for us.

Here are a few responses to this question that you can ponder:

+ The point of life is life.
+ The point of life is to accept all of life as a gift—with gratitude.
+ The point of life is to be fully alive, fully present, with open eyes, ears, hearts, and mind.

- The point of life is to have a full life, full of being the person you were created to be.

- A full life is not full of material stuff, but the stuff of the spirit.

- The spirit of God calls us to lives of honesty, integrity, dignity, and maturity.

- The spirit of God calls us to learn, grow, change, become, be transformed, be wise, be holy.

- The spirit of God calls us to live to love, and to love to live.

- The spirit of God finds ultimate expression in the life of Jesus, the Author of Love.

- Our love of life must embrace death as a natural and normal aspect of our existence. There is nothing to fear.

- The resurrected Jesus holds forth the promise of eternal life.

- Resurrection is not immortality. Resurrection means we really do die. We go to the grave, dead as a doornail. It is God who gives us back our lives.

- Life constantly reveals the nature of eternity.

- The fullness of time, life, and eternity is revealed at the point of death.

CHAPTER RESPONSE BY RABBI ASTRACHAN

Pastor Grimbol has decidedly given us great things to consider regarding the importance of our existence. In this chapter, Pastor Grimbol remarks that *being* is of great significance—our very existence is what God expects of us. While this is certainly an important part of who we are, I would like to suggest furthering this notion—that *being* is one important component that makes us who we are but only serves as one of a multitude of the pieces of the jigsaw puzzle of our lives.

According to Jewish thought, *being* allows us the opportunity to fulfill a particular mission. That, really, is what our lives are for—not for ourselves so much as for others. When we have lived out our allotted days, others must be able to look back on our lives and say, with certainty, that we have made a difference. That is, what have we *done* with the time God gave us? Did we squander it away for our own selfish tasks, or did we use our talents and our mind to improve this world in some way, for some other person?

How we approach life demands our attention to the 613 *mitzvot* (commandments) given by God. By these rules for living are we to govern our lives. Fulfilling them, then, gives us a certain strategy which, when followed well, leads us to not only *be* but also to *do*. It is a widely held Jewish belief that our legacy is left through the actions which created the person who we were known to be. Did we perform acts of kindness, or did we willfully wrong others? Did we create a warm and loving home, or did we beat down the spirits of those who trusted us most? Did we raise up the hopes and dreams of others, or did we act selfishly in order to climb the corporate ladder? Did we pick flowers, or did we plant them?

The actions we undertake in life are the things we will be remembered by and that will live on in the memories of those we have left behind. We have only truly lived when our legacy of action is so strong that when we are gone, people are so moved to act in righteous ways on our account.

WHAT IS TRUTH?

Pastor William R. Grimbol

What is truth? What a huge question! What an enormous field of investigation. Isn't such an inquiry futile? Doesn't the question beg a million other questions? Do we dare to answer? How could we be so grandiose? Why would we even bother trying?

Why? Because it is such a good question. A really good question demands to be asked. It makes us think hard. It makes us feel deeply. It makes us believe. A good question is alive. It is alive with possibility and choice. It is flexible and creative. It makes us feel alive. It takes us on a journey.

In this chapter we will look at ways to locate the truth. We will examine the experience of finding a truth. We will explore the mystery of how silence speaks, and why stories are frequently coated in the gospel truth. Most of all, we will see how the truth makes itself known. How it reveals itself to us. Truth is not passive. Truth seeks us out. It is looking as hard for us, as we are for it.

WHAT TRUTH IS NOT

Like all good questions, one is wise to begin by answering in the negative—what truth is not. I would contend that ...

+ Truth is not fact.
+ Truth is not fixed or rigid.
+ Truth is not a noun.
+ Truth is not confined by time or place.
+ Truth is not a possession.
+ Truth is not private property.

- Truth is not to be grasped.
- Truth is not to be imposed on others.
- Truth is not to be used to harm anyone.
- Truth is not finished.

As is the point of the exercise, putting forward what we suspect truth is *not* magnifies what we believe truth to *be:*

- Truth is faith-based fiction—the gospel truth.
- Truth is flexible and fluid.
- Truth is a verb.
- Truth is eternal.
- Truth is the presence of God.
- Truth is the experience of the Grace of God.
- Truth is heartfelt.
- Truth pricks the conscience.
- Truth keeps maturing.
- Truth is the movement of the Holy Spirit.

The quest for the truth is invigorating. The adventure itself is inspiring. The hot pursuit of truth leaves us sweating with satisfaction. I have come to cherish those friends who share the chase. I love to swap stories about the hunt. The truth does indeed set you free.

On the other hand, there is nothing duller than the pompous soul who believes he owns the truth. Those who talk as if they have truth in their hip pocket leave me yawning for less. Facts make lousy stories. Folks who claim the truth as private property make rotten storytellers. The difference between a lecture and a good story is infinity. To be a captive listener to a know-it-all gives new meaning to the term *slavery.*

TRUTH KEEPS QUIET

I went to New York City two weeks after the twin towers tragedy. The quiet was eerie. It was also quite pleasant. The big city seemed to have become a village. Folks nodded hello. There was a bit of chatter but no yelling. Not one honk. As a fire department funeral procession moved down Fifth Avenue, the scurrying crowds stopped and stared in silence. For 15 bloated minutes, one could feel the reverence in the air. I could hear the flapping of the seagulls overhead. When the truth is near, even a brutally painful truth, it is human nature to be quiet. Like a good host, quiet greets and receives the truth.

We live in a noisy world. Nonstop television programming, news, and music channels, music as we shop in malls and supermarkets, headsets for when we fly or jog or drive—noise is piped in everywhere. Any resemblance it had to music is lost in the onslaught. Noise is hard to escape.

Americans appear to mistrust silence. I recently walked the picturesque streets of my hometown, Sag Harbor, New York. It was August, and the streets were jammed with folks trying to capture a bit of the country. I would venture a guess that well over half the people I passed were talking on cell phones. Noise must make us feel important, as if we're part of the hustle and bustle. How sad that folks cannot come to the country without dragging along the racket.

What is it that we fear in silence?

+ The sound of our very own thoughts.
+ The sound of our needs and wants and wishes.
+ The sound of our longings.
+ The sound of our yearnings.
+ The sound of our cravings for forgiveness.

- ✦ The sound of our soul asking good questions.
- ✦ The sound of our God providing momentary answers.
- ✦ The sound of the truth.

Although we tend to use noise as a means of locating ourselves, the truth is that noise keeps everything at a distance. We lose our selves. We orbit our world. We are detached from our lives. The noise becomes an effective means of removing ourselves from life.

Noise—the sound barrier to the Word of God. Most of my mornings begin with a ritual: large coffee with cream from Seven Eleven, a bagel, *no* newspaper, and a brisk walk around the perimeters of Trout Pond, which is about three quarters of a mile. For whatever reason, there is never anyone else there. I can hear the wind, birds, or the scamper of a squirrel or deer, but all else is silence. Beginning my day in silence sets a healthy, if not holy, perspective. I have framed the day in the truth that all is grace.

Each night as I return from work on Shelter Island, I ride the ferry. Most evenings I get out of my car to see the sky and again listen to the silence. It is only a three-minute ride, yet it often feels as full as my eight-, nine-, or ten-hour day. The day is wrapped up with the same awareness with which it began—that all is gift.

Silence invites the truth. Silence searches for the truth. Silence seizes the truth. When we are truly silent, when we can hear stones shout, we are dumbstruck. No, we did not go suddenly stupid; we are just wise enough to keep our mouths shut to hear the Word of God. The silence is sacred. It forms the canyon walls off which God's expressions of love can be heard to echo.

TRUTH TAKES OUR BREATH AWAY

I have been a photo-taking fanatic for the past five years. I create photo cards for use as gifts at my church. I am not a professional photographer, but I have a good camera and a good eye. I leave all processing and developing to others. I just love chasing beauty around on a regular basis.

This morning, before writing these pages, I took a leisurely drive along the Mohawk Mountain Trail in western Massachusetts. The autumn light was flickering with fast scudding clouds, and the early October foliage was as breathtaking as always. I drove to a favorite overlook and stepped outside into the nippy frosted air. The mountainside was ablaze in color. The red-splashed oranges were at their brief peak. As I knew it would, the view took my breath away. I snapped a whole roll of film.

When beauty takes our breath away, we die a little. We die in knowing that the view cannot ever be fully grasped. We die in the awareness that our lives are as fleeting as the seasons. We die in the consciousness that we cannot imagine not having just one more look, one more chance to see, one more opportunity to behold such grandeur. And yet, tucked snugly into the bed of beauty is the revelation that what's beyond will be grander still. The moment falls fast asleep, and we move on.

To behold beauty is to stare in to the eyes of God. As is the case with all eyes, they are our best means of seeing the truth. Look me in the eye. The eyes reveal it all—honesty, fear, courage, love, passion, compassion, forgiveness, and being possessed of a dream. The eyes tell the truth. The eyes of God do as well.

Truth Loves a Good Mystery

I have a children's club called Imagine. It is for first, second, and third graders. I use the arts as a means of introducing the kids to what they think, feel, and believe. We may do a watercolor painting of our fears or a collage of freedom or a clay sculpture of heaven. It is always delightful to teach kids without the pressures of tests or grades or competing with each other. All children start with an A. They also finish with an A. All they need do is be present and create—like we adults before we were brainwashed into believing that life was an endurance test that nobody passes.

On one warm Saturday last spring, I took the kids to the beach to look for shells. The kids quickly found a treasure chest full of all sizes and shapes and coral colors. One little boy, Shane, took notice of the big fluffy clouds that exploded overhead. I remembered how as a child I loved to look for animals and faces and objects in the clouds, and so I invited the kids to do the same. Twenty-three kids, two moms, one dad, and a pastor laid down on the sand, with eyes gazing heavenward.

I'm not sure why, but I always see Abe Lincoln in the clouds. Maybe because clouds make such great beards and top hats. The children were far more original. Rachel saw a camel eating popcorn. Ricky pointed out five big toes. Martina saw ghosts playing ring-around-the-rosy. One mom saw Jesus—I am afraid she was working way to hard on that one. The dad saw his grandmother's lap, and by the way he said it, I was quite sure he now sat upon it. Soon our cloud-viewing turned to cloud-questioning. "Why did God make clouds?" I asked. "Because he got bored with blue," Michelle said without missing a beat. "Why did God make the sky blue?" I retorted. "He didn't. Not all the time. Some days it looks like mud or wet clay," responded Josh. For the next 20 minutes we bounced from one question to another. It was like being wonderfully trapped inside a pinball machine, lights flashing, gongs sounding, racking up points. Delightful.

"But Pastor Bill, what is the real answer?" Shane inquired. The ball rolled between the flipping levers and into the pit. "I don't know," I said calmly. "But you are supposed to know, Pastor Bill. You are the minister," Shane continued. "I know, Shane, but even ministers can't explain life's many, many mysteries." "Good," he said with a grin. I grinned as well. Good is right.

As we mature, the mystery expands. We know more and more and less and less at the very same time. The truth comes to us only in paradoxes: life and death, love and hate, joy and sorrow. All of life is woven together in a checkerboard pattern. Wisdom can only point to the paradox, like watching a sunset or snowfall. Wisdom "oohs" and "aahs" as it beholds a truth tied in a knot, never to be undone, rarely loosened. Paradox. The essence of faith. The core of the Christian faith.

Jesus the human. Christ the divine. Free to obey. First are last. Last are first. Lose your life to find it. Befriend the friendless. Love the enemy. Turn the other cheek. Forgive and forgive and forgive again. Worship and bow down. You shall be as gods. Be disciples. Disciples deny, doubt, and betray him. Good Friday and Easter. Heaven and hell. The first coming and the second. All of my faith is built upon the twin towers—I recognize the choice of image—of truth, the fusion of opposites, words that express the inexpressible.

TRUTH TELLS A GOOD STORY

People remember stories. Stories stimulate the brain. Stories carve their initials on the heart. Stories inspire and ignite the soul. Little stories have big meanings. Simple stories crafted from daily life, manage to put their arms around eternity.

I preach in stories. About 10 years ago I realized that not one person ever said, "Geez, I loved that sermon about Pentecost or
sanctification or the will of God." People primarily commented,
"Do you remember when you told about the time ..." "I could
really relate to that story about ..." "I was so touched when you
shared about how ..." Stories grasp the listeners by the shoulders,
sit them down, and make them listen—with their hearts.

I am going home to Racine, Wisconsin, for Thanksgiving. It will
be my first Thanksgiving at home in 16 years. I can't wait. I am
so excited, as is my son. We both admitted we could hardly wait
to hear all the stories again. The stories of my childhood pranks
and antics continue to delight Justin. My personal favorite is
about how I sold tickets for a dime to see my father, who had
painted himself into a corner of our basement and refused to
come out until it dried. There were others that would be dragged
out of the attics of our memory: Jackie's first boy-girl party and
how the boys stole a $500 bottle of champagne; the day Grandpa
died suddenly of a heart attack and the garage caught fire; my
Uncle Bill's murder in England and the call from Scotland Yard;
my mother's appendicitis attack and how a tissue wall formed to
stop the spread of poison; my wedding; the birth of Justin;
Grandma and Justin's forts underneath the kitchen table; and the
Christmas Eve when 18-month-old Justin crawled under the pews
and up to the pulpit to join his dad. This year there would be
many stories of Christine. Her magic and power. Her huge heart
and laugh. Stories that try to capture the truth of her spirit.

We need to keep track of our stories. Our stories are our piece of
the pie, the dessert of truth. We need to record them: Write them
down in journals and letters, tape them or keep them on video,
tell them again and again, and provide occasions for their telling.
We must not lose them. Our children and grandchildren need

them. They declare roots. They ground us in grace. They define us. They impart the wisdom of the years and the unique perspective of our family—our history—our testament. Don't neglect them. Don't let them fade or wither. Keep them safe. Keep them near.

What stories you ask? That is easy. Whenever you have a lump in your throat, write down why. If you are moved to tears, take note. When life gives you a shiver up and down your spine, make sure you pay attention. Our bodies are telling us when the truth is here. Our job is to listen and record, to take our lives and our stories seriously. We write the fifth gospel with our lives. Our stories are portions of the Word. They may not be factual history, but they contain the gospel truth, which is the core of life, truth, and faith.

TRUTH IS FAITH-FULL

I am not sure who said it, but I agree. Some things have to be believed to be seen.

I saw New York City on a recent visit through the eyes of faith. The sadness was everywhere, like another thick coating of ash. There was fear in some eyes, pain in others, grief in most. Those of Arab descent felt watched. Those of Arab descent were being watched. There was little tension in the air. The flow was smooth. The activity was energetic but slower. The conversations were less animated and loud. The feel was one of closeness and community.

The imprint of evil was upon this place, but so was the hand-mark of God. People were working at being good neighbors. Kinder. Gentler. No shoving arms or words. No running. A holy hush shrouded the city. I was so conscious of the presence of grace. People were cherishing the cool fall air and trying to savor the sweetness of the day. In truth, love was everywhere. New York City was alive with the look of love. Neighbors were trying to love neighbors as they loved their own lives. The love was as obvious as the grief.

Faith allows us to see the truth, to see inside, to check out the beating of its heart. Faith freed me to see inside New York City that day, to see the contorted face of pain as well as the calm face of compassion. People walking through the dark valley of death without fear. People who had dwelt in darkness but still led by a great light. The good folks of New York City picking up their crosses and following.

Faith is full of the sights of truth. Faith envisions the truth. The truth is the vision of a faith believed.

Truth Leaves a Trace

As I boarded the bus to Manhattan, I took note that the driver was probably of Arabic descent. I tried to look like I didn't notice. I think every passenger did the same. As the bus chugged off, our hostess announced, "Hi, my name is Sheila, and our driver today is Abdul." With that, a young man with a pony tail and pink shirt, blurted loudly, "We love you Abdul!" There was a wave of gentle laughter. Abdul came on the speaker system. "I love you, too," and then he laughed.

The mood on that bus was electric. Love had won. We became a tiny village being transported safely by our beloved driver, Abdul. It felt a bit like Christmas on that bus, and did we ever need it right that very minute. Folks were cheery. Conversations and laughter were rampant. People noticed the beauty of the day outside—the cobalt blue sky and the first colors of autumn. I doubt there was a single departing passenger who did not thank Abdul for the joy of the journey.

The truth leaves a trace. It makes a mark on the human heart. It fills the soul with gratitude. It grants a fresh perspective. It unleashed a healthier and holier attitude. The truth was victorious that day. It came with a shout and a laugh. It was announced on a speaker. It said what all truth manages to say ... "I love you, too!"

CHAPTER RESPONSE BY RABBI ASTRACHAN

I'm so glad that Pastor Grimbol talked in this chapter about paradox as a means to faith. I don't think we could call the following paradox "Jewish," per se, but certainly it lends itself to a system of accepted questioning, which Pastor Grimbol also alluded to early in this chapter. During one of my many courses in philosophy at the Hebrew Union College-Jewish Institute of Religion in Cincinnati, Ohio, I was faced with the question, "Is it possible for God to construct a boulder so large and so heavy that even God can not move it?"

Think about it for a moment before you try to come up with a flippant response. Of course, telling you that it is a paradox sort of spoils the punch line—there *is no* answer, only questions. You see, if you believe in an omnipotent God, then surely God can do anything God wants to do. For instance, God could create a rock any size, shape, and weight that he wanted to create. But if God couldn't move it, then God would not be omnipotent. If God couldn't create a rock that he couldn't move, then God wouldn't be omnipotent. If our God is truly omnipotent, then we're stuck!

Pastor Grimbol and I are completely on the same page here: Religious faith is not infallible. It has so many holes in it the Swiss could use it as a model for a variety of cheese. But the holes should not be seen as problematic to our belief. Rather, the holes allow each of us to climb inside, get cozy with our own particular notions, become intimate with God, and ask whatever questions are on our minds. It is only when we *stop* asking the questions that we find ourselves in trouble.

I can't really speak to Christianity, but Judaism demands that we question. Who is God? What does God really want from us? Where will I go after I die? Did God cause the terrorists to invade our country? Does God make children die? As Pastor Grimbol told his student, we certainly have more questions than we have answers. That's okay. Questions keep us interested and intrigued. Would we rather the questions not have to deal with such horror and grief? Of course. But we take comfort in the ability to question, the power to react, and the wisdom to rely on others' strengths to help see us through the difficult times in our lives.

I suggest we all lay down in the sand, look up to the sky, and find whatever we find in our mind's-eye. It just might be God.

What Is My Purpose?

Pastor William R. Grimbol

I hate committees. One main reason is that committees always want to draft a statement of purpose before they do anything. After hours of haggling, the committee finally agrees on some lengthy manifesto as bland as unsalted oatmeal. Worse, every member of the committee knows full well that whatever they do accomplish will have little to do with their declared purpose.

Is it always futile to craft such a statement? It's as though it is worn like a straightjacket; used to smother the spirit; more important than the work itself. A statement of purpose is effective only if it expresses hope. This can usually be accomplished in one or two sentences and crafted in under an hour. Such a statement is simply a restatement of the need that called the committee into being. That is truly all that is needed.

In this chapter I will share those purposes I have found to be of great significance in my own life, as well as those I have heard named most often in my ministry. I would ask you to note that these purposes are not about doing, but about being. Purpose is not a task or job to be done. Purpose is a journey to be lived.

To Be an Individual

Now, what about individuals? Should we each have a statement of purpose? Again, only if it claims our hope. Purpose is not a list of goals. It is not a detailed outline for living. An individual statement of purpose need only be a summation of what matters to us most.

My statement of purpose is plain and simple. It's nothing fancy. It's just what I believe is essential to a life well lived. It is a decent summary. It reflects 52 years of seeing what matters. For today, I would say my purpose is ...

+ To be human.

+ To be my self.

+ To be real—genuine.

+ To be creative.

+ To be holy.

Clear. Simple. Honest. My understanding of the good life.

"Then God looked over all he had made, and he saw that it was excellent in every way. This all happened on the sixth day." (Genesis 1:31) I would hope my life reflects such excellence. That is my perspective on purpose. A personal conviction. A tenet of my faith. My purpose conforms to this belief. As always, you may not see it my way.

To Be Human

I hold these two truths to be self-evident: It is the will of God for humans to be human, and we humans spend a lifetime trying to be anything but human.

What is it that we find so abhorrent about being human? If we're honest, the list could be endless:

+ We often fail.

+ We grow old.

+ We lose many people we love.

+ Many of our dreams die shattered.

+ We get hurt.

+ We get depressed.

- We say and do stupid things.
- We can act like a complete jerk.
- We have bodies that wither.
- We vomit.
- We get diarrhea.
- We may know the heartbreak of psoriasis.
- We are not in charge.
- We can become addicts.
- We catch cold.
- We get green with envy.
- We lie.
- We hold grudges.
- We can be bigots.
- We can be selfish and arrogant.
- We can be fierce critics.
- We can't handle most criticism.
- We are capable of violence.
- We can be wicked.
- We get hopelessly lost.
- We whine and complain.
- We can be so negative.
- We tease.
- We could care less.
- We die—at times horribly.

There. That is enough. Case closed. To be human is to claim our imperfections. It is to know one's flaws. It is to be Peter Pan with the shadow sewn back on. Yes, I could rattle off a slew of our good points, a list of like magnitude, but that is not why we struggle with our humanness. We find humanness unacceptable because it demands the acceptance of our whole selves.

To be human is to give up any notion of perfection. The pursuit of perfection is demoralizing. Perfectionism is a key component in depression and a serious factor in most suicides. Perfectionism is the opponent of creativity, the curse of relationships, the cancer of the soul. Religious perfectionism often leads to self-righteousness and a venomous spirit.

The attempt to be perfect negates the presence of grace. Grace can only be experienced by those wise enough to know they are not God. Grace is the exclusive domain of the human being. When we know our need for healing, the heart's desire for wholeness, the soul's yearning to be God's beloved, then we are truly human. The seeds of God's Grace must be planted on human soil. It is our humanity that makes this soil fertile. It is God's purpose to plant. It is our purpose to blossom.

Jesus was human. He embraced fully being a human being. When he got angry at seeing people ripped off, he tipped over a few tables. When he lost a friend, he wept. When he prayed in the garden, he asked God to take away his pain and suffering.

"Why hast thou forsaken me?" can only be heard as a shout of doubt. Jesus was tempted. He knew loneliness and despair. He felt pain. He thirsted. He died. All that makes us human, Jesus knew.

It is our purpose to be human. God knew what he was doing. We were meant to experience life on God's terms. God the creator; we the creature—those are the terms. Just human? Think about it.

For all our imperfections, we remain the pinnacle piece of God's creative magic. We are 99 percent miracle. The real mystery is just how wonderful we can be.

TO BE YOURSELF

To be yourself. How difficult can that be? Should be instinct. Should come natural. Should flow like the river—right? Nope. Somewhere along the line, perhaps when we're very young, the flow of the river gets dammed. It gets blocked by the need to conform and please others; barricaded behind the need to belong and fit in; clogged by the longing to be safe, popular, perfect.

At some point, our lives make a dramatic shift. We move from living to performance. Our performance is finely crafted by a large backstage crew. Families are in charge of wardrobe and makeup and helping us learn our lines. Sets and lighting are done by friends. The culture serves as producer. Unfortunately, the audience is both director and cast. Though the show may run a long time, it never feels right. The plot is chaotic. There are huge patches during which nothing happens. Most nights we cannot wait for the curtain to come down.

Though we long ago wearied of our performance, we can't seem to figure out how to get off the stage. Then suddenly it dawns on us. We walk. We walk off stage. Maybe for just a moment, a whole day, a month, or a lifetime. The relief is immense. We breathe. We feel life rush in. No spotlight. No lines to remember. No place we have to be. It feels divine.

It is. It *is* divine. It should feel heavenly. Ordinary living that is not a performance is extraordinary. To just be yourself is to be free. Freedom is found in obeying God's singular command to be who God created us to be. Once God is back in charge, the show mercifully closes. The sets are dismantled. The wardrobe is sold. The cast scatters. We are invited to leave. We are sent packing with our lousy reviews in hand—just to remind us that we were not meant to act.

To be yourself begins and ends with questions. The self dares to daily ask:

- ✦ What do I want to do and be today?
- ✦ What are my longings and yearnings?
- ✦ What am I feeling and thinking?
- ✦ What do I believe matters?
- ✦ How can I love?
- ✦ Where can I find love?
- ✦ When will grace tap me on the shoulder?
- ✦ What miracles will I witness?
- ✦ How can I make a difference?
- ✦ What revelations are in store for me?

The true self lets these questions take center stage. The play to be performed is all improvisation. The questions inspire the action as well as dictate the direction. A river of energy begins to flow through the self. The curtain goes up. Before one word is spoken, the audience—God—stands and applauds. The show is a hit. The reviews—God's—are fabulous.

To Be Real

To be real is the sole purpose of the self. What we long for most in life is to reveal who we really are. The problem is that this is also our greatest fear.

To be real is for the self to find its voice and vision. It is the actualization of the human spirit. It is the becoming of the soul.

I recently finished a collection of stories called *Growing Up in Grace*. The stories sought to trace how grace was dabbed onto the surface of my childhood and adolescence, like dots on a connect-the-dots picture. As the adult writer, I connected the dots and hoped to share with my readers the face of God that appeared.

I liked the book. I still do. But then I did a dumb thing. I gave the book to a half dozen people to edit. I then took the six edits and reworked the entire manuscript. I reread it. The reading felt cumbersome, odd. Something was missing. Me. The writing may have improved, but the book had lost its voice and vision.

That is the risk of living—that we will let everyone edit our lives to such an extent that we lose our real selves. Let's face it, the world is loaded with critics. I have to admit that I find it much easier to solve someone else's issues than I do my own.

If we allow ourselves to be shaped and formed by the wishes and wants of others, we wind up looking like a sculpture with six heads.

I had a woman come into my office who had just been named vice president of a major bank. She appeared distraught. I asked her what could possibly be wrong. She told me that she had just realized that being a bank vice president was not her dream, but her father's, and worse yet, she suspected that it had been his hope for the son he never had. There is nothing quite as tragic as living out someone else's dreams.

TO BE CREATIVE

I truly believe that God created us to share in creation. We are, in effect, co-creators. This faith-fact gives me goose bumps. But like all goose bumps, they express both ecstasy and panic. The ecstasy is the result of sharing in such sacred chores. The panic is that the work is done in a room called chaos.

Creation begins in chaos. The context of creative expression is conflict. It is conflict that arouses passion and gets the proverbial juices flowing. It is conflict that pricks the mind, pierces the heart, and empowers the soul. Wind and wing in conflict create soaring. Not all conflict is battle, and not all conflict destroys. Conflict conducted in safety, ringed in grace, can yield more life.

Still, to be creative requires risk. The risk is naming and claiming the conflict. It's entering the turbulence and creating the calm. This is the flightpath of every dream, the requirement of spiritual growth, the essence of maturation. The risk is to go deep. The conflict is the digging—going down inside yourself. Creativity is never shallow. It cannot be done on the surface. Whether it is to write a play, paint a picture, build a friendship, raise a child, or worship God, the essence of creativity is exploring new depths.

Think of the difference between a celebrity and a hero. A celebrity is known for being known. What they have accomplished is being noticed. When they stop being noticed, they are gone.

People magazine will do a story on them 20 years from now, asking the silly question, "Where are they now?" A celebrity makes a mark in sand, but when the sands shift, the signature swiftly disappears.

A hero is also known for having made a mark. A hero creates a safer and saner world, a better place to be alive. A hero eternally alters the face of the planet. They have changed the world by some significant display of love, forgiveness, or courage. The initials they carve pierce deep into the bark of the tree of life.

Creativity requires us to dive in, to go deep, to touch bottom, then to rise like a phoenix to the surface and share the treasure we have found there. The treasure will appear to be anything but. It will be covered in the mud and muck of living.

It will bear scars and stains. It will be cracked. Yet treasure it is, and the shine will be unmistakable. Like all treasure though, it will take many dives to locate.

To Be Holy

"And so, dear Christian friends, I plead with you to give your bodies to God. Let them be a living and holy sacrifice—the kind he will accept. When you think of what he has done for you, is this too much to ask? Don't copy the behavior and customs of this world, but let God transform you into a new person by changing the way you think. Then you will know what God wants you to do, and you will know how good and pleasing and perfect his will really is."

—Romans 12:1–2

In this passage, Paul admonishes his readers that a holy life is one that conforms not to the ways of the world, but is rigorous in its allegiance to the way of God. Paul is clear here. The path followed by the world is a dead end. He declares that God's path leads in the opposite direction. A holy life is to closely follow this path. For Paul, the world is seen as the opponent of the holy life. For this reason, a holy life requires genuine sacrifice. What must be given up is the opinion of the world.

For much of my life, I thought of holiness as way, way out of reach. To be honest, I had no interest. I had zero desire to be a monk or saint. Holiness was reserved for the pure of heart, mind, and, especially, body. I was polka-dotted with impurities. To be holy was out of the question. To work at being holy—I'd have to be out of my mind.

I have matured. I no longer think of holiness as the pursuit of perfection or the state of purity. To be holy is to put God on and to wear him like a cloak. Holiness is to look through God's eyes, hear with his ears, and touch with his hands. It is to allow the heart of God to beat in my chest. It is to let my mind take root in his. Holiness is not work. It has nothing to do with *my* efforts. It is opening myself to the presence of God. Holiness is to be received.

Crazy as it may sound, we need to see ourselves as the Virgin Mary. We must be open to the Holy Spirit. We must possess a faith receptive to being impregnated by the spirit of God. As the Christmas carol sings, we must let Christ be born in us this day. Once we begin to act as if we carry the seed of God inside us, a miracle occurs and the child will have his way—he will be born.

The work of being holy is surrendering, waving the white flag, letting go. Trust me, this is no small or easy task. It is, however, our only access to holiness. If it is anything, it is a decision— deciding for God, deciding that our way does not work and that God's way might, deciding and then turning it over.

> "Since God chose you to be the holy people whom he loves, you must clothe yourselves with tenderhearted mercy, kindness, humility, gentleness, and patience. You must make allowance for each other's faults and forgive the person who offends you. Remember, the Lord forgave you, so you must forgive others. And the most important piece of clothing you must wear is love. Love is what binds

us all together in perfect harmony. And let the peace that comes from Christ rule in your hearts."

—Colossians 3:12–15

In this passage, Paul seems to acknowledge that there are times we cannot be like God. We may lack the energy, courage, or even conviction. At these times he invites us to wear God like a cloak. To put him on. We let God do the work for us. I find this to be most true in the arena of forgiveness. I am always conscious of how mightily I struggle to forgive. Even when I choose to forgive, I am keenly aware it is God who does the actual forgiving. The choice is mine. The power to forgive is God's.

To Be Perfect

"Come to me, all of you who are weary and carry heavy burdens, and I will give you rest. Take my yoke upon you. Let me teach you, because I am humble and gentle, and you will find rest for your souls. For my yoke fits perfectly, and the burden I give you is light."

—Matthew 11:28–30

This passage is stating that the burdens of the world are heavy. If our purpose is to be perfect, please everyone, and perform to packed houses, we carry the weight of the world on our shoulders. At some point we will collapse from fatigue or fall in painful failure. We cannot do it. We were never meant to. It is not our purpose at all.

Jesus asks us to take on the yoke of being human. He calls us to be real, to be true to our selves. He promises that this is the yoke that will fit perfectly. He teaches us how to be co-creators, how to help him fill the world with graciousness and mercy.

Jesus requests that we carry one burden—grace. It is a light burden. It is a load of light. In carrying this load, we become holy. In holiness, the burden is eternally lifted. Upward.

CHAPTER RESPONSE BY RABBI ASTRACHAN

Pastor Grimbol has certainly approached the holiness in a wonderfully universal way. Of course, for Jews the only difficulty with his theology is the personal relationship with Jesus that adherents of Christianity feel. I often marvel at how beautifully Christians who are true to their faith embrace the theology of Jesus as Christ (Messiah) and all that it entails. It is majestic, really. To be sure, someone looking at Judaism from the outside might question what Jews have to hold onto in the absence of a *Jesus* figure.

With the single exception of *being received,* I would put Judaism's concept of our relationship with God in perfect harmony with what Pastor Grimbol states as his concept for his relationship with Jesus. For me, substitute his use of the word *Jesus* with the word *God,* and we have a theological match. That is, Judaism, too, speaks of opening oneself to the holiness of God and to being cloaked in God's presence.

For Jews, too, there is a certain degree of anthropomorphism that attaches to the theology of God. We listen for God's voice. We wait for God's touch. We feel God's presence within us. Some more observant Jews even wear certain religious garb that helps them enhance their connection to God. A *yarmulke* or *kippah* is worn as a symbol of devotion and of respect for God. A prayer shawl is worn to wrap oneself in the presence of God. Traditional body motions accompany many prayers that we recite, developed as a means of bringing the whole self to God through our worship.

In essence, much of how we approach God is similar except for some of the semantics. It is no secret that Jews do not believe in Jesus as the Messiah. (The explanation for this deviation of our two faith systems would fill too great a space to include here.) But this is not to say that Jews have any less a connection with God.

Many times I have been asked how I connect with God. Kids and adults both seem to think that clergy have the absolute answer to these kinds of questions. It is as if they think "If the rabbi wears green pants because green pants bring him closer to God, then I must wear green pants, too!" The fact is, I don't own green pants. I don't believe that there is one *right* way to approach God, either. How we define *holiness* is our own business. So long as it stays within certain faith-centered parameters that don't conflict with the broad strokes laid out by our particular religious traditions, we have quite a range of latitude to figure out how best to connect with God.

PART 3

THE WHEN QUESTIONS

When questions seek to locate us in time. When questions establish our relationship to time. Way back when is clearly the past. When? When then? Whenever?—all focus on a foggy future. The question of when is erased by the present. Now removes when.

When questions often sound hostile because our relationship to time is frequently adversarial. We buy time. We spend time. We waste time. We kill time. We speak of time as enemy or private property, neither of which is true or healthy.

Our open hostility toward time creates lives that are rushed, desperate flights from the absence of time—death. With time as our opponent, we are the hare stuck in a futile race against the wiser turtle.

The simplest and surest way to improve our relationship with time is to seize the moment. Living fully in the now keeps the question answered. Being fully awake to the day, aware of its potential for miracles, in awe of its mysteries, occupies the soul in observing eternity. All questions of when evaporate under the bright sun of eternity.

When Is the Right Time?

Pastor William R. Grimbol

My son, Justin, asked me a question with a look on his face that was both wince and wonder. "When will I know?" His inquiry was about love. It was a question, like all good questions, packed with other questions. When is the right time to tell her I love her? Is this the right time to make love? When do you know if this is the real thing?

Questions that lead to other questions also offer a multiplicity of answers. There is no single answer. The answers change by history, circumstance, and perspective. Our answers do not come with warranties or guarantees. No refunds. No returns. Our answers are our choices.

This chapter will present time, not as an opponent to be conquered, but as a companion with whom to share the journey. We must make our peace with time. We must learn to live within its borders. We must accept the reality of its rules. It is my hope that this chapter will help you come to terms with time—to be on intimate terms.

The Choices We Make

Life is all about making choices. Some of them are sweet and simple, but many are complex and confusing. "When" questions address these tough choices:

+ When is the right time to start or finish?
+ When is the right time to stay or walk away?
+ When is the right time to accept or reject?

+ When is the right time to compromise or change?

+ When is the right time to fight or surrender?

When is the right time focuses on life's most difficult choices.

These questions demand decisions—decisions that require the investment of our whole being—heart, mind, and soul. These are decisions that make or break lives, create ease or dis-ease, and shatter dreams or free them to soar.

Questions that ask about the *right time* also pose a moral dilemma. They require making good choices. They ask for goodness to be a major player in our decision. Right time questions necessitate discipline. Goodness takes work. Doing good is a serious craft. Being good is an art.

The disciples made a choice to follow Jesus. They made this choice because they knew they had no other choice. Their only involvement in the decision was surrender. They followed.

The following required daily decision. Each day they had to decide for Christ. Every dawn brought the question of "Where do we go from here?" Each dusk was answered by having followed. Following is my discipline. Following makes my decisions. Following mandates the choice of goodness.

GOOD TIMING (MAKING GOOD CHOICES)

At times, making a good choice is luck. Occasionally a good choice falls in our lap. But most of the time it is hard work. Knowing when the time is right is what makes most choices good. Timing becomes everything. Like a good comedian, knowing when to deliver the line is all important.

Good timing has nothing to do with doing better, but everything to do with being smarter. Smart means knowing when the time is bad:

- ✦ Don't make a decision in the midst of a crisis.
- ✦ Don't make a decision when angry, depressed, or exhausted.
- ✦ Don't make a decision that seeks escape or to get even.
- ✦ Don't make a decision that feels rushed or forced.
- ✦ Don't make a decision that repeats a previous mistake.
- ✦ Don't make a decision in an arena in which you are prone to bad judgment.
- ✦ Don't make a decision that does not have love somewhere in the equation.
- ✦ Don't make a decision without significant time for prayer.

Smart also seeks counsel. Smart requests input from trusted friends or mentors. Smart is never embarrassed to seek or receive help. Smart strives to become wise. While the world shouts that we don't have all day, smart knows we do. While the world tells us to leave our hearts out of it, smart gives the heart veto power. While the world says that we must make this decision on our own, smart knows that there is no such thing as a good choice made in isolation.

Smart is also obedient. Smart follows a higher power. Smart knows that God knows what is best. Smart prays. Smart worships. Smart seeks the sacred space of silence to listen for the Word of God. When God is silent, smart waits. When God speaks, smart listens. A smart choice is a good choice. A smart choice knows that a good choice takes time to make, and once made, takes time to feel right. A good choice is willing to make good, to put forth the energy required to make the choice work, to let the choice settle. Making a good choice at the right time remains a process. The process is completed when the choice finally feels like no choice at all.

Having a Good Time

As a minister, I do a good deal of pastoral care. I am not a counselor per se, but I am a spiritual mentor. A big chunk of my work
with folks is to help them make good choices. I help them focus
on their choices, weigh the pros and cons, look at the matter
through the eyes of Christ, pray, meditate, factor in those who
will be impacted by the decision, and then ... decide.

In my work with people on making good choices, I find one glaring omission. No, not God. People come to me looking for God to
be a central character in the process. What is missing is often
themselves. They do not factor in who they are, or more important, what makes them happy. Maybe it is our neurotic religious
habit to believe our happiness does not matter, but I find many of
my congregants omitting a key piece of evidence in making their
decision—will it make them happy.

Making a choice should have something to do with our state of
mind and being. A good choice would not leave us depressed. A
good choice should not create added conflict or chaos in our
lives. A good choice has a lot to do with having a good time. A
good time is always open to the possibility of joy. It is a time
being enjoyed. It is time being with good people or doing something we love to do, something we are good at.

I find that good choices usually produce the following results:

+ We feel good.
+ We are in better health.
+ We have a good time.
+ We make good friends.
+ We do good more often.
+ We have the best brought out of us.

The most glaring result of making a really good choice is the time that is freed up to lose track of. Losing track of time is the presence of joy. When the clock disappears from our minds, eternity has entered. Timelessness is the state of God being happy with who we are.

When is the right time? It is the right time if you know the choice has something to do with you and your happiness. I am not talking about Mouseketeer happiness—I am happy as can be. I am talking about Christ happiness, when we know what we are doing and being is pleasing in the eyes of God.

In Good Time

"There is a time for everything, a season for every activity under heaven."

—Ecclesiastes 3:1

In this passage, Ecclesiastes is asking his readers to refrain from any futile efforts to control time. Life is a dance with time, and time always takes the lead. We need only go with the flow, because time is the flow. Ecclesiastes suggests here that we need only follow time's rhythm and beat and then wait, wait for the next step, twist, or turn.

Timely. A timely fashion. All in good time. This language speaks to making decisions on God's timetable. It expresses a belief that the right time will appear, that the answer to our when questions may have nothing to do with our work, but with the toil of God. This belief is rooted in the conviction that many when questions are seasonal.

Life, like nature, does have its seasons. The when questions of childhood are filled with wonder and imagination: When is my birthday? When do I get to go to school? When can I go out and play? The when questions of adolescence are haunted by fear but futilely attempt to sound unafraid: When can I stay out past midnight? When can I be home alone? When can I move out on my own? Some of the when questions of adulthood are coated in urgency: When should I get married? When will I be a success? When will I be ready to have a family? Others are more solemn: When will I feel secure? When will I be free of that burden? When will I be ready to see my kids leave the nest?

The Christian church also has seasons. I find these seasons tremendously helpful with all the when questions. They offer us a unique perspective on the art of making good choices. They enable us to relax both with and in time. They ground us in grace. Each season of the church year has a spiritual function. Each reminds us how we must prepare our answers to life's when questions:

+ **Advent.** The season of waiting. A time of wondering. A time bloated with expectation. Advent is a time pregnant with possibility. We patiently wait until we are full of our wishes and dreams. We let our hopes rise to the surface. Advent is a time of preparation. We prepare the way for the arrival of Jesus. We ready the nest. We become host to the Holy Spirit. We let God in—inside. Advent is a good time to ready a good choice.

+ **Christmas.** The season of birth. Christ is born in us this day. All things become new. Joy has arrived. Birthing begins. Giving birth to the real you. Labor pains. Born in a barn. Born out back. Often our best choices are made in the most unexpected places and times. Life at its most ordinary can squeeze out the most extraordinary decisions. Christmas marks the birth of a great decision—God's radical affirmation of life—your life.

✦ **Epiphany.** The season of wisdom. A time to risk following stars. Three wise men travel far to kneel and worship an infant. The world is turned upside down. The wisdom of the world bows before pure innocence. Epiphany is, for me, a reminder: All choice is risky; following the wisdom of the world is a bad choice; kneeling is a good position from which to make a good choice.

✦ **Lent.** The season of examination. Rigorous honesty is required. The soul must be searched. The spirit is often scorched by blistering truths. When questions must be raised with passion, and the crucifying absence of answers must be faced. Lent is a season of hard work, a time to face life's hardest issues. Lent picks up the cross of "when" and carries it forward. Lent marches into the future without fear.

✦ **Easter.** The season of rebirth. Jesus is resurrected. Jesus conquers death. Jesus becomes timeless. Jesus remains in time—the presence of the Holy Spirit. The Holy Spirit promises a life full of such "easterings." As a Christian, Easter daily calls me to new life, to face all when questions with the Holy Spirit at my side. I am not alone. My choices must seek to conform to Christ's choices. I am God's beloved child. I graciously accept all parenting.

✦ **Pentecost.** The season of the light. The Holy Spirit explodes before our eyes. The fog lifts. We can see clearly. Choices are made in an instant. We feel sure. Certain. Positive. Right. Pentecost is the time when *when* vanishes. The moment is so full of grace that we need only be. The choice has been made for us. We can simply live and reflect the light—aglow.

The seasons of the church year anchor life and give perspective to all the when questions. Anxiety is relieved and calm is restored as "when" is yearly encased in the promise of grace. Grace cannot be rushed. It offers us glimpses and glances as it will. All we can do is watch and wait and be prepared. Such preparation fills our days with good things. Such preparedness becomes our holy purpose. Getting ready for God is always right.

THE RIGHT TIME BOTTOM LINE

For me and my faith, there is a bottom line. The right time must be a good time. The right time must enable a good choice. A good choice is for all time.

For all time becomes the Christian standard. I seek to leave a lasting legacy, a legacy that matters: good family, good friends, good deeds, good times, good news, and good faith. A life well lived.

For the Christian, eternity answers all our when questions. Eternity is the frame and focus. We live in the eternal now. We face all "whens" with the assurance of an eternal beyond. We build our faith upon a foundation of the timeless presence of God's Grace.

As a Christian, there is no such thing as a best time or the best years of our life. All time is good time. All time is bursting with grace. Any time can be the right time. In no time at all—that is how long it takes for God to answer our when questions.

Time was there from the beginning. Time is always at its best. Time only asks the best of us. Our best behavior. Our best wishes. My faith is that the best is yet to come.

Chapter Response by Rabbi Astrachan

Seasons are important occurrences. Each brings with it joys and sorrows. Every year, with the arrival of the JCPenney fall/winter catalog, I spin into a mild depression knowing that the days will start getting shorter, the temperatures colder, and the trees more barren. I await with eager anticipation the arrival of the spring/summer issue, knowing that nature will awake once again to renewed life and verve.

The same holds true with religious seasons. Pastor Grimbol describes six such seasons in this chapter—each of which lends itself to enhancing the joy of a Christian's faith and connection with God. Judaism also maintains a specific system of religious *seasons*. For Jews, the seasons that accompany life from birth to death are as important as the seasons that carry us throughout the year. As Pastor Grimbol has shared some of the annual seasons he believes to be of particular significance to Christianity, I also would like to share some of those of significance to Judaism. First, I will share four annual holiday seasons then two lifetime seasons:

✦ **Rosh HaShanah.** The beginning of the 10-day season called the *Days of Awe*. Rosh HaShanah, considered to be the first day of the Jewish New Year, also is described as a time of deep introspection. It is at this time that we consider our deeds of the past year, the wrongs we have committed, and how we might work to correct our path. On Rosh HaShanah God opens the *Book of Life* in which our days are recorded and considered for another year of life.

✦ **Yom Kippur.** The conclusion of the season of the *Days of Awe*. Yom Kippur is also called the Day of Atonement. A day of fasting, prayer, and personal reflection, this day is often referred to as the Sabbath of Sabbaths. It is among the holiest days of the entire Jewish calendar. We are told that on this day, more than any other, we are to reflect on our own deeds and misdeeds, the rights and wrongs of the past year, and the ways in which we will strive to improve our lives and the lives of others in the coming year. By observing a 24-hour fast, we allow our minds to focus only on what is truly important: how we are living our lives and how we connect with God.

✦ **Simchat Torah.** A season of renewal. On Simchat Torah, Jews celebrate the annual renewal of the cycle of reading the Torah (the five books of Moses). This festive season reminds us that there is no ending and no beginning to God's universal message. During the celebration, we dance and sing with the Torah scrolls throughout the synagogue. (Some congregations even take their celebrations into the streets.) We are to consider the omnipresent messages of Judaism and to rekindle our spiritual connection with God and God's instructions for living (the *mitzvot*).

✦ **Chanukah and Purim.** These two holidays, very distinct in their placement within the calendar, are both celebrated as seasons of freedom. The story of Chanukah teaches us about the small band of Maccabee soldiers who, around 185 B.C.E., defeated Greek tyranny and oppression. The story of Purim teaches us about the strength of one person—Esther—to make a difference in the lives of many. Both seasons are joyous occasions that allow us to consider who we are and what we are capable of accomplishing despite odds being against us. They remind us that all things are possible when we believe in ourselves and in the goodness of others.

+ **Bar/Bat Mitzvah.** Literally, Son/Daughter of the Commandments, this season is generally one of the most celebrated in all of the Jewish life cycle. At age 13 (12 for girls) children are called to the honor of reading from the Torah for the first time. In most congregations this honor comes only after the child has completed many years of dedicated study of Judaism and has fulfilled a number of other growth activities. Students learn that by becoming a bar/bat mitzvah, doors within Judaism open to them. They are considered full members of the community and may be called upon to participate in other service roles within the congregation.

+ **Death.** Not every season is joyous. Death, especially, brings us great sorrow and begs questions of God's mercy and compassion. Nevertheless, we cannot escape the inevitable. Death teaches us that we must cherish all that we have and continually remind ourselves not to take anything for granted.

Life is short. The seasons change quickly. Regardless of which religion we ascribe to, let us utilize our time wisely that each of the seasons will be celebrated fully, without regret and with our most complete being.

WHEN WILL IT END?

Pastor William R. Grimbol

At first it was a gaping hole. Then fire engulfed the hole. Then the second airliner hit. The explosion grew larger and the fire more intense. Then the shudder and the smoky collapse. Steel, glass, bodies, memories, and so much love came crashing to the earth. First one and then the other. Like a brokenhearted wife who passes on within days of her husband. The billowing clouds of ash pouring through the channels of Manhattan streets. The stunned faces of people running in every direction. The incessant TV coverage. The images hammered into our collective psyche.

September 11, 2001, was an ending for America and for every American. No matter how deep or strong the faith; no matter how many valiant pep talks from Mayor Guiliani; no matter how often we recounted the stories of true heroes, the NYC firefighters, or the passengers who wrestled their aircraft to the ground near Pittsburgh, there was an ending. Innocence went down for the count. Now security is exclusively a spiritual matter. Our homeland is no longer seemingly invulnerable to attack.

This is not to say that there have not been myriad wonderful beginnings. There have been: unprecedented outpourings of compassion and mercy, an influx of human kindness and civility, a renewal of sensible patriotism. United we stand—and we believe it. But there will be no forward movement or rekindling of hope without first embracing the ending. If we are to write a happy ending to the events of September 11, it will be a rewrite because the first draft was pure tragedy.

Terrorism is the culprit. Terrorists stole our sense of security, and with it a good many of our freedoms. We are furious with them. Christ's call to love our enemies never sounded more foolish. This is evil. These are folks who long to die. How do we deal with religious fanatics who find the *end* to be the *hope?* How do we respond in faith to what seems to be Satan's handiwork? Won't there always be one more martyr for the cause?

When will the terrorism end? Life has added another frightening question to its already formidable arsenal:

- ✦ When will the pain end? When will the grieving be over?
- ✦ When will I stop feeling guilty?
- ✦ When will I be free of this nightmare?
- ✦ When will I be able to relax?
- ✦ When will I quit feeling so uptight?

Life is riddled with such yearnings, yearnings to see life's pain and suffering and sorrow taken away. Many of us wish daily for an ending. We want an end to what complicates our lives or paralyzes us in fear. We want the fog of anguish to lift. We want blue skies, nothing but blue skies.

There will be blue skies. There will be sun. There will also be storms, some of them violent and destructive. Endings are a major aspect of life's weather. We may be doing a better job in forecasting dangerous weather, but like September 11, there will still be the tornado that savagely and unexpectedly drops out of the sky. Maybe these terrorist attacks on our country are another perfect storm—a coming together of all the right forces to produce terribly wrong results.

This chapter is focused on how we respond to endings. It will not offer solutions. It will provide no easy answers—there are none.

This is a "how to" chapter: How to cope with the reality of endings, even the loss of our spiritual footing. As the world trembles and rolls beneath our feet, we must still walk. This chapter attempts to offer insight on changes we can make in the way we think, our attitude, and our perspective, as well as the way we behave.

I am encouraging us all to cultivate a more sacramental existence, a life grounded in grace, a lifestyle rooted in making a habit of hope. Hope is our last and best option. Hope is the only place we can turn. Faith finds hope. Love builds hope. Courage creates hope. If hope can become our purpose, our lives may not be free of terrorist threats, but they will be void of fear. Fear has never been a match for genuine hope. Hope is what we do when there is no end in sight. Hope is who we are, a people who do not find the end to be our hope. Our hope remains firmly fastened to life.

LIVING WITH LOOSE ENDS

I am anal-retentive, a neat freak, a control freak. I have always struggled getting work done on a desk that isn't tidy. I don't like clutter. I hate leaving a mess. I will probably clean this hotel room before I leave. I know—sad.

However, I am better. Much better. I have worked hard to accept the reality of clutter. I have spiritually struggled with the notion of letting go and letting God. I have all but stopped trying to keep everyone happy. I'm much better at knowing when I need to slow down or even stop. I give myself daily gifts of grace, times of doing nothing or times to do something good just for me— which is usually one and the same. Most of all, I have learned to live with loose ends.

My wife Christine was my tutor in what I call "loose-end living."
She was always telling me to loosen up. She would regularly
remind me that life was unpredictable. She would point out my
efforts to tie a knot long before it was wise to do so. She patiently
taught me how to parent and to realize that raising a child is
loaded with loose ends—ends that can only be tied by the blessing of maturation. She even got me to enjoy the dander and dust
of two pet shar-peis.

She once told me, and I paraphrase and summarize, "You live
your life, Bill, as if it is a checklist. Each thing you check off, and
you feel relief. Getting things done. Putting them neatly in the
past. That is no way to live. That may be neat and tidy, but it is
also boring as hell. Try being married to it. Do you know how
many days I feel like I have been checked off? Many! I hate feeling like I am just another chore. Do you want your son to feel
like an item on a list? Aren't you sick and tired of living life as if
it were a chore? I would think you would find it exhausting. By
the way Bill, the two things missing from your checklist—you
and Christ. You may be getting a lot done, but I doubt you enjoy
much of anything. Bill, you really need to have a little faith. You
really do. A little faith."

Ouch. But true. Only a wife can hit you between the spiritual
eyes. I miss that. Rigorous honesty is the lifeblood of a strong
marriage. Christine was right. I often need just a little faith. A
mustard seed of faith. At first I found it funny to think of faith
and loose-end living in the same breath. My catechism training
made me think of faith only in the strictest terms. But I knew
that mold was old. I long ago knew I needed out of the confines
of such a rigid religion. Christine was the catalyst. She freed me
to actualize what I knew in my guts.

This is what Christine taught me about loose-end living:

+ Learn to accept imperfection, clutter, and loose ends.
+ Learn to surrender to a power much higher than ourselves—for me, Christ.
+ Rigid expectations produce stress and strain.
+ Hard-line theology is eventually destructive.
+ Staying loose is knowing we are not in control.
+ Staying loose gives grace room to roam.
+ Magic, mystery, and miracles cannot be tied up.
+ A rigid faith will only tie us up in knots.
+ Our faith needs to be flexible and free to change.
+ Our faith must be tender and tolerant.
+ Life is tough enough. We don't need to have a faith that beats us up.
+ Scripture is not a book of laws.
+ Scripture is a patchwork quilt of faith, and all the thread is grace.
+ Loose-end living celebrates tolerance.
+ Loose-end living celebrates change.
+ Loose-end living celebrates diversity.
+ Loose-end living is inextricably bonded to maturation.
+ Loose-end living is like a dance. The Holy Spirit is our partner.

Follow the leader. Go with the flow of the music. Listen for the beat. Hear the rhythm. Loosen up and let go. We have to be flexible. Our bodies must be free to move. Our feet quick. Our spirits open. The dance is best enjoyed when we invent a few new steps. Kick up our heals. Get a bit wild. Offer our own unique vision.

Dances have steps. The best dancers know these steps by heart. After they have the steps memorized, they are free to interpret. They can put their whole being into their movement. The spirit so dominates the steps that we cannot tell if different dancers are doing the same dance. The dance, even when carefully choreographed, looks fresh each time it is danced.

I credit Christine with getting me on the dance floor. She taught me many of the steps. She also felt the Holy Spirit tapping her on the shoulder, and she introduced me to a new partner. I am becoming a pretty good dancer. She would be proud.

JESUS AND LOOSE-END LIVING

Jesus was a master of loose-end living. He literally wrote the book on the subject. He preached a message of tolerance and mercy. Like the creation itself, the hallmark of his ministry was a celebration of diversity and change. To celebrate diversity is the essence of loose-end living. To accept change is its foundation.

When Jesus selected his disciples, he chose 12 guys who could not possibly agree on a thing. By history and heritage, these 12 could not have been more different. They may have spoken the same language, but they saw the world through a dozen different sets of eyes. Jesus knew that diversity is the best context for creativity and that true community is never the result of cloning.

Jesus and the disciples never had a conversation that was wrapped up neatly. There were always loose ends. Reading scripture, we get the sense that there were more than a few furious debates—debates never finished. Had Jesus cloned himself 12 times, chosen folks of like heart and mind, and demanded a duplication of his faith, the Gospels would be full of nice, tidy conversations, rather than frustrating encounters which often left Jesus feeling his disciples still didn't understand.

Jesus' whole ministry was soaked in tenderness. He was constantly asking his followers to loosen up. To turn the other cheek. To forgive repeatedly. To love the outcast. To love the enemy. To touch the untouchable—the leper or the individual with demons. At the core of Jesus' message was a call to tolerance. Jesus' tolerance was as wide as the world. His patience unlimited. His steadfastness complete. He asked us to be the same.

Jesus' greatest anger was saved for the religious elite. The Scribes and Pharisees bore the brunt of Jesus' spiritual wrath.

Jesus loved these men of the law, and he deeply appreciated their desire to know the law. However, their study of the law had become so all-consuming, so fanatical, that they had no time or energy to do justice, bind a broken heart, or love their neighbor. The law, like a boa constrictor, was squeezing the mercy from their souls. Their inability to accept any loose ends had them hopelessly and endlessly tying knots.

The law was never meant for worship. The law was never intended to replace life. Ironically, the effort of the religious elite to digest the law whole had ultimately made them spiritually sick. In this powerful passage from Matthew 23 (which I encourage you to read in its entirety), Jesus scolds the religious for their rigidity:

> "How terrible it will be for you teachers of religious law and you Pharisees. Hypocrites! You are like whitewashed tombs—beautiful on the outside but filled on the inside with dead people's bones and all sorts of impurity. You try to look like upright people outwardly, but inside your hearts are filled with hypocrisy and lawlessness."
> —Matthew 13:27–28

Jesus pulled no punches. He attacked the religious elite for having hard hearts and for being drained of the mercy, tolerance, and love that would free them to minister to those folks in dire need. The religious elite needed to loosen up and take their religion and themselves less seriously.

DEAD ENDS

The week after the World Trade Center and Pentagon bombings, I took off for a few days. I felt a need to get away and get my head on straight. I needed to relocate my heart and revive my soul. I was overwhelmed, and knew I had to be in focus. I also knew full well that I was escaping. I was not ready to minister to my flock. I was not feeling full of love and leadership. I felt as empty as an abandoned well.

I drove to the Berkshires, a favorite haunt of mine. The foliage was ablaze but failed to ignite the usual "oohs" and "aahs."

On the drive I listened to tapes of Garrison Keillor's *Lake Wobegon,* but this time it was hard to follow the stories. The farther I drove, the more aware I became of what I was really doing—running away. That knowledge deadened me further. I felt numb and miserable—like my whole body had been to the dentist.

I pulled into a small diner in a small town, Stephentown, New York, for some lunch. I was seated by a doughy waitress with a kind smile. I began to read and jot notes for upcoming sermons.

Nancy, the waitress, quickly noted that I wasn't a regular. She asked me where I was from. I told her. She reported the news of my living close to NYC to the entire kitchen staff, who emerged from out of the kitchen and gathered at my table. They wanted to know if I had known anyone who had been lost or harmed.

I explained that I was a minister, and that yes, some of my members had experienced the gruesome horror firsthand. It was then that I noticed the cook, a big burly guy. He had a kid's face but a man's body. His eyes were wet. He said, "Will you tell those folks in your church that we have them in our prayers and that we are collecting as much money as we can?" I promised I would. I ate my lunch and left to a flurry of hugs and kind words.

As I drove off, I said out loud to myself, "Man, there is no escape!" It was then that I realized I was right: I was feeling better. I had found my focus in the eyes of a weeping cook. There is nowhere to run or hide from life. All escapes are dead-ends. They lead only to despair. I turned the car around and headed home. I needed to dive into my ministry. I was being called back to life— the place where Christ is always found.

Dead-ends are escapes, the means of denial, the refusal to live on God's terms. We live in a culture that gives us directions down dead-end streets all the time. Sadly, many of us love to grow-down. Because spirituality and maturation are pretty much synonymous, this means that we are literally selling our soul.

On September 11, many of our busiest American streets revealed themselves to be nothing more than dead-ends. There is no way to deny the transformation of our world, our lives, our spirits. We can't keep ourselves occupied with work. We can't keep ourselves perpetually entertained. We can't ignore what happened by pursuing some trivial pursuit. We can't believe it will all get better soon. We cannot make the world go away. Even our myriad addictions cannot protect us from the pain of this formidable foe—terror.

Dead-ends are paths paved in fear. Fear numbs us. Fear deadens us. Fear paralyzes us. Terror leaves us gasping for breath. If we choose to travel these routes, we will know only a withering of the soul. If we try to escape our new reality, we will be swept up by anxiety. If we attempt to ignore the new state of our world, we will swirl down a drain of despair.

What can we do? How do we choose roads that lead us back to life? How do we travel with courage and enthusiasm? We go back to the basics—the basics of the real good life:

+ We work on having good families and friendships.

+ We work on having good conversations—intimate, honest, challenging, and spiritual.

+ We chase beauty.

+ We play and dance and soak in good books and good music.

+ We stay healthy. We exercise our brains and bodies on a daily basis.

+ We build strong communities.

+ We pray and worship as often as we can.

+ We pick up the cross of our terror and follow Christ.

+ We feel deeply and let our hearts fill with compassion.

+ We have a good laugh and a good cry.

+ We celebrate birthdays, anniversaries, weddings, baptisms, and holidays.

+ We send cards, make calls, and give gifts and hugs and kisses.

+ We remember.

+ We create memories.

Jesus Christ was born into a bleak and battered world. Bethlehem was a tiny village situated in a ragged landscape of hunger, poverty, immorality, greed, disease, violence, war, and despair. It was a time of chaos. Fear filled the air. Everyone lived in terror. It was as if the whole world was shouting, "What next?"

What was God's response to such a shout of hopelessness? A baby. A tiny shivering infant born in a barn. A single star illuminating a black, black night. Wise kings kneeling before the wisdom of God—a child. What was God's response? It was life. A single life. A child. Life's most basic and precious gift.

God brought the world to its knees by laying a babe in our spiritual lap—life at its most fragile and glorious. God's reply to a world gone mad was more of the same. Back to the basics. Back to life. Back to the sweet awesome goodness of a child.

So it is for us. We are called to turn around, to leave the dead-end alleys, and return to those paths that will bring us the hope we seek. Get back to the living and the loving. Head home to the children. Care for them. Protect them. Inspire them. There we will find the bright star of our hope.

Bittersweet Endings

"When will the sadness end?" I was recently asked at a gathering of high school youth. It was a great question. Real. Honest. Tough. Unanswerable. We juggled our responses back and forth. We sought comfort. We searched for hope. I could see the yearnings in their eyes for not just relief, but some semblance of certainty. Had terrorism left us permanently emotionally disabled, forever coated in sad?

I asked them, "Is it so bad that we are so sad?" The question quieted the discussion, and there was an interior acknowledgment of the importance of sadness. But why? We explored this new terrain, the rugged landscape of sorrow. It soon became apparent to these young people that sorrow serves a sacred purpose. It is the fertile soil of faith. Sorrow yields a rich harvest of joy. It is the ground of grace. It is the place where the precious can be found. Sorrow gives perspective. Sorrow is maturing. It is often in the midst of great sadness that our true greatness emerges.

Courage blooms. Compassion blossoms. The fruits of faith literally fall from the tree of sorrow.

That night I introduced the youth group to the old term *bittersweet*. I told them that the gospel truth is bittersweet. I reminded them that the story of Jesus Christ was one of bitter betrayal and sweet rebirth. We talked about the bittersweet events of September 11 and how such tragedy had yielded so many stories of courage and compassion. We talked about how good it had felt for these young folks to see adults weep and pray and how the gloom of terrorism was penetrated by the rainbow of faith. We talked about how they believed the germs of anthrax would be thwarted by the even faster spread of grace.

All losses hurt. All endings include suffering. Saying good-bye is never easy. Whether it is a broken heart, a shattered dream, a death or divorce, a planned or unplanned departure, or the loss of health, happiness, or hope, each knows his fair share of pain. Life is not easy. Life is damn difficult. Even at its best, life is bittersweet.

Bittersweet is the taste of the gospel truth. Bittersweet is the frame of the life of Christ. We are free to obey. We follow and suffer. We serve to know joy. We sacrifice to find faith. We triumph over tragedy. We call the day of crucifixion Good Friday.

We know the downward ascent of Lent. We lay claim to an "eastering" that flies like an eagle out of the ashes. The bottom line of faith—without the bitter taste of loss, we will never know the sweetness of finding ourselves full.

A Good Ending

I remember taking a group of seniors from my church to see the blockbuster film *Titanic*. For three plus hours, two dozen of us sat riveted to the screen. More than a few tears were shed. Many of the men pretended to have caught colds while viewing the film.

We left drained but happy and boarded our vans. One of my favorite elderly ladies, Edith, said, "What a good ending!"

The van erupted in laughter. The ship sank! I asked, "What was good about it?" Edith joined in the laughter, but then replied, "Yep, the ship sank, but our hearts didn't."

How true. That is a good ending. A good ending is when we plant just a seed of faith, when a remnant of hope remains, and when a few loose ends are left dangling for the next generation to tie. A good ending is not always a happy ending. It is not an ending that answers all questions or resolves all conflicts. A good ending is one we can believe. It is an ending that leaves us with a good taste. It is an ending that leaves us wanting—more movie, more life.

The account of the life of Christ has a good ending. Yes, there is abundant pain and sorrow. Many of the villains are also the heroes. There is a plot filled with greed, hatred, doubt, despair, envy, disappointment, and betrayal. But there are also moments of extraordinary joy. There are miracle stories. Jesus' whole ministry is soaked in love and mercy. His message calls his followers to extravagant love, a celebration of radical equality, and tolerance of all that is human. His is a story that ends with abundant tragedy and a slight sliver of hope. In the end, we know in our heart of hearts that goodness will emerge victorious.

CHAPTER RESPONSE BY RABBI ASTRACHAN

I was deeply moved reading the words and thoughts of Pastor Grimbol in this chapter. In the face of the terror that erupted suddenly upon our country and our hearts, Pastor Grimbol has shared with us a ray of hope and vision for a future exemplified by the glass being half-full rather than half-empty.

Absent of the references to Jesus as the one who gives humanity that hope and that vision, we are all able to come together to share in the feelings stated here: We all are capable of love. Each one of us can find a faith—not only in God—but in others, which allows us to find the strength to continue to worship life and all that God has given us to enjoy.

As Pastor Grimbol stated so eloquently, when we are faced with despair, anxiety, terror, and a withering of the soul, *we go back to the basics* of living well. We are all living in these times right now more than ever before. There are none among us who feels nothing from the tragic events of September 11. Each of us has been cast into a black fog of unknowing and uncertainty. Still, it is our task to lift the fog from upon us, to come closer to each other, and to hold fast to the people and the ideals that may have only been tangential to our lives before the attacks.

Jews, too, consider life to be God's most precious gift. Not the life of Jesus, as we know, but life, in general. Each one of us is to be cherished for who we are, for the life we live, for new life we help to create, and for the renewed life that we help build out of the ruins and out of the ashes. When we do this—when we continue to do God's work of continually re-creating the world around us—then we have begun to fulfill God's desire of us. Then we have really begun to live.

When Is Enough, Enough?

Pastor William R. Grimbol

"If you would be perfect, go, sell what you possess and give to the poor, and you will have treasure in heaven; and come, follow me ... Truly I say to you, it will be hard for a rich man to enter the kingdom of heaven. Again I tell you, it is easier for a camel to get through the eye of a needle than for a rich man to enter the kingdom of God."

—Matthew 19:21–24

What can I say? These are truly amazing statements. They are also radical and offensive. Jesus seldom minces words. I would venture to say that if you have ever wondered what God thinks about money, just take a look at who he gives it to. Jesus sees money as the chief obstacle to a spiritual life. Wealth and discipleship seldom work in cooperation.

When is enough, enough? I believe this is the question of our age. It is the question that will frame our future. It is the question that most defines and divides our world. It is certainly the most disturbing question haunting our American culture. It is also at the very heart of the Christian gospel.

A majority of the world's population lives without enough. They do not have enough food, clothing, health care, work, or income. A few of us have way too much. We have closets full of clothing for every season. We dine on daily feasts. We travel the world in jets and complain about the food or onboard movie. We drive luxurious cars. We own spacious homes. We have big toys—boats and computers and gadgets of every kind.

The disparity between rich and poor is growing. The word *enough* has different meanings depending on where you live and the color of your skin. The question of enough remains at the core of the relationship between the "haves" and the "have-nots." Not enough is the base of poverty. More than enough is the foundation of wealth. It is just that simple and just that obvious. Closing that gap remains as difficult as ever. We simply lack the will or conviction to do so.

In this chapter we will take a serious look at our culture's need to speak the word *enough*. We will also reflect on the importance of "enough" to the spiritual life.

ENOUGH SPIRITUALITY?

The spiritual gap, however, is narrowing. Those who are poor are growing weary, frustrated, and anxious by the seeming hopelessness of their lives. Those who are rich are growing weary, frustrated, and anxious by the seeming hopelessness of their lives. Both know an emptiness. Both desire something better. Both search for home; one seeks physical shelter, the other longs for a spiritual dwelling in which to find rest. Neither has what he needs. Neither claims much hope. Neither seems happy. Satisfaction is scarce.

The line of demarcation has gained clarity and focus. The haves must struggle with enough in terms of quality. For the have-nots, enough remains fundamentally a quantity issue. The line in the sand is both border and bond. The haves will never know the joy of being enough until the have-nots have enough to live in genuine dignity.

We also live in world that is running out. We are running out of numerous resources. We are running out of room. We are running out of time to address many of our major environmental issues.

We are running out of hope that we can heal the gaping wounds of our world or that our lives can make much of a difference. We are running out of faith in the future. We are running out of the will to transform tomorrow into something livable. In a world that is running out, enough takes center stage. The spotlight is on enough.

As a Christian, I am challenged by Christ to honestly address the issue of enough in my life and world. Enough is, for me, a concept measured by the cross. Jesus' ministry and message calls me to preach good news to the poor. To wash feet. To serve and sacrifice. To give away the extra coat. To invite the outcast to my table. To pay the bills of the beaten stranger at the side of the road. To build the Kingdom of God with bricks of justice.

I am taught that charity means justice. I am confronted about my worship of money. I am informed of the blessings of generosity and the curses of greed.

My faith in Jesus Christ does not indulge me. It does not let me off the hook. I know how rich I am. By any standard in the world, I am fabulously wealthy. I am only middle class in America. I own more than I need. I know I could dig deeper into my wallet and still not hurt. I know that I, too, make Christ a bottom priority.

I know that my checkbook has some sad things to say about those priorities. My faith reminds me daily that the good life is all about goodness and that goodness is still about narrowing the gap between rich and poor.

WHAT TRICKLES DOWN IS NOT ENOUGH

"There was a rich man, who was clothed in purple and fine linen and who feasted sumptuously every day. And at his gate lay a poor man named Lazarus, full of sores, who desired to be fed with what fell from the rich man's table; moreover the dogs came and licked his sores. The poor man died and was carried by angels to Abraham's bosom. The rich man also died and was buried; and in Hades [hell], being in torment, he lifted up his eyes, and saw Abraham far off and Lazarus in his bosom. And he called out, 'Father Abraham, have mercy upon me, and send Lazarus to dip the end of his finger in water and cool my tongue; for I am in anguish in this flame.' But Abraham said, 'Son, remember that you in your lifetime received your good things, and Lazarus in like manner evil things, but now he is comforted here, and you are in anguish. And besides all this, between us and you a great chasm has been fixed, in order that those who would pass from here to you may not be able, and none may cross from there to us.' And he said, 'Then I beg you, father, to send him to my father's house, for I have five brothers, so that he may warn them, lest they also come to this place of torment.' But Abraham said, 'They have Moses and the prophets; let them hear them.' And he said, 'No, father Abraham; but if one goes to them from the dead, they will repent.' He said to him, 'If they do not hear Moses and the prophets, neither will they be convinced if someone should ride from the dead.'"

—Luke 16:19–21

The message in this passage is clear. The poor were never meant to live off the scraps of the rich. The Kingdom of God has no have-nots. In the Kingdom all folks would have what they need to survive in dignity. The rich man is punished for failing to invite Lazarus to his table—it is a punishment conducted in eternity. Again, Jesus is amazing in his willingness to risk offending the religious elite.

The trickle-down theory is still a major player on the political scene and a long-held, not-so-secret belief of many conservative economists. The premise is simple: The rich have so much that their excess will trickle down to the poor. It has never worked. It never will work. The fact that it doesn't work is seldom noted, though, because nobody admits to being an advocate of the philosophy.

Jesus found the trickle-down philosophy to be spiritually bankrupt. In fact, he called it sin. In the brutally revealing story of the rich man and Lazarus, Jesus finds the whole trickle-down notion worthy of landing a soul in hell. From Jesus' perspective, it was the rich man's responsibility to invite Lazarus to his table. He needed to serve Lazarus, to send him home with leftovers, to make sure he had enough to eat on a daily basis, to treat Lazarus as an equal!

The Christian faith advocates equal distribution of wealth. It is a faith built on the premise of shared blessings. A Christian believes that it is the will of God for all people to have enough. Enough is not excess. Enough is not luxury. Enough is necessity. Enough is what it takes to live with self-respect and dignity.

Christ was not a capitalist. He clearly did not believe in private property. The notion of profits would have been foreign to him, even absurd. Competition was not the way of discipleship. Power was not to be ranked. There was no hierarchy of disciples. Christ was not a champion of the free-enterprise system. His values would have been more along the lines of a cooperative or a kibbutz. His economics had a distinctly Amish flavor—work hard, own little to nothing, share all, and see everything as God's blessing upon you.

Jesus asked his disciples to trust their hearts to determine when enough was enough. He taught them to live simply and avoid what could be called extravagance. He taught them to sacrifice on behalf of the needy, practice hospitality, and celebrate equality and diversity. It was his conviction that we know exactly when enough is enough. We also know when we have too much. Our souls, like our stomachs, tell us clearly when we are empty, full, or bloated to bursting.

Jesus despised the concept of a trickle-down theory. His was a ministry of lifting up, of raising spirits and hopes, of bringing those in need to the table, of empowering the powerless. He was for raising children of mercy and generosity, reminding us that we will reap what we sow, and telling us not to forget that there is a heavenly reward system. Jesus' idea of the good life and the one advocated by our culture bear little resemblance to each other. Culture wants us to believe that we never have enough of anything. Jesus wants us to believe that with God, we have all we need.

Way Past Enough

America is a culture that does not seem to know the meaning of the word *enough*. We are told in a million different ways that we are just not enough. We don't own enough. We're not smart enough. We are not successful enough. We're not rich enough to be secure. Our fences are not high enough or thick enough to keep us safe. Nothing is fast enough. Our marriages are not enough. Our children don't measure up to the Japanese. We are forever playing catch-up. Perhaps the dominant emotion of our culture is being burned out—the spiritual equivalent of feeling you are never enough.

America is a culture built on a foundation of addiction. Addiction is what the Bible called idolatry. Being addicted to something means we believe we cannot live without that something. Addiction is the name of the game in America. It is the price we pay for selling our souls. Addiction is the malignancy I see spreading throughout our nation and our spiritual lives.

We are addicted to accumulation. We never have enough stuff. We must buy to feel good. Purchases equal power. The state of the union is the state of the economy. Greed remains our chief and central sin. We all know that. We all deny that. Denial is a symptom of addiction. Case closed.

We are addicted to adolescence. We never seem to resolve that identity crisis. We are forever looking to find our selves, while all the time never asking how or where we lost our selves. We appear shamefully inept in the intimacy department. We have a tough time with loyalty. We struggle with keeping commitments. Vows and covenants are thought to be old-fashioned. Even the declaration of independence, a hallmark of the transition from adolescence to adulthood, is receiving fewer and fewer signatures. The addiction to staying forever young has become a huge industry. Folks will pay almost anything to have a taut stomach, or no wrinkles or extra chins. Trim it. Tuck it. Suck it up. Whatever it takes, we Americans will pay the price.

We are addicted to being entertained. We watch endless hours of television. Our children play video games with a crazed look on their faces. We pay our athletes salaries so ridiculous that we can't even imagine what God might think or say. We worship Tiger Woods as if he had cured cancer or saved a child from a burning building. Our movie stars demand—and get—millions per role. Scads of magazines record their every move. We treat celebrities as royalty, and royalty as celebrities.

We are addicted to religion. We love black-and-white, easy answers, all the answers, a heaven-just-for-me religion. We love to hear about how good we are and how bad *they* are. If you watch many of America's leading TV evangelists, you will hear about a white, Southern, American, Protestant, Republican Jesus. Many American Christians have indeed successfully cast Jesus in their own image.

These same evangelists, as well as many fundamentalist preachers, hawk Jesus as if he were the newest Corvette. Their television shows are nothing more than infomercials, and sweet Jesus is the product being sold. His name and Norwegian image is emblazoned on mugs, T-shirts, place mats, and bumper stickers. The campaign for converts spares no cost. This is big business—an all-American Jesus is one big seller.

We are addicted to pain-free lives. We like cool, calm, and collected. We want no hassles. We avoid conflict at all costs.

We don't like struggle. We refuse to wait. We keep ourselves pleasantly numb. We have many drugs of choice. Booze remains number one, but we have food, prescription and designer drugs, gambling, and sex, all readily available. We want life to be smooth—like a flat line on a heart monitor.

We are addicted to work. We must be busy at all times. Busyness is equated to importance. We are what we do. Our value is measured by work. We say we are a workaholic with a smirk of pride. We love to think the world couldn't go on without us. We are frightened by the thought of slowing down and terrified of stopping—we might have to think or feel or reflect or even pray—we might have to get in touch with what really does matter.

I could go on. So could you. Addictions are rampant in America.

We are all addicts to some degree. We are a culture that thrives on excess. We have built our reputation on abundance. It should come as no shock that the terrorists went after America's symbols of power and wealth. That is, unfortunately, where our heart is—far too much of the time. This in no way condones the evil of these terrorist acts, but simply acknowledges the obviousness of their choice of targets.

Addiction avoids life's big questions. Addiction enables us to skirt the whole issue of enough. When we are enmeshed in addictions, we have no time to question. In fact, it is the nature of an addiction to demand abstinence from questioning our behavior. Addiction is rooted in denial. What we deny are the questions themselves. What we keep out is the significant matter of when enough is enough.

Just Enough

Jesus Christ has a unique take on enough, both in terms of quality and quantity. The Gospels speak of a radically new perspective on determining enough. Less is more. Gain is loss. Weakness yields glory. Suffering yields joy. All the values of the world are turned upside down. Jesus preaches and teaches a message of grace as the one true source of enough.

The world teaches us from a perspective that we are never enough: We never own enough. Big is better. Faster is better. Easier is better. Honesty is seldom the best policy. Don't let them see you sweat. We cannot reveal our humanity. Remember Edmund Muskie running for president? He cried. He lost. He lost because he cried. Again, humanness was found to be intolerable. The world would tell us that only power and money create enough.

Let me review with you how I believe Christ defines the concept enough.

Small Is Big

Jesus was a big advocate of small. Jesus' gospel was small. The message was small: Preach good news to the poor. Build the Kingdom of God on this earth. You are my beloved child; with you I am well pleased. I will be with you always. Don't be afraid.

In a world where size matters in everything, Jesus was the champion of a little. What a difference a little kindness ... forgiveness ... laughter ... hope ... love ... can make. A faith the size of a mustard seed can move mountains.

Jesus was not much for appearances. He was not impressed by power or wealth. He could have cared less about size. He was a David to the world's Goliath. Jesus cared about the spiritual innards. It was a person's perspective that mattered. Their values, ethics, morality, and belief system—this was how you knew an individual. Appearances said nothing; attitude and actions said it all.

Less Is More

> "And why worry about clothes? Look how the wild flowers grow; they do not work or make clothes for themselves. But I tell you that not even Solomon, rich as he was, had clothes as beautiful as one of these flowers."
>
> —Matthew 6:28–29

As you can see in this passage, Jesus simply expends little to no energy worrying about external things. He sees no spiritual function in worrying about anything that is of trivial importance, or beyond our control.

Jesus was a big advocate of simplicity. If you don't need it, give it away. Don't clutter your life with stuff. Don't fill up your lives or your schedule with what does not matter. Don't measure your success by how much you own or how many you know.

God pays little attention to much or many. God pays attention to those few things that truly matter.

Could this be the real reason why we feel good when we clean out a closet or drawer or room? It is clean, and we feel the relief of ridding ourselves of that which we don't need.

Isn't this the same principle behind removing a bad habit or attitude or even relationship from our lives? Our lives become cluttered by excess. No matter how we arrange it, clutter is a mess.

This is also true for our insides. When we are swarming with worry or anxiety; when we carry the excess baggage of guilt, shame, or fear; or when we drag around a trunk full of grudges or disappointments, we are carrying internal clutter.

Our souls often need a good cleaning to remove the excess emotion that has been gathering the dust of despair for far too long.

Loss Is Gain

> "If you cling to your life, you will lose it; but if you give it up for me, you will find it."
>
> —Matthew 10:39

This passage is the forerunner to the idea of letting go and letting God. The truly spiritual life begins with stop. We stop trying to be in control. We cease the futile effort to be in charge. We wave the white flag. We surrender. In surrendering, we ironically find our freedom, the freedom to be the people we were created to be.

Surrender. The world despises that word. Our American culture holds it in contempt. Surrender is for losers, for the weakest links, for the unfit. We are encouraged to avoid surrender at all costs.

Surrender is the loss of everything, but from Christ's perspective, it is the loss of all that which does not matter. When we have the spiritual courage to wave the white flag of surrender, to turn over our lives to God's care, we have gained access to the one thing that does matter. We become God's beloved children again. We surrender our ego's pretensions to being a somebody without God. We forego our human desire to play God. We free ourselves from our cultural compulsion to be self-sufficient.

Jesus was a loser by most American standards. He had no wealth or power or position. He considered himself a servant to all. He spent far too much time with those the world despised. He went so far as to wash the dirty, smelly feet of others. He was the victim of mocking and persecution. Jesus won only one fight—the one for the human heart.

WEAKNESS YIELDS GLORY

The Widow's and Widower's Workshop was held on a Sunday afternoon in March. The day outside was as gray and dreary as the 12 faces that gathered with me inside. A gloomy day was matched by a gloomy gathering. We ate our soup in awkward silence, punctuated only by an occasional smile or acknowledgment that the soup was delicious. After lunch, I asked everyone to join me in the lounge. Ten women and two men reluctantly followed me to an oval of couches and chairs.

"How do you feel about being here?"

Silence. Stones shouted. It was first meeting of Mutes Anonymous.

"Please ... be honest."

At last "Hank" broke the silence. He had lost "Marie" to cancer about seven months earlier. His regal baritone spoke succinctly,

"I really didn't want to come. I didn't figure it would be much fun sitting around with a bunch of folks just as miserable as I am. I came because I hate to cook. Plus, anyplace at this point feels better than being home alone."

Suffice it to say, this one brief, direct, honest response opened up a dynamic exchange. Feelings and stories and remembrances were swapped. Tears were shed. Gales of laughter filled the room. The seeds of friendship were planted. At the end of the workshop, the group quickly planned their next gathering. They didn't seem to care if I could be there, which was a good sign.

This group became a real ministry, not only to one another, but also to many others for many years to come. By sharing the fragileness of their lives as widows and widowers, they managed to reinforce their will to live and love again. To the glory of God, they came in weakness and created strength. Blest be the tie that binds. It is a strong, sturdy knot.

Suffering Yields Joy

I arrived home at about nine. There were several cars in the driveway. There were kids in the front yard. There were kids in the kitchen and the living room. Funny, I didn't remember planning a party, and I couldn't remember inviting anyone over tonight.

My son Justin spotted my arrival. He maneuvered his way out of a clot of youth in the front hall and ran over to intercept me. As I looked around the room, several faces did become recognizable. They had been members of my wife's youth group. The last time I had seen most of them was at her funeral.

"Dad!" Justin said with anxious enthusiasm.

"Yep! It's your dear old dad. I guess I got home a little earlier than I said … or you hoped."

"Oh, you mean the group?"

"Geez, I can't remember sending out the invitations."

"You know, Dad, they are still grieving pretty hard. So I thought it might help if they came over for a bit."

I looked at my kind, sweet, lying-through-his-teeth son and said, "Justin, that is the most pathetic excuse I have ever heard. Even your mom thinks you have hit a new low."

We both erupted in laughter. We hugged. We both asked the throng to disperse and head home. I told them all I hoped the evening had helped with their grief. Several stared at me with puzzled looks smeared across their faces.

Suffering often produces joy. Since Christine's death, a remarkable intimacy and honesty has developed between Justin and me. We've been through so much together that we would not consider inflicting any more pain on the other. Our relationship has known more anguish than we ever imagined, but it has also known incredible joy—the joy of memories shared and created. The joy of being clear on what matters and what does not. The joy of knowing the gospel truth when you hear it, and especially when you don't!

JUST A PINCH

"All things are possible to him who believes."

—Mark 9:23

This one line says it all ... faith makes all things possible. Faith is the force of freedom. Faith is the author of all discipleship. Faith alone can build the Kingdom. Just a pinch of faith can make a miracle.

The only time I truly feel at ease is when I have just enough faith, which in turn yields just enough forgiveness, to believe and to be forgiven. This dynamic duo defines enough.

Faith states clearly that God alone is enough. We are never enough without God. We are more than enough with God. God is the key, the one true source of enough.

Forgiveness is the gracious gift of faith. Faith receives and gives this gift. When we feel forgiven, and we offer others forgiveness, our day is open to all possibilities. To live life to the fullest requires both feeling forgiven and offering forgiveness.

Faith and forgiveness. They both come solely from God. One cannot live without the other; they are soul mates. Their intimacy could scorch the sun. They are the width and the length by which a Christian measures enough.

Chapter Response by Rabbi Astrachan

For most of my adult life (and for all the years I have spent either studying to be or practicing as a rabbi), I have preached to both my co-religionists as well as my Christian neighbors and clergy that there are few issues which separate "us" from "them." Jesus, of course, is the biggest. The entire concept of *messiah* is a significant branch shooting off toward Christianity, which deflects away from Jewish theology. With some other, less glaring differences, Judaism and Christianity share so much in common it is really a shame that more Judeo-Christian adherents don't come together on a more regular basis to interact. In so many ways we share common goals and philosophies of life.

In this chapter, Pastor Grimbol focuses almost entirely on what some might call the sin of gluttony, or as he puts it: the haves and the have-nots. Which category we put ourselves into is really up to us. The problem, though, is that too many of us forget that while we always think we don't have enough, making us the "have-nots," there is always someone who has less than we do, making us the "haves."

For a long time, Judaism made great distinctions between classes of people. If you were a descendent of the Priestly line of Aaron, called the *Kohanim,* you were given top billing. If you were a descendent of the Priestly attendants, called the *Levites,* you were second in line. If you didn't qualify for either of those, you were simply an *Israelite* and basically got what was left. Modern Jewish movements that subscribe to a more liberal interpretation of historical lineage have done away with this class-system in favor of a much more inclusive, nonbiased system in which all are treated with complete equality. At least in a religious sense, we do not accept a notion of "haves" and "have-nots." Still, as Americans, this unfortunate dichotomy exists among nearly every schism of our culture.

When I lived in and served a small congregation in Macon, Georgia, for three years, I was confronted with an array of garments, bumper stickers, and jewelry that had emblazoned upon them the acronym, "WWJD?" which I learned quickly stood for the phrase, "What Would Jesus Do?" This was to serve, apparently, as a reminder to the wearer of his "Christian" obligation to do what would be right, noble, generous, and socially responsible in every possible situation. The funny thing about this was that long before I ever saw my first "WWJD," I had long been confronting injustice with the phrase, "What would be the Jewish thing to do?"

The fact is, all of us are obligated (religiously, morally, and ethically) to "do the right thing." The fact that we attach a religious caveat to this decree lends a particular weightiness to it. Of course, we want to do what is right *in the eyes of God.* But let's remember: God doesn't have eyes! But people do. And people see all and hear all. We know when we have done right and wrong. We know when others have done right and wrong. What it really comes down to, quite simply, is why do we do wrong when right is right?

Pastor Grimbol has given us great fodder to digest in so many ways. Let us all strive to give of ourselves in every way we can. But let us not only do so because it is what God wants. Let us do so because it is what humanity needs us to do. It isn't just the Christian way. It isn't just the Jewish way. It is the right way.

PART 4

THE WHERE QUESTIONS

Where questions ignite life. They give life zest. They spark the imagination, embolden the heart, and tantalize the mind. Where questions add flavor to our lives. The quest salts life. The hunt peppers life with mystery and wonder. The whole experience of looking gives life the aroma of fresh baked bread.

Where do I find faith? Where do I find hope? Where do I find love? These questions call us to a quest. The treasure has been hidden by God, who is also not much of a "hider." If we are possessed of the spirit of a child, we will thrill to the hunt. We will seek knowing that the treasure will be found. We will hunt for treasure that is never buried, but hidden out in the open. We just have to look. Look with our whole being. The joy is in the search.

The central issue of all where questions is whether we trust the map. God provides the map. The map is accurate and quite detailed. The map is our life. Our lives contain all the clues. Our lives ceaselessly attempt to point us in the right direction. If we pay attention to our lives, if we bother to notice what our hearts and minds and bodies are telling us, if we are open to receiving the endless messages of a gracious God, and if we embrace the fun-loving nature of the hunt, the treasure will be ours.

WHERE DO I FIND FAITH?

Pastor William R. Grimbol

I believe faith to be our nature. I believe that faith is divinely planted, like a mustard seed rooted at the core of our being. I believe that faith is our original blessing. Like the bird that knows exactly when to fly south, I believe our souls possess such spiritual instincts. Our hearts and minds are inclined to God. Our bodies ceaselessly inform us of a Higher Power. We are never meant to be away from God. God is home. Home sweet home. No place like home.

I have never believed in original sin. It has never made any sense to me. When I hold a babe for baptism, all I am aware of is the awesome call to love without conditions. Each child is such a blessing. We cannot look into a child's eyes and see evil.

We cannot behold a child's face and witness sin. I believe with my whole heart that we are born in blessedness. We are God's beloved children. God is well pleased with each of us. We carry within us the awareness that we are loved beyond measure. That is the foundation of faith, the ground of grace in which we are rooted.

Therefore, I don't believe that faith is ever lost. It may be buried under a pile of worries or fears, hidden in a cave of despair, enshrouded in the fleshy folds of laziness and luxury, or cast off in the pursuit of power and wealth or we may be too busy to even notice its presence, but our faith is there. Always. Eternally. Like the sky. Like time. Like our very own breathing.

Where do we find faith? Often we must uncover our faith. We must surrender our piles of troubles to God. We must let go of the burdens that clutter our lives. We must accept God's presence and his power to dig us out of the traps that bury us. At times we must recover our faith. We need to go back to the basics. We need to work on the loving and forgiving, the praying and worshiping, and the serving and sacrificing that fuel the engine of faith. On occasion we must discover our faith. We must see it through fresh eyes. We must embrace it like a newborn babe. At these times our faith must be allowed to consume our whole being, to become who we are and what we do. At these moments, we are indeed born again. God's will becomes our will. Being born again is a daily decision.

I think of faith as being dabbed onto our lives by a generous and gracious God. The dabs are like the dots in a connect-the-dots picture. As we begin to connect these dots, a face begins to emerge. It is the face of God. For me it is the face of Jesus Christ. Each of us has different dots. Each connect-the-dots picture contains a unique image. Each of us sees the face of God with different features. Each of us has an original faith—like a snowflake or fingerprint.

In this chapter, I will share with you some of the places I have found faith being dabbed onto my life, sacred spots on the map where I have witnessed God's unmistakable signature. These are holy places, places filled with the presence of God, places that bear the brushstrokes of God's artistry. The dabs or dots are the footprints of God and offer me a path to follow. When I have chosen to follow, which is my only real choice, I have always been led to treasure—never buried treasure, but treasure always sitting out in the open, right under my nose.

FAITH IS FOUND IN LIVING

The clues are all found in our lives. The map is drawn on the landscape of our existence. The dots are dabbed upon the canvas of our experience. To look for faith is to look at life, to recognize life for the miracle it is. It is to be vividly aware of the importance of paying attention, to be conscious that God's will for us is to take note of all that matters.

Faith is to accept being fully human. To be human occurs only in the context of life. This is our life; we have no other. This day is all we have. This moment is all that exists. This reality is the one we struggle hardest to accept.

We often look to the past for clues. Many of us secretly believe that the treasure is permanently buried in the past. Sometimes we are certain that the map will appear in the future. The dots will all magically connect some day soon. The faith fact is that all clues—all dots, all maps, all treasure—can only be found in the *now*. The issue is receptivity. When we are combing the past for clues or preparing for the future arrival of our map, we pay no attention to the kingdom that exists in our midst.

Faith is found here and now. The issue for us is to be awake, aware, and alive. If we are open and receptive, the dot will be dabbed, the map will yield directions, and the treasure revealed.

It is just that simple, and yet many of us go for months, maybe years, without allowing ourselves to experience such a moment.

COMING TO OUR SENSES

Our bodies are informants. They tell us when God is present. We get a lump in our throat and feel the breath of God warm our being. We have goose bumps and know of God's wisdom. We get a shiver up and down our spine and feel the awe of God's presence. We are left dumbstruck and are finally quiet enough to be able to hear the Word of God. We are blown away, and all that remains standing is what matters. We lose track of time and enter eternity.

Our daydreams speak to us of our longings. Our dreams either unravel the worries of the day or foreshadow our hopes for tomorrow. Our fantasies are filled with our humanity and our divinity. Each and every morsel of each and every day is jammed with messages from God. Each message is sent without code.

Ironically, each message is basically the same: I am God, and you are not. You are mine. You are my beloved. You shall be as gods.

Coming to our senses, we are free to the degree we are aware. We are free to become the people God created us to be. Our senses give us spiritual feedback. They are homing devices. They receive messages from God and show us the way home to God.

Faith Is Found in Doubting

Doubts. Questioning if anything matters. Wondering about the point and purpose of life. Trying to figure out if there is a rhyme or reason to it all. Asking if there is a God.

Doubts are not denials. Doubting does not deny faith, nor does it prevent its formation. Doubting is where the seeking starts. Doubting is essential to the whole spiritual process. A doubt is the match that is thrown onto the kindling of faith.

Faith is not a certainty, warranty, or guarantee. Faith is not a dogma or doctrine or a collection of rules or regulations. Faith is certainly not some religious hierarchy. Faith is rooted in mystery. The mystery is shaped by doubts. The doubts become the ground in which true faith is grown.

A faith without doubts is a blind faith. It is faith without eyes or ears. Without doubts, faith becomes nothing more than a religion that calls for the removal—not the renewal—of your mind. A faith void of doubt is the product of indoctrination, not inspiration, and becomes a faith without a leap. Without a leap of faith, which crosses the chasm of doubt, faith just stands still. Such faith is lifeless, clueless, and hopeless. Jesus did not want slaves who had no choice but to follow; he wanted disciples, free to choose and willing to take the leap of faith.

Doubting directs our seeking. Doubting motivates our maturing. Doubting dabs on the first dots of the painting.

Faith Is Found in Maturing

I believe that maturation and spirituality are one and the same. If you are maturing, I believe that God is alive and well within you. Maturation is the art of the soul. It is the soul that can resolve the conflicts and challenges of maturation.

I recently met the father of a young man I was counseling. He was in his mid-40s but acted 16. He was still stranded in the pursuit of his identity and hopelessly stuck in the need to prove his manhood. The net result was the experience of a man who had no spiritual tools to raise a teenager. He lacked perspective, patience, and perseverance. He made everything a battle. He disparaged his son into submission and unknowingly fostered a relationship built solely on fear. Although he saw himself as a good man and as a good father, he was neither.

Maturation is work. It is not simply aging. It is not having a license to drink or smoke. It has little to do with having sex or making money. Maturity is all about …

+ Knowing our strengths and weaknesses.
+ Knowing our dreams and limits.
+ Facing and handling conflict.
+ Overcoming obstacles and fears.
+ Learning to compromise and build consensus.
+ Relinquishing power to a Higher Power.

- Conforming our will to God's.
- Aging with grace and gratitude.
- Learning how to live well.
- Learning how to die well.

These are all matters of faith. They address the subject of our longings and yearnings. They are the issues of being human and being alive. They are the topics that haunt and hallow our days.

They are the passages of maturation. Maturation is movement forward. It is circular. It is a spiral, like strands of DNA. The movement must be headed somewhere, to someplace. I believe that maturation is headed home. For me, Jesus is home, the one place where I truly belong, the place where I can be ordinary. Jesus is a place of quiet rest, as well as the joyful noise of intimate chatter. He is a holy habitation where I get to be and become myself.

Faith Is Found in Praying

Christine and I were having problems. Our marriage was in trouble. We had let things get so bad that our last conversation was about dividing up the furniture. We decided to seek counseling. We chose a pastoral counselor. Because we were both ministers, this seemed a logical decision.

At the conclusion of our first appointment, which had pretty much been *Hiroshima the Sequel,* Dan, our pastoral mediator, asked us to pray together. We were stunned. When did prayer become part of the deal?

I know. We're ministers. Aren't we used to praying? Well, yes, but for others, not to and for one another. This was new. This brought forth all kinds of anxiety.

It took us a full five minutes to decide who would start the prayer. We were like two awkward 13-year-olds negotiating our first kiss. It was humiliating. It was revealing. I cannot tell you anything of what was contained in the prayer. I don't remember the words. What I clearly recall, though, is the experience.

The anger melted. The need to prove my point evaporated like a morning mist. My disdain for Christine's behavior was suddenly replaced with the recognition of how much she loved me and how much I adored her. The prayer transformed us from a pair of warring partners, hell bent on beating each other up, back into two lovers and friends struggling to be happy together.

In that moment of prayer, we discovered a few faith facts. It was life that was difficult, not the marriage. Chris was not responsible for my boredom, and I was not responsible for her fears. Blaming one another was pointless. Building a case against one another was a pure waste of time. It was hard to have someone know me so well that none of my convenient excuses worked.

It was hard to see the reality of who I truly was in my wife's face. Her eyes knew my gospel truth.

Prayer isn't magic; it is not some instant miracle. However, I do find it to have awesome and mysterious power. Prayer has the uncanny ability to ...

+ Focus us on what truly matters.
+ Dissolve anger, fear, and guilt.
+ Reduce tension.
+ Unleash love.
+ Create hope.
+ Encourage forgiveness.
+ Center us in patience.
+ Grant a fresh start.

Prayer brings us back home to God. Prayer brings God into the equation. Prayer invites God in. Prayer affirms our ultimate desire to behave as God would wish us to. Prayer offers us the strength to admit our flaws and failings and to claim our need to be forgiven. Prayer erases our worst and brings out our best.

Prayer is a discipline. It requires daily practice. It is the art of listening and waiting to hear God's word. It is the craft of whittling away at our worries and fears, our grudges and jealousies, and our anger and rage and replacing them with the calm of a Christ-centered soul. Prayer is one sure way to experience that peace that passes all understanding.

Jesus prayed often. He utilized prayer as a means of releasing fear and expressing hope. Prayer was his way of removing himself from a world whose neediness threatened to suffocate him. In prayer he reestablished his spiritual connection. He found support and strength. His spine and spirit grew firmer. His intimacy with God deepened.

Prayer is my greatest homing device. It brings me back to God. It clears away the clutter of the world and the fog of my own pride. Prayer locates my faith. Prayer, without exception, moves me in the right direction. It may be no more than a spiritual inch, but at least I know I am headed somewhere I want to go.

> "Truly, truly, I say to you, if you ask anything of the Father, he will give it to you in my name. Hitherto you have asked nothing in my name; ask, and you will receive, that your joy may be full."
>
> —John 16:23–24

Prayer is faith in action. The action we take is to claim God. Prayer seeks joy. The source of all joy is in relationship to God. We may not want to think of prayer as simply asking God for help or healing or hope, but it is. It is just that simple. Prayer is often more than enough.

Faith Is Found in Loving

"To him who strikes you on the cheek, offer the other also; and from him who takes away your cloak, do not withhold your coat as well. Give to everyone who begs from you; and of him who takes away your goods do not ask them again. And as you wish that men and women would do to you, do so to them.

"If you love those who love you, what credit is that to you? For even sinners love those who love them. And if you do good to those who do good to you, what credit is that to you? For even sinners do the same. And if you lend to those from whom you hope to receive, what credit is that to you? Even sinners lend to sinners, to receive as much again. But love your enemies, and do good, and lend, expecting nothing in return; and your reward will be great, and you will be sons and daughters of the Most High; for he is kind to the ungrateful and the selfish. Be merciful, even as your Father is merciful."

—Luke 6:27–36

In these passages of Scripture, Jesus stresses the demands of loving. To love in faith demands us to be at our best. Jesus calls us to the difficult task of loving those that the world rejects. We are asked not only to love extravagantly, but to do so even when we might be provoked to hate, or to respond with hostility. Love is hard work. In the eyes of Jesus, it is the hardest work we will ever do, as well as the most rewarding—eternally.

For me, the Bible is a constant and dependable source of faith. It is within the domain of Scripture that I hear Christ's incessant call to love. It is here that I learn that Jesus is the author of love. Jesus tells me the gospel truth, that love is all there is and that God is pure love. Jesus challenges me to a love that is extravagant and bold, a love that embraces the outcast and courts the enemy, a love that stretches to the width of the cross. Jesus calls me to a love that knows no end, a love that risks pain and hurt, a love that is willing to suffer, a love that accepts compromise and change, a love that is grown best in the garden of commitment.

Jesus advocates a radical love, a love with a bleeding heart, a love that has no concern for what the world thinks and could care less about playing the fool. This is a love without conditions and that asks for nothing in return.

This radical love goes against every notion of our American culture. We are the culture of pre-nuptial agreements. We are warned not to let anyone take advantage of us and that to be tenderhearted or merciful is to be played the fool. Our culture asks what is in it for *us*—this question is thought of as key, as a sign of wisdom. Not to ask about the personal benefits is considered downright dumb. Our culture loves only on condition.

We know when we are being truly loving. We also know when we are being manipulative or trying to be in control. We know the difference between loving graciously, without conditions, and loving by the book, where there are all kinds of conditions.

We are aware that one feels right, even holy, and the other feels false, even phony. It is genuinely hard to lie about loving. We have to really work at it or have had to made it a habit.

The heart informs us when the love is real. The heart knows when we are coming from a place of grace. We know the gospel truth when we hear it. The heart offers a foolproof lie-detector test.

Create in me a clean heart. A clean heart is a loving heart, a heart that is not soiled by the desire to have its own way and that is not stained by any playing of games.

When we love, we come alive. Our loving enables God to move in and through us. Our loving locates our faith. One cannot love without deepening one's faith. All love yields faith. It is impossible to genuinely love without believing that somehow we were meant to love. Loving reminds us of who we are and who we were created to be. Loving illuminates and guides our faith. Loving is both the means and the ends of faith.

Our loving bears the imprint of God's love. We are God's students. We bear witness to God's artistry. Like those painters of the Rembrandt School who worked tirelessly to mimic Rembrandt's style, we of the Christian School are equally disciplined in our efforts to recreate the love we have first known in faith.

Loving takes place in relationships. Relationships are the context in which faith is grown. Faith does not blossom in isolation. Faith bears no fruit alone. The Scripture tells us that Jesus sought disciples. He did so, I believe, because it was his need. He needed followers. He needed friends. He needed a spiritual family. He needed to pass on his legacy of love.

Faith is at its very best in community. True community is a celebration of diversity. Community thrives on difference.

The disciples were 12 guys who, by heritage and history, would struggle to agree on anything. The disciples were a community of faith. Twelve versions of the same story. A dozen different viewpoints. Twelve men held in community by the power of their love for one another and for Jesus Christ.

FAITH IS FOUND IN FORGIVING

> "'You wicked servant! I forgave you all that debt because you besought me; and should you not have had mercy on your fellow servant, as I had mercy on you?' And in his anger his lord delivered him to the jailers, till he should pay all his debt.
>
> "So also my heavenly Father will do to every one of you, if you do not forgive your brother from your heart."
>
> —Matthew 18:32–35

This passage places a focus on forgiveness. Jesus demands that those who follow him, fully comprehend that they, too, were forgiven. He asks them only to give what they first received.

Jesus is enraged when those who claim him as Lord, fail to reflect his commitment to forgiveness. Jesus simply demands that mercy be seen as integral to faith. One cannot function without the other.

Jesus performed miracles. He healed the sick. He gave sight to the blind. He enabled the lame to walk. He restored hearing to the deaf. He rid many souls of their demons. He brought the dead back to life. These miracles are all matters of faith. In faith they are believable; without faith they are fabrication.

At the core of most of these miracles is forgiveness. It is the forgiveness of sins that forms the foundation upon which the miracle is constructed. The forgiveness comes first, then the miracle. Forgiveness heralds the arrival of the miracle. Why?

What is it about forgiveness that has such miraculous healing powers? How about the following:

+ Forgiveness releases energy.
+ Forgiveness untangles the knots of anxiety and fear.

- ✦ Forgiveness heals the wounds of hurt and disappointment.
- ✦ Forgiveness brings grieving to closure.
- ✦ Forgiveness creates calm.
- ✦ Forgiveness puts us at ease again.
- ✦ Forgiveness sets us right with God.
- ✦ Forgiveness restores respect.
- ✦ Forgiveness restores faith.
- ✦ Forgiveness renews our intimacy with God.

When Justin was five, we put in a pool. It was an above-ground pool that we had dropped into the ground. The day the hole was dug and the pool liner placed, Justin's mom told him to stay away and to throw nothing into the hole that might rip the liner. The next day, Christine saw eight good-size stones in the bottom of the would-be pool. Christine was as mad at Justin as I had ever seen her. He got his first swat on his bottom and was placed in his room for a few hours.

That night when he emerged for his supper, he was as pale as a ghost. His eyes were red rimmed from crying. His breathing was huge and heavy. His mother melted—as I knew she would—as she knew she would. It was only Justin who did not know. She took Justin in her arms and told him it was all over. He was for-given, and she was sorry for having been too angry.

She explained that it was big investment for us to put in a pool, and she was frightened that the pool liner had been ripped. She made it clear to Justin that he was far more important than the pool, and though she deserved to be mad, and he deserved to be punished, she had overreacted. She said she was sorry.

The look on their faces was unforgettable. Justin wore an expression of such raw relief and joy. Christine was ablaze with love for her child. The look revealed the heart of forgiveness.

Forgiveness creates the context in which grace is known and faith is found.

Over my 25 years of ministry, I have rarely seen that look. Forgiveness is not only hard work, I believe it is the most neglected aspect of our faith. We live in a culture that advocates getting even. I suspect that most of us see forgiveness as giving in, surrendering, losing. Forgiveness somehow means weakness. We would rather hold a grudge or simply walk away than to forgive.

Forgiveness takes a strong faith. Forgiveness is the acid test of faith.

I watch couples divorcing over the silliest of issues. I hear of fathers who will not talk to their sons, or sisters who cannot be seated together at a wedding, or the uncle who will not be allowed to attend a funeral. I listen to sad stories of friendships dissolved over trivialities and families broken apart by money or gossip or childhood rivalries. If there is one great sadness I have known in my ministry, it has been my inability to communicate the centrality of forgiveness to the Christian faith.

Jimmy Carter said, "Forgiving is one of the most difficult things for a human being to do, but I think it means looking at some slight you feel, putting yourself in the position of the other person, and wiping away any sort of resentment and antagonism you feel toward them. Then let that other person know that everything is perfectly friendly and normal between you."

Faith Is Found in Believing

Seeing is believing. How true. This morning at 5 A.M., I headed to the beach to watch a meteor shower. It was breathtaking. Streaks of light flashed across the sky in a God-made fireworks display. I could not imagine how anyone viewing this spectacle could not believe in God.

I feel the same whenever I witness a first snowfall, or the lime lace of spring, or the pumpkin innards of autumn. I am in awe of how the sky and sea reveal the myriad moods of the creator. I see the face of God in every sleeping child—pure peace.

To behold beauty is to have our breath taken away. A brief death. This mini-death yields a sudden rebirth. A rekindling of faith. A reconnection with the artist behind the beauty. A reawakening of belief in the awesome splendor that is God's creation. Beauty teaches us to believe in a creator. Beholding beauty is like catching a glimpse or glance of God's grace.

Believing is seeing. To believe enables us to have insight and to live with vision. There are many days when I do not feel like being Christ-like. I am lazy. I like easy. I resist conflict, confrontation, and, often, maturation. I have, however, learned to act as if the faith is there. I choose to believe. I wear Christ like a cloak. I look at life through Christ's eyes, and I can see the truth. I can see what I need to be and do.

Believing creates faith. To choose to believe, even in the absence of faith, will miraculously and mysteriously create the faith needed to conform to God's will. Let me put it this way: Believing is trust. Choosing to believe is surrendering our will to God's. If I have decided to trust that Jesus Christ knows what is best for me, I surrender, I let go, I let God. God enters my life and world. God creates and inspires my faith. My faith, a gracious gift from God, animates my being.

If this sounds like talking in circles, well, it is. All talk of faith is talking in circles. All faith is paradox and irony. All faith is the fusion of human and divine. Faith is the expression of the inexpressible. Believing often comes before faith. Faith follows belief's lead. I don't know why. I just know this to be true in my life and in my faith.

Choosing to believe opens the eyes of my faith. I see with honesty. I see inside myself and others. I see clearly, as if my world has been suddenly illuminated. I have a vision, a hope.

I have a view of where God is sending me and why. Believing frees me to be aware. Awareness reveals the nature and will of God. Faith is all about such awareness, and a lived faith is to be conscious of what I see. The hope of faith is to see what God sees.

WHERE DO WE FIND FAITH?

We find faith everywhere, in everything, in everyone. It's in life, in death, in the seasons, the skies, and the seas. It's on the face of humankind and on the face of God. We are granted numerous glances and glimpses of God's grace, moments when we know that life is too good *not* to be true. These moments, events, and experiences are times when the gospel truth has pierced life's hide, when it has cut it and made it bleed. These are the revelations of God. What is revealed is our part in the play, our role in the mystery, our connectedness to the author and artist.

To find faith we must look closely and attentively to our lives. We must be awake, aware, and alive. God arrives on every dawn. Faith is the wisdom to greet the dawn.

CHAPTER RESPONSE BY RABBI ASTRACHAN

There are a lot of religious people in the world. If you consider yourself Jewish or Christian or Buddhist or a member of any recognizable faith, you are, by definition, religious. Few who are religious, however, are observant. Last year during the period Jews refer to as the High Holy Days (the period of time between Rosh HaShanah and Yom Kippur, usually in September in the secular calendar) I preached a sermon on the differences between being *religious* and being *observant*. I think most of those listening (not all in attendance were listening, I'm sure) were confused by my remarks. You see, in my years as a rabbi I have been confronted with the following situation:

I receive a call about a funeral, often from a family who is unaffiliated with any synagogue in the area. I am, therefore, performing a ceremony for a person I never knew, speaking with family members of the deceased whom I do not know, and trying to not only offer comfort and consolation but also to learn about their loved one in order to adequately prepare a personalized eulogy and service. In almost every situation, among the first words out of the family's mouths are, "Rabbi, we aren't very religious people. Please keep the service short."

Of course, that moment is not the time to contradict what they've just shared with me, but the fact is, they are religious. They consider themselves Jews, they want a Jewish burial service, they want a rabbi to officiate. They are religious. The distinction, however, is that they are not particularly observant. They do not belong to a synagogue. They do not pay heed to the Sabbath. They do not attend worship services. They are not *observant*.

Something about their lives, however, has still guided them toward a *faith* that demands an appropriate farewell to their loved one who has passed on. That faith may be immature. They may have given little attention to how faith must grow with an individual throughout his life, but still there is a faith that demands they make arrangements in accordance with their religious background, whatever that happens to be.

Faith is an illusive presence in our lives. It is a gift, really. Not everyone has it. Some have only a basic concept of what it means to be faithful. Some have what they believe to be a mastery of faith; for them it is unwavering and undeniable. Wherever you happen to be with your faith, I encourage you to continually evaluate your connection with your faith every day. Do not take for granted that it will simply be there for you when you need it. You must hone it, shape it, and mold it to be what you want it to be. If you don't, you might find it to be, like an old box of opened cereal left open in the back of the cupboard, just a stale mess with nothing decent to offer you. Therefore ...

+ Have faith in others.
+ Have faith in God.
+ Have faith in yourself.
+ Allow others to have faith in you.
+ Be faithful to your spouse and to your family.

But beyond faith, observe. Be everything you can be to the faith you maintain. If you are going to consider yourself part of a religious tradition, whatever that tradition may be, do it with every ounce of who you are. Live your life with the knowledge and the comfort that *faith* is what is driving you to make yourself a better person and this world a better world.

WHERE DO I FIND HOPE?

Pastor William R. Grimbol

The Scripture tells us that hope is found where we least expect it. Hope was found in a manger. Hope was found in a brood of 12 guys who were known to doubt, deny, and betray their friends, as well as compete for the affection of their leader. Hope was found beaten and robbed at the side of the road. Hope was discovered at a pig trough. Hope was revealed in the eyes of a leper. Hope was even found on a bloodied cross. Hope arrives when we are sure it is too late. Hope occurs in situations that the world deems hopeless. Hope is indeed found where we are certain it cannot be.

In this chapter we will see how one family became a beacon of hope for a whole community. In the midst of great tragedy, this family chose to make hope their habit. This very personal story will reveal the very personal nature of choosing to live a life in hope.

FINDING HOPE

One week ago I received a phone call from Marion, a woman in my congregation. She does not live on Shelter Island, but each Sunday she drives over from Amagansett, New York, a neighboring village—which requires a trek and ferry ride. Marion is a good friend, a remarkably gentle and gracious presence, and a sweet soul. She told me that Tess, a little girl who had valiantly fought cancer of the brain for 21 months, had died. Marion and her family were summertime neighbors of Tess and her family.

Marion made a request. She asked if I would be willing to coordinate the funeral service. I reminded her that I had not known

Tess nor ever met the Ryan family. I said that I would be glad to help but asked if she was aware of the family's wishes or plans. She said that the family was not religious, but she found them to be overwhelmingly spiritual. I understood. She said she thought they would welcome my assistance. I said I would do whatever I could, but I would need to hear directly from the family. I did not want to assume anything in such a delicate situation.

Later that day I did hear from the Ryan family. We agreed on a date and time for the service and set up a meeting to plan the celebration of Tess's magical life. As I drove to that appointment, I felt anxious. I knew that Tess's battle with cancer had become a "cause" on the East End of Long Island and that her passing would be powerful and painful for literally thousands of folks—especially children. I felt hopelessly inept as I drove into the driveway. I could not imagine a more difficult or depressing task. How do you bury a child who everyone fought so valiantly to keep alive? Tess had touched so many lives with joy. How could her death and funeral be anything but gut-wrenching? I entered the house and was introduced to Dianne, Tess's mother.

Dianne is truly one of the most impressive spiritual souls I have ever encountered. Her every word and action radiated her devotion to Tess. Her heart had been ripped out by Tess's death, and she held it out before her without fear or reservation. The only entry into this family would be through the doorway of Dianne's raw grief. It was instantly clear that I could not know Tess without first knowing the lava flow of Diane's love.

Gordon, Tess's father, wisely asked me to look at all kinds of photos of Tess. I saw Tess in all her blonde ringlet glory, splashing in pools and playing in the sand, wearing costumes, singing songs, and dancing up a storm. I also saw Tess with a bloated face—a face contorted in pain but one that still radiated a hint of joy.

Gordon is a lawyer. He is quieter and much tighter-lipped than Dianne. Still, his eyes were wet and reflected the anguish of a daddy.

We sat in the living room. The fire was blazing. Above it hung a recent painting of Tess, a magnificent rendering by David Joel. In it, Tess was aglow and serene and smiling softly, monarch butterflies flittering about her face and body. It felt like an altar. Tess's sisters joined the gathering—Robin, all quiet and stoic dignity, and Loralee, all spunk, spark, and fire. A few friends of Dianne's and Gordon's completed the group.

I asked them to tell me about Tess. Then I listened. I listened with my heart. What I heard was truly inspiring. What I heard gave me such a powerful sense of hope. Hearing all about this beloved child—this little Auntie Mame, this kid with a smirk and a smile and a sigh, this angel unaware—gave me more hope than I had felt in months. I want to share with you what I heard, because I believe it will tell you a great deal about where to look for and how to find hope.

Trust me, the last place I thought I would find hope was in planning Tess Ryan's funeral. I never expected her funeral celebration to be one of the most powerful spiritual events of my life. I had no idea that a child I never knew would manage to restore my faith and renew in me a bright burning hope. Who would have thought it? Only God ... and, as I came to know, Tess.

Hope Is Found in Joy

Every word spoken about Tess was coated in joy. Joy was the essence of Tess. It was that word—joy—that kept coming up in every description, story, and anecdote, over and over again like the refrain of a favorite song. Tess enjoyed her life. Tess brought joy to life. Tess took joy from life.

When Tess was forced to leave school to see the doctor, she did something quite remarkable. She first said good-bye to each and every child in her class. She said their name. She said good-bye.

Did she know that the doctor would have bad news? Was she spiritually aware of how sick she was? I do not know those answers, but I have my beliefs. What I do know is that Tess knew how to get the most from her days. She dove into life. She made a huge and joyous splash. She sprayed all who came near her with energy and exuberance.

Isn't this the case with all children? I wish that were true, but the answer is no. Many children are emotionally or spiritually shut down. They seem encased in worry or fear or approach life as if it were a fire that can only burn them. Tess knew life to be a fire that offered her light and warmth, and around it she gathered all who loved her.

Tess was an inspiration to the hundreds of folks who attended her funeral. Tess savored every morsel of her time here on Earth. In fact, she literally got her good friend Johnny, a landscaper, husband, and father, to bring her a gourmet menu of tasty treats.

Each day Johnny was given a list of delights to bring to Tess. Tess would have just a bite, knowing that her system could not handle too much. She only had a taste, but she had a taste of everything she could think of. Tess died the way she lived. She saw life for the feast it was, and she headed straight for the dessert table.

What brings you joy? When was the last time you experienced joy? What were you doing? Who were you with? Anyone? What were you feeling? Why? Did you notice a transformation in yourself? I suspect you did. The transformation was a dose of hope. Hope is produced by joy. Joy knows no other way to feel than hopeful.

When we know joy, hope gains access to our soul. Joy pries us open. Hope fills us up. Jesus' singular hope for us is that we enjoy our lives. Tess enjoyed each of her days to the max. In this one gesture, Tess proved to be more of a disciple than most people who claim to be on intimate terms with Jesus are. Jesus applauds and affirms a living faith. Tess lived what she somehow knew to believe.

At the funeral, Tess was called an old soul. I think this was a reference to her wisdom. Tess was truly wise. She was wise enough to receive life as a precious gift to be enjoyed.

Hope Is Found in Despair

The news of Tess's cancer spread like wild fire. The prognosis was dire—only a few months. Dianne and Gordon were devastated. Robin and Loralee were numbed and shocked by the news. Tess's school was swarming with sadness. It was February, a perfect month to know despair, a time of slush and drab gray, a time when the whole earth appeared as bleached and empty as the hearts of thousands of folks on the East End of Long Island.

I doubt there was a soul in Amagansett, East Hampton, or Montauk who was not angry with God. The question on everyone's lips was the proverbial "Why?" Why such a beautiful, joyous little girl? What can we do? How do we respond? Can we help? Just as Jesus shouted long ago, I imagine the sky filling with the words "Why hast thou forsaken me?" I can see many an angry fist aimed skyward at a seemingly indifferent God.

Nobody felt the pain deeper or stronger than Dianne. It nailed her to a cross of fear for her child—but only for a brief time. Dianne dug down deep inside herself, or maybe it was in response to Tess's indomitable spirit, but somewhere, somehow, out of the despair arose a ferocious determination to fight. Dianne and Tess led the battle and the charge. The Ryan army was quickly gathered. Out of the ashes of a diagnosis came a swift flying eagle of hope, an eagle that flew on the wings of a mother's love. Dianne made a decision. Gordon followed her lead, as did the kids, extended family, neighbors, and friends. If death was coming, it was in for one hell of a fight.

My ministry has repeatedly shown me that hope is grown in the "crap" that life dispenses. Like fertilizer, despair is often the rich soil of hope. Despair is the absence of hope. Despair confronts us with a demand for an answer. What will we do? Will we fold and run, or will we decide to fight? Will we shrivel and shrink and fade away, or will we rise to the occasion? Will we fly straight into the storm? The choice is ours. For Tess there was no question. This was all Dianne needed. The fight was on, and battle plans were quickly drawn.

There is a story in Scripture that tells of a night spent in despair. It is the tale of the Last Supper. Jesus gathers his disciples in an upper room. The wind whips, and the room is lit only by candles. Fear is thick in the air. They break bread together and sip wine. It is here that Jesus informs his spiritual brothers that their ministry together will soon be over. He tells them that three years of ministering in the spirit of mercy and love would soon come to a horrifying conclusion. Jesus makes it clear that he will be a sacrificial lamb. He will be savagely nailed to two beams of wood.

Can you imagine their despair? Can you feel their pain on that black night? Can you sense what it must have been like to hear your leader announce the demise of everything that had once given your life meaning and purpose? Hope must have rushed out of that room like fresh gossip. Twelve bewildered souls sat in silence, wondering what to say or do or be. Twelve wounded men ironically looked to Jesus for an answer.

The only answer he gave them was a promise, a promise that his legacy would live on, that his love for them would continue. They would not be alone. They would find the courage to minister again. They would lead the battle for the Kingdom. They would wage the war for justice. This promise may not have seemed like much to the world, but to the disciples it proved to be enough. It gave them just enough hope to move on and told them that life and love and faith would continue. It was a hard hope to cling to, but it was all they had.

The Christian people see themselves as a people who have known great darkness but who have also seen a great light. It is that black backdrop that makes the light so bright. It is the cross of Jesus that gives such richness to the new life of Easter. Easter without Good Friday is a hollow event. We call the blackest day of the spiritual year "good," because it is on that day that genuine hope took root and thrust itself up and out of the soil and into the light.

Hope Is Found in Community

Tess's 21-month battle against cancer was waged by an army. A whole community gathered to fight. Tess was the magnetic force that united these folks. No matter how brief, her life would matter. This was the catalyst that fueled the formation of this sacred group.

I believe even the community itself was stunned by their spiritual strength. Villages on the East End are often rife with division, saturated in petty jealousies, laden with long-held grudges, and struggling with a growing sense of class warfare. All divisions melted. Boundaries and class borders were crossed. A true community took shape, a community with a focus and a purpose, a community called into being by the plight of a little girl and her family.

For 21 months hundreds of people were willing to do anything to help. They made meals, sent cards, delivered gifts, made phone calls, and gave hugs. They prayed. They prayed in different churches and synagogues. They prayed on the beach.

They cared. They shared one another's pain. They became better parents. They became better teachers. They became better kids. They lifted up Tess with their compassion. The tears of the Ryan family fell down their cheeks.

Hope is never found in isolation. Hope requires relationship. Hope is best achieved in community. True community in America is hard to find. We certainly know it when we experience it. New York City became a true community on September 11, 2001. Amagansett, East Hampton, and Montauk became a true community in February 2000. In each case, hope was born in despair and claimed by folks determined to know joy again.

I have worked with teenagers for the past 25 years. I am often asked what makes today's adolescents different from those 15 or 20 years ago. I know *my* answer: Today's teens do not appear to be hopeful. They are cynical and often claim to care about nothing. They don't feel they matter. They don't feel that they make a difference. They don't think adults offer them much inspiration or hope. They don't see adult life as all that appealing. They are pessimistic and negative. They know the price tag of everything but the value of nothing. No, not all teens, nor all the time, but far too many youths, far too often, act hopeless.

I have come to the conclusion that one of the chief factors behind the pessimism and hopelessness I see in teenagers is their lack of belonging to any true community. They seldom see adults willing to drop their differences and band together around a common cause. The community often comes together only to complain or say no. Communities gather to express what they are against but rarely name what they are for. It is rare to see a community inspired and motivated by love.

I believe today's youth might find genuine hope in the experience of true community—community with a cause, community inspired by love and motivated by goodness, community that thrives not on anger but compassion, community that shouts not at one another but for a common hope. We adults owe it to our youth to teach them how to make hope a habit. To do so, we must work hard at forming community. Our families, our neighborhoods, and our churches and synagogues must all function as true communities, as places to belong, places to find meaning, places to locate hope.

Jesus formed the church to be a true community. It was his hope that the church would be a gathering of folks committed to ministry, inspired by love, and compelled by compassion. He hoped for a church of folks determined to build a kingdom of justice and equality, of people who worshipped and prayed to find the strength of faith to face the issues and crises of their world.

Admittedly, far too often the church is anything but a true community. It often functions more like an exclusive club. It can be brutally self-righteous and the last place on earth a lost sheep would hope to find help. The church is frequently motivated by the human need to be superior and judge others. The church is far too often better at producing shame and guilt than hope.

For 21 months, the communities of Amagansett, East Hampton, and Montauk functioned along the lines of what I believe Jesus intended for his church.

HOPE IS FOUND IN COURAGE

Dianne tells a splendid story of Tess's courage. After the cancer returned, Tess went swiftly downhill. Her sight diminished. Her speech slowed to almost a halt. She was weak and tired and suffering. Dianne took her for a swim. Tess loved the water. She floated there at her mother's side, enjoying whatever respite the water provided. Dianne noticed her straining to speak. With every fiber of her being working to shape the words, Tess asked her mom, "Are you still fighting?" Dianne assured her beloved daughter that she was and that she would not stop.

Hope is a choice. It is a courageous choice. It does not come cheap; it often exacts a huge price. Gordon told me that for 21 months, Tess did everything she was told. She never complained or resisted treatment. She waged a valiant fight.

She chose courage. That courage inspired hope in her parents, family, and friends. Tess's defiant display of courage kept the hope alive in the hearts of hundreds of East Enders.

Courage is contagious. When a choice for courage is made, all of life expands. When a decision is made to deny the truth, or to run and hide, all of life shrinks. I have heard it said that the difference between a hero and a coward is just one step taken sideways—getting out of the way and not facing the pain or problem. Courage is facing it. Courage comes face-to-face with the worst life has to offer and simply stares it down.

Tess faced her cancer. She looked it straight in the eye. She defied her cancer to beat her. The cancer may have won the physical battle, but on a spiritual level, Tess proved the victor, the far superior force. Her courage inspired her mother and father to a strength they never knew they had. Her courage created a community with greater compassion than they dreamed possible. Her courage demanded all who met her to believe that there is no such thing as false hope. All hope is hope. All hope is true. All hope is the gospel truth.

Jesus faced the cross. He wavered. He asked to have this terrible task removed from his life's journey. He ultimately accepted and carried his cross. He faced the pain and persecution of the world with courage. He held his head high against the world's mocking words, "Well, if you really are the Messiah, then come down off that cross." Christians believe in him because he did not get down. Our faith is built on his courage to come face to face with the world's evil. His courage to meet the cross is our courage to live a daily Easter. His courage became our hope.

HOPE IS FOUND IN CELEBRATION

Tess's funeral celebration was like nothing I have ever experienced. It was held at the Old Whaler's Church in Sag Harbor, New York, the parish my wife served for some 16 years. The last time I had been in the sanctuary to lead worship had been for Christine's funeral. The irony of this situation was not lost on me, nor I suspect, on Christ, Christine, or Tess.

I was moved from the moment I entered the sanctuary. Jacqui Leader, a woman of enormous talent and gifts, had transformed the church into a vision of heaven. There were stars and butterflies hanging everywhere. David Joel's extraordinary painting had now fulfilled its destiny and had become the altar. The flowers were bright and glorious. There was a huge sun made by Tess's class. The music played and the children chattered. Even before the service began, the holiness could be felt in the air.

The service started with a processional of children. They carried paintings, photos, and candles, all of which would soon adorn the sacred stage. They arrived to the sounds of "Dancing with Angels," and the congregation immediately began to clap. It was clear: This would be a service that would shake the foundation of the church and our very souls. We would be moved. We would be moved to a better and holier place.

We heard speaker after speaker tell us of how Tess had changed their lives. Tess the Tessinator had forced folks to see the world with fresh eyes. From Johnny Muse, her butler and buddy, to Alec Baldwin, her movie star pal, each adult acknowledged what they had learned from Tess. Tess the spiritual tutor. Tess the wisdom guide. Each speaker revealed the nature of Tess's mission on this earth—to teach us about the real good life, the one that is all about goodness.

We sang songs. We listened to everything from Julie Andrews singing "My Favorite Things" to "Love Potion #9." Diane Westbrook, of the First Baptist Church of Bridgehampton, sang "Amazing Grace" with such passion that for a time the whole congregation felt airborne. Loralee belted out "I Will Survive" and brought down the house. The congregation stood and cheered. Music is such a powerful way to communicate and celebrate.

For nearly three hours time stood still. A celebration of a life was being held, and we were held in the embrace of our awe for what one little girl can accomplish. The recessional was to the sounds of the First Baptist Church of Bridgehampton's choir singing "Swing Low, Sweet Chariot." There was not a dry eye in the house. The tears were tears of joy. We had all been changed. We were all new people. Celebration creates hope.

When the Christian community celebrates communion, we are once again called to hope. We are reminded that to live in the spirit of Christ will require everything we have. It will take our whole body and being. The bread and wine symbolize the sacrificial nature of true love, as well as the true heart of Christ's ministry. Christ died for loving extravagantly and boldly and for embracing the outcasts and the misfits.

When the Christian community celebrates baptism, we are equally called to hope. Baptism is the celebration of a new beginning, a once and forever fresh start. In baptism we celebrate the precious gift of both the child and our commissioning to surround the child with grace. The celebration of baptism is a symbol of the eternal hope of faith. Each child is seen as a sure sign of the infinite love of God.

There are only two sacraments in the Christian church: communion and baptism. I think of sacraments as sacred moments, times that are bloated with the presence of God. Each of these sacraments is designed to offer hope. The congregation is gathered to be inspired, moved, and called forth to lives of renewed strength and spirit.

Tess's service was a sacrament. Her life had been one long communion. Her death was a baptism into a new life.

Chapter Response by Rabbi Astrachan

As I understand Christian theology, its adherents await the "second coming" of Jesus. That is, for Christians, Jesus—the messiah—lived on Earth once, died, and will at some point in the future, return to walk on Earth once more. Judaism does not share such a concept. In fact, for Jews, it is believed that the one true Messiah has not yet come but is something for which we await with anxious anticipation.

From either perspective I think we can examine our religious lives with equal concern. Were Jesus to come back *or* were there to be a Jewish Messiah suddenly appear, what do you think that messiah would have to say about what we have done with our world? In general, I think that messiah would be aghast, at best, with the disaster we have made of God's world. We ought to be ashamed, every one of us, with what we have allowed to come to pass with each day we exist on this planet.

We all know that we have done despicable things in the eyes of God. We have all said horrible things about others for God to hear. We have cast aside and left untouched that which God would long to touch and care for and comfort.

Pastor Grimbol focused, in this chapter, on an extremely emotional, beautiful, and heart-warming story of a girl who fought valiantly to hang on to a world filled with such cruelty. She, herself, was a victim to it. Yet those around her came forth in droves to ensure that her final months on Earth were the very best that humanity could offer. People of all faith traditions and backgrounds rallied to offer their support and their prayers.

I realize that this situation was particularly sad because of the grave circumstance. But I believe it is also tragic because it took an illness to bring out of people what should be coming out of all of us all the time. We wait. We stand by idly, doing nothing at all, going about our daily routine.

Each time it happens, I'm sure there are those who say "I'm going to commit the rest of my life to making a real difference. I'm going to donate money to research. I'm going to donate my time to a cancer hospital. I'm going to ...." And maybe some actually do what they say. Most do not. And again, they wait.

It's time we woke up, people! All of us. Myself included. Just because Pastor Grimbol and I are clergy doesn't mean we are *holier than thou*. We're human beings like everyone else. And we, too, wait. It's time we stood up, gave everyone we know (including ourselves) a swift kick in the backside, and started doing something to actually make a difference in this world of ours.

Pastor Grimbol spoke in this chapter of *hope*. I think too many of us consider our role in *hoping* to be a passive activity. *Hope* is not going to get us very far if we don't do something pro-active to make it happen. Hoping is good. But if all we ever do is hope, we might as well just close our eyes, make a wish, and blow out the candles on the cake. No difference.

Where Do I Find Love?

Pastor William R. Grimbol

Love. So much has been said on the subject, yet so little of it has had much to say. We all act as if we have a Ph.D. on the subject, yet down deep we know that we are still waiting to graduate from kindergarten. Most of us claim that love is life's primary purpose. Most of us see love as just about all that truly matters. And yet few of us spend much time on learning the art of loving. Few of us seem to recognize our own need to improve and develop our skills as loving human beings.

We get an A in the "falling-in-love" department. Of course, that is a course we only need to audit. We all will fall in love. We all will know the wild, weird, wonderful sensation of losing control. We may not be good at the landing part, but most of us are reasonably good at the falling. We seem to understand that falling in love is all about chemistry and sex and timing. We also recognize that the experience is as brief as a passing comet. Though many of us keep on looking to repeat the experience, for most of us it is a one-time event.

The sad part is that many of us end our education on the subject after getting our guaranteed A. Even if we have had our heart badly broken or keep on entering disastrous love relationships, we remain paradoxically convinced that we know all we need to know about love. If ever there was an area of blind pride, it is in the arena of loving. We all tend to think of ourselves as experts in a field where few of us have passed Love 101.

The search for love is all too often the hunt for the experience of the fall. As I said, that is a one-time event. Yes, we can and often do fall in love with more than one person. No, it is not an experience on which we can improve. We cannot become better fallers. The experience remains pretty much the same. The fall may have softer or harder landings, but the fall of love is an event out of our control.

Where do I find love? This is not a question that hunts for a fall. This question addresses the topic of loving on a much deeper level. This inquiry is about how we can improve our skills as loving human beings. Though our American culture has hundreds of books on how to become better sexual lovers, it has few on the subject of how to improve our loving. Many of us may know many exciting positions to enhance our sexual lovemaking, but few of us know many ways to become more spiritually gifted at loving.

Loving is hard work. Jesus makes that clear by framing the topic of love with a call to love our selves, our neighbors, our God, and even our enemies with our whole heart. Loving an enemy? When was the last time that happened in your life? What would it take for the people of America to love the terrorists who attacked our country? Jesus makes it abundantly clear that he is not speaking of love in the falling sense, but love in the stand up and be counted sense. Loving the enemy is central to Christ's message and ministry. It spells out the discipline of loving. It advocates a love that will take artistry and courage and abundant effort.

If life allowed us to fall in love with the same person on a daily basis, there would be no need for covenant. The fall would seal the vow. That is, however, obviously, not the case. The person with whom we fall in love may also be a person with whom we will share great conflict and pain, and the relationship itself may often be stretched to the point of breaking. We will question the wisdom of our choice. We will get bored to tears with those we love. We will fantasize escape. We will yearn for something different.

I found marriage to be terribly hard work. I loved Christine to pieces, but we were remarkably different people. I was a neat freak; she loved a good deal of clutter. I enjoyed isolation; Christine despised it. I enjoyed a long ride down a country road and staying in inns with no TV or phone; she loved quick rides down a freeway to hotels with room service and saunas and multichanneled TVs. I was ambitious; Christine could have cared less. I was often moody and depressed; Christine was as steady as the rising of the sun. Christine loved a good fight; I avoided an argument at all costs. I loved to read a good book; Christine loved having me read to her.

Our marriage was a rocky ride. What held us together was the covenant we took seriously. We had taken vows, and we meant them.

We had promised to work out the kinks. We had pledged to muscle our way through the tough times. The covenant became the glue that allowed us to push and pull without breaking apart. The covenant reminded us of why we had married in the first place.

The covenant spoke. It told us of the joys of the fall as well as the oft-expressed desire to grow old together. The covenant created and renewed our love for one another.

Covenants are pledges. They are a vow of loyalty. They are a wise acknowledgment that this thing called love will not be easy. They are symbolic reminders that life will change, as will we, and that compromises will have to be made. For richer and poorer, in sickness and in health, in good times and in bad—the vows tell a story. They speak of lives that will require acceptance and a willingness to face times of adversity. A covenant is an expression of faith. It is a statement of hope. It is a promise to love, even when the love cannot be felt.

Jesus made covenants on many levels. He worked hard on his covenant with his disciples. His words at the Last Supper are a clear declaration of covenant. He asked his followers to be committed to one another, the vision of the Kingdom, and the God who was their creator. Christ used prayer and worship as a means of renewing vows. He saw service and sacrifice as a statement of faith commitment.

Love is found within covenant. Covenant is the context in which love grows full and strong. Covenant grants the atmosphere of grace in which human love can blossom. One of my favorite children's sermons is to bring in a potted plant and to cut the flower off in front of the children. I then ask what will happen to the flower. The kids know. It will quickly wither and die.

It is such a stark and simple image, yet it makes its point. Covenant is the soil in which the flower blossoms. If we cut the flower off from its covenantal roots, it, too, will quickly unravel and collapse.

Love Is Found in a Child

There are few guarantees in ministry. Ministry, like life, comes without directions, and the unexpected is the one thing to expect. I have found one sure thing in my 25 years of ministry, one experience that I can count on, one event that is predictable.

After each baby baptism conducted at our church, I take the child in my arms and walk down the center aisle. There are always a chorus of "oohs" and "aahs." I watch the faces of the adults as they gaze at the child. They are truly in awe, mesmerized. They are so uncannily aware of just how precious is this child. Their reaction is the same regardless of the color of the child or their feelings about the parents. The sight of the child induces an expression of reverence, an "ooh" or "ahh" that speaks volumes.

A child is a gift. A precious gift. A gift that matters. When we gaze into the innocence of a child's face, we are swept by the beauty of life. In that face we so clearly see the image of God. That image is dazzling, haunting, and inspiring. That image ignites our desire to love.

Loving is human nature. I am well aware of how many obstacles there are to our being true to that nature—the abuses that can kill the spirit and the encouragement to play it safe or care only for family. Still, when we encounter a child, when we look, and look deep into that sweet face, I defy you not to be moved. Our eyes moisten. Our hearts grow tender. Love is born in us.

Could this be why God saw fit to respond to a loveless world with the gift of a babe? Could it be that God heard the human question "Where is the love?" and answered with a child born in a manger? However we choose to understand the Christmas story—as literal or symbolic truth, as fact or faith-fiction—the meaning of the story is clear. Into a world void of hope, a world at war with itself, God came in the form of a child. God was certain that only a child could inspire the faith, hope, and love needed to build the Kingdom.

Love Is Found in Gratitude

How many times have I heard the phrase "Count your blessings"? How many times have I casually thrown that phrase into a sermon or prayer? How many times have I actually counted my blessings? Far too few!

Gratitude is a powerful force. It creates an attitude and a perspective. It releases energy and excitement. It is a reminder. It focuses us on what matters and what makes a difference. It gives us a boost, it lifts up our heart, it clears our mind, and it restores our soul. Gratitude leads in one direction. The destination is love.

Corny as that may sound—even trite—try it. Try counting your blessings and not feel moved to love. Try to give thanks and not feel love welling up in your heart of hearts. Try to offer praise to God for all that you have received and not be filled with the desire to share your love.

I am not sure how this works. I am not even sure why. What I do know is that in my life, gratitude makes a bee line for love. A grateful heart is a loving heart. The attitude of gratitude transforms relationships.

I love working with children. I cannot imagine doing ministry without having ample exposure to kids. Children are so honest. They are so inspiring. They ignite so much energy in me. My ministry to all ages would fall flat were it not for the time I spend with children. Recently, at a gathering of my 456 Club, which is for fourth, fifth, and sixth graders, I asked them to list their 10 favorite things. For a full 15 minutes they composed their lists.

They had no trouble answering the question. The only difficulty appeared to be limiting their responses to 10. Their lists were magnificent. They spoke of pets and parents and favorite frostings on cakes. They mentioned holidays and birthdays and their favorite season. They celebrated best friends, teachers, neighbors, aunts, and uncles. Almost every child named a grandparent— what a wonderful retirement-free job. They even mentioned things like backrubs when they have a bad cold, or cold showers after a hot August day, or the thrill of swinging and closing their eyes.

Then the question came: "What about you? What about you, Pastor Bill? What are your favorite things?" I smiled and started to answer, but stalled. At first they thought, and so did I, that I was having a tough time locating my answer, but the truth was that I have so seldom asked myself the question that I was startled by the ease of the answer.

"I love to write and paint. I love to read a really good book. I love to take photographs and make photo cards. I love to take walks in the snow and in falling leaves. I love skies. I love the smell of cinnamon. I love the taste of mashed potatoes and homemade bread. I love everything about being a dad. I enjoy time talking with my son, Justin. I love my church family, and I enjoy preaching. I enjoy all of my ministry to kids, and I love …."

"Wait a minute, that is way more than 10," they chanted. We all laughed. It was a loving laugh. Love filled the air and animated my being. Love was smeared across all their faces. Counting our blessings was like devouring a huge piece of cherry pie. The red remnants remained on the face and spoke glowingly of the love that went into the making and eating of the pie.

Love Is Found in Action

Love is a verb. Love must be expressed in action. I cannot be loved by a feeling. Love may be expressed in words. It may be shown in acts of kindness or generosity or mercy. It may be displayed in the giving of a gift or in the contents of a letter. It may come in the form of a hug or a kiss. It may be offered as a compliment or even a critique. However it arrives, it must arrive. It takes action. It necessitates movement. If love is to move us, it must be moving itself.

There was nothing passive about Jesus' love. His love was spoken, declared, and lived. He preached good news to the poor. He built the Kingdom with acts of justice. He gave coats away. He shared his faith and his food. He touched the leper. He embraced the mentally ill with forgiveness. He brought the lost home. He bound broken hearts. He restored sight. He picked up his cross and carried it. He made faithful choices. He erased fear. He lifted up the soul.

Many of us have grown lazy in our loving. We are flabby with inactivity. We fail to get our love moving. We resist love's call to action. We are often filled with the best of intentions, but we fail to act. We are excellent at procrastinating. We love only when it is easy and only those who are easy to love. We never love the enemy. On a scale of 1 to 10 in terms of improvement in our loving skills, with 10 being the highest, most of us are hopelessly mired at 2 or 3.

Loving requires exercise. Our love needs a jog. We need to let our love have a daily walk or run. We need to put our love out there in the world, in our relationships. We need to risk pain and fear and even loss. Our love needs to be stretched and flexible. We need to run the race of life and let love set the pace. Many of us choose to sit out the race or only cheer the heroes we see crossing the finish line. We need to get back in the race. If we run, we win.

LOVE IS FOUND IN WORSHIP

Now, this one is tricky. I have been to many worship services that were duller than dull and left feeling deflated. I have heard messages that have upset my stomach more than stirred my soul. In a nutshell, worship can be deadly.

I have also experienced worship that is exhilarating. Worship has the capacity to be transforming. Worship can be an experience of grace. The recognition that God is love and that we are God's children. The revelation of our status as beloved. The basking in a new identity. A showering with both meaning and purpose. The celebration of a new way of being.

What makes for such a worship experience? What is it in worship that can fill us with the knowledge of the unconditional love of God? What must happen within worship to free us to become the loving creatures we were created to be? Here is what I believe is necessary, in no particular order:

- ✦ We must be ready to worship.
- ✦ We must be ready to receive, feel deeply, think creatively, and above all else, listen.
- ✦ The worship must acknowledge the mystery and create an atmosphere conducive to the experience of holiness.
- ✦ The silence needs to speak.
- ✦ The worshipping community needs to feel intimate.
- ✦ There needs to be time to claim one's pain and offer up one's joy.
- ✦ The message needs to inspire faith, not fear.
- ✦ We need to feel that all that is said is from the heart and genuine.
- ✦ We need to be fully present and fully human.
- ✦ We need to soak in a bath of forgiveness.
- ✦ We need to ask God to enter the experience.
- ✦ We need to take note of God's arrival.
- ✦ We need to celebrate the arrival of pure love.

I readily admit that my concept of worship is quite traditional. I still think of worship in the context of a sanctuary, a choir, a minister, and a liturgy that moves from confession to praise. I am still quite devoted to the notion of a church family, and I am reliant upon hearing a spoken message.

This does not, however, rule out the possibility of worship in the woods or by the sea. It does not deny the potential of solo worship or the worship of pure silence. It does not mean that worship must take place in a sanctuary, or have a leader, or even have a liturgical format. Worship is whenever and wherever we choose to invite in the presence of God and faithfully wait for the arrival.

I often hear folks complain that worship is boring. I know this can be the case. I wonder, though, if at times the real issue is that people attend worship without really being present. They bring a closed heart and mind. They have no desire to feel. They are unwilling to contemplate life's mystery or seriously entertain one of its biggest questions. They have no wish to meet their God. They are uncomfortable praying.

Could it be that worship is boring because we are boring? Could it be that worship demands an authenticity we fail to live? Could it be that to enter worship means to face one's true self and that we have no desire to reflect upon such a reflection?

For me, personally and professionally, worship has been a tremendous source of love. I find love in gathering with folks whose sole purpose it is to become more loving. I find love in the laughter and tears that lace the service. I find love in the words and the silences. I find love in the looks of the older members when a favorite hymn is being sung or a child belting out the chorus to a new song. Most of all, I locate love in the belief that God is there. Even when I have delivered a lousy sermon or the whole service falls flat, I never fail to sense that God still radically affirms our efforts.

Love Is Found in Beauty

An autumn night lit by a golden moon. Leaves fluttering to the ground. Winter trees coated in fresh snow or ice. A child playing with bubbles. A soft serene sea at sunset. The lime lace of spring. The face of a parent greeting a child coming off an airplane. Christmas lights and sounds and smells. Purple mountains. Brooks. Old, tree-bark hands. White beards. A long view. A romantic kiss. A sky made alive by fast-moving clouds. A wink. An apple. A snowman. Any flower. A storm with lightning. Fog. Candlelight.

Each of us finds beauty in different places and faces. Our experience of beauty is, however, remarkably the same. Beauty makes us fall in love with life. Beauty beholds the creator. Beauty inspires us to cherish and protect. Beauty sings praises.

Beauty releases the love we feel for just the chance to be alive. Beauty is the handiwork of God. Loving hands. Creating hands. Tender and tough hands. Hands that touch us with grace and squeeze out the love within us.

Chapter Response by Rabbi Astrachan

Pastor Grimbol, my friend, has conjured up many wonderfully warm thoughts within me with the words written on the preceding pages. My response to this chapter will be significantly more brief than the others that I have written. I would, however, like to add a few additional thoughts about the things that bring wonderful thoughts of love and comfort to my life:

+ A hot bowl of matzah-ball soup at Passover
+ A tuna-melt sandwich made just like Grandma's: a perfectly toasted English muffin topped with mayonnaise and

tuna fish, a thin slice of tomato, and a piece of "melty" American cheese

✦ Chasing my children around the house, then catching them, tossing them to the floor, and tickling them until they roll with laughter

✦ A quiet night out with my wife

✦ A member of my congregation jotting a note to tell me that I brought them comfort in a time of need

✦ The smell of a baby's head

✦ The scent of Chanel No. 5: Grandma's only perfume

"Love is a many splendored thing." This we know so well. What brings out those feelings for me may not be the same for you. I hope, for your sake, you've got your own. Make a list, like Pastor Grimbol did with his kids. It's not just for kids, you know. Try it. In this trying world of ours, it sure made me feel good.

PART 5

THE WHY QUESTIONS

How often has something happened in our lives—something so overwhelming—that the best we can do is mutter to ourselves, "Why me?" No one ever said life was easy or that we would not face repeated challenges along the journey. What we are told, however, is that we have the strength and the resolve to pick ourselves up and deal with the mess. In these three chapters, I will focus on questions that beg answers. Unfortunately, to the questions raised here, there may be no single, satisfying response.

In this part of our book we will explore the realms of death, evil, and the self as the central character in life faced with the challenge of coping with life when all hope seems to be lost. How we respond to the difficulties and the stumbling blocks, how we rally our senses to come to terms with illness, grief, pain and an array of other emotions felt at times of weakness, these are the mechanisms with which we have been endowed to combat the slings and arrows which we daily face.

WHY ME? NOW? HERE?

Rabbi Jeffrey R. Astrachan

In previous chapters I shared with you thoughts about how we find our way in life as a part of something greater than just individuals going about individual tasks. The fact is, we can each be likened to a gigantic jigsaw puzzle, where each piece is equally important. If we are missing even one piece of a 1,000-piece puzzle, the overall integrity, not to mention the inherent beauty, of the puzzle is degraded. And what do we do with that puzzle? We throw it away. It is simply discarded because all the pieces were unable to come together to form the whole.

What then, can we say about our obligations to the rest of the world? In the grand scheme of the workings of the universe, it is easy to forget—or simply to disbelieve—that anything we do could possibly make a cosmic difference. Black holes will still swallow up planets and stars. Our sun will eventually cool off, and our planet will, some day, cease to exist—regardless of whether or not we are good people, regardless of whether or not we help a nice lady across the street, regardless of anything we could possible consider doing or not doing during our allotted days on Earth.

Wow! What a mind-numbing thought to think that in the greatest scheme of universal events our lives might actually be meaningless. How disturbing. How unsettling. But we know that although we might not be able to move worlds, we might be able to move something of our world. We learned long ago that the earth is not flat and that the planets in our solar system actually rotate around our sun, not around the earth. We learned that gravity affects all objects relative to our planet. We learned that the earth is *not* the center of the universe.

In this chapter we will explore ways in which we might see ourselves as the *center of our own universe*. In a great many ways, much of life does, in fact, revolve around us. We must begin to see the value of accepting our responsibility as that single, most reliable puzzle piece. Without us, the world as we know it would lack its integrity and its worth. Everything we do has an effect on those people and objects that surround us.

THE SELF AS CENTER

Each one of us—while part of something much larger than ourselves—must act as if we are the center of our own universe. Everything we do and everything we are to become must revolve around what is inside: our soul, spirit, and conscience. In "Who Is My Enemy?" I talked about the role our conscience plays in determining how we interact with the world around us. I raised the questions of good and evil, of choosing to act kindly or wickedly, and of how we make choices that effect relationships and events.

What then, of soul and spirit? How do these reflect a center and a centering of belief, organization, responsibility, and commitment? The challenge for many of us lies in the intangible nature of the soul and the spirit. We cannot touch them with our hands. We cannot see them with our eyes. None of our senses can approach them. We simply must have faith that they exist. Like so many other issues of the metaphysical world, it is our faith alone that guides our understanding of this otherworldly context.

For those who doubt their existence, I point to the common metaphor of God represented by the wind blowing through the trees. We cannot see God, but we can see the results of God's actions. We can feel God enveloping us. We can smell God's scent as the aroma of fragrant blossoms is carried through the air. This is the God we cannot see. So, too, this represents the soul within us which we must reach inward to find.

In Psalm 103, King David (the author of the Psalms) said, "Bless the Lord, O my soul." In this text we find a beautiful place to begin our journey of the soul, to explore the possibilities that lie within each one of us as we try to connect with the God who made us who we are. In interpreting the message of this first verse of the Psalm, there is an understanding that the connection between God and the individual is inseparable. When we read the text just as it is, we find a wonderful message of God's inherent presence within us. Allow me to rewrite the verse while gleaning its message as I see it: "Bless my soul, which is the Lord." (This interpretation may be different than one you may be familiar with. When most translate the text to read "Bless my soul, O Lord," we lose a deeper sense of the text.)

With this understanding of the Psalm's opening verse, we are then able to proceed with a greater concept of God's presence and the greatness of the self. King David must have been talking about his own inner self (his *soul*) when he wrote this verse. In a section of the Talmud called *Berachot 10a,* we find a wonderful discourse, which critically analyzes this text as a measure of five qualities shared both by human beings and by God. In this text we learn that as God fills the world, the soul fills the body. As God sees but is not seen, so the soul sees but is not itself seen. As God feeds the world, so the soul feeds the body. As God is pure, so the soul is pure. As God abides in the innermost regions, so the soul abides in the innermost regions.

Let us not misunderstand the implication of this analysis. What the rabbis of the Talmud are telling us here is not that God *is* the world or, for that matter, that we are God. More accurately, we learn that God is the soul of the world and our souls are the God-like in each of us.

In our understanding of God as the master of all things, we must then relate that to our own being. In the commentary of Psalm 103, it is clear that our own being is relevant to the world just as God's being is relevant. If God's existence is to have meaning for us as a central focal point of life, our own existence must have similar meaning.

All of this goes to rebut that wonderful cliché, "So do you think *you* are the center of the universe? Do you think the world revolves around *you?*" I suppose now we can say "Yes" with great certainty that, indeed, it does.

UNQUESTIONED BLESSINGS

Feeling left out or left behind is a common personal shortcoming. For many of us, a sense of belonging is of tremendous importance. Very few people are able to live a healthy life without the comfort of friends, family, acquaintances, and associates. In speaking with family members about a loved one who has just passed, I am almost assured of hearing about various clubs and organizations to which that person belonged or, perhaps, even attained a certain level of leadership and prestige. Not only do we want to belong in life, but also in death we wish to be remembered as having been a part of something larger than ourselves. Some people actually feel guilty about how they are living their life if they are not extending themselves into extracurricular events.

For a long time I was under the mistaken impression that Jews had the market on guilt. In fact, we find it going all the way back to the Bible. We learn all through the Book of Leviticus about various kinds of animals and grains we had to bring to the Great

Temple in Jerusalem in order to expiate some sense of guilt. Throughout the ages our mothers have been most closely identified with offerings of guilt—though, to be sure, in a wholly different manner.

There's a wonderful story about a mother who repeatedly called her son's answering machine to leave messages about how hungry she was, that she had not had anything to eat for days. She called again and again, leaving similar messages, aching over her hunger. Finally the son checked his messages and, feeling greatly concerned, called his mother and asked "Why are you so hungry? Aren't you eating? Do you need me to call a doctor?" To this, his mother simply replied, "No, dear. I'm fine. I just didn't want to have anything in my mouth in case *you* decided to call!"

Come to find out—according to my wonderfully ethnic Italian neighbors—guilt is something that knows absolutely no religious or ethnic bounds. Theirs is a multigenerational household, and I have heard many stories of how much a part guilt plays in the fabric of their lives. But the wonderful thing about guilt, of course, is that it's the gift that keeps on giving. When we are the recipient of some off-the-cuff comment such as the mother in the preceding story, we know that the reason we feel the guilt (and that its intended message is so stingingly felt) is because we are fortunate enough to be the object of some person's caring and affection.

In fact, we could make the case that guilt is a form of blessing. We offer blessings to those we love and to those about whom we care deeply. Religion, in general, is filled with a multitude of personal blessings (it happens to be filled with wonderful curses, as well, but that will have to wait for another essay). In Judaism, for example, we find such blessings as "May your eternal knowledge of God lead you always in paths of peace," or even "May a nice, hot bowl of chicken soup cure your cold." You see, blessings do not have to be complex. Perhaps, however, the greatest blessing of all comes from the tradition of the ancient Hebrew Priests spoken in the Book of Numbers, Chapter 6:22ff:

> "And the Lord spoke to Moses, saying, 'Speak to Aaron and to his sons, "Thus shall you bless the people ..., saying to them, 'May God bless you and keep you; May God's face shine upon you and be gracious to you; May God's countenance be set upon you and give you peace.'"'"

Blessings of peace reign supreme, though closely followed, perhaps, by blessings for health. What we seek through blessing is, in essence, the opportunity to be made whole. In Hebrew, the word *peace* is the word *Shalom*. The deeper meaning of the word, however, goes far beyond simple peace. Shalom comes from a root word that is more accurately translated as "completeness" or "wholeness." Therefore, when we wish someone Shalom, we are asking for their lives to be made whole or complete, perhaps then providing that individual with peace.

The word must be parsed further, though, so as to leave no confusion with the matter. Blessings of Shalom, peace, or wholeness should not be confused with a vain blessing for perfection. Although there are some who wantonly and brazenly proclaim their own personal greatness, there is none among us who reaches the truest level of perfection. That we leave to God alone. We can, however, strive to attain that unreachable level of goodness and wholeness that completes us as human beings in the eyes of others.

When we seek wisdom through those who are wise and seek comfort from those who have it to give, we grow toward perfection. When we avail ourselves to the love of our friends and our family, we grow toward perfection. When we give freely of ourselves with the noblest of intent, we grow toward perfection. When we realize that we are perfect in God's eyes, we grow toward perfection.

Each one of us is blessed with God's unquestioned blessings because God sees in us our greatest potential to succeed and to share with the world. We are endowed with the power to command our destiny and provide blessings to others.

WHY *NOT* YOU? NOW? HERE?

So if we are endowed with such power to command our destiny, why is it so difficult to actualize our fullest potential? For many of us one of the major stumbling blocks comes in the form of self-doubt. We so often fail to see in ourselves what others see in us. How many times have we heard phrases such as "He's not living up to his potential" or "I know she is capable of so much more"? If we looked inside ourselves—soul-searched, as it were—we might find something wonderful and unexpected waiting for our discovery.

In the Book of Genesis we find a wonderful example of discovering the unexpected. Jacob awakens from a dream that had been filled with tremendous imagery of angels ascending and descending between Earth and the heavens. In the instant of his waking, Jacob declares "The Lord God was in this very place and I did not know it!" (Genesis 28:16) What happens in this fantastic Biblical moment is a sudden realization by Jacob that things beyond perceptible reality are possible and plausible. Beyond what we think we know to be true lies the potential for unimaginable possibilities—enter God.

There is a wonderful lesson we can derive from an early verse in Genesis. In fact, from a single word we learn much about the potential that lies within each of us. Genesis 2:1 contains the word *vaye'chu-lu*, which is usually translated to mean "were finished," as in the verse, "The heaven and the earth *were finished*." But because the traditional Biblical text is not written with any vowels, the reader is sometimes left to consider possible alternate pronunciations and, therefore, meanings, for words. In this case, according to section *Shabbat 119b* of the Talmud, we learn that it is possible to pronounce this word as *va'ye'cha-lu*, which means "and they finished." Here, *we* now become an active part of the creative process. The great rabbis teach us that the "they" to which this new translation refers is each one of us, that *we* are participating—with God—in completing the unfinished works of creation.

Why not us? Do we think that we are incapable of living up to the expectations of God? Far too many of us cower at the thought that we might actually be here to fulfill a Godly purpose: to complete the works of creation. This, then, must be the rationale for our own creation according to God's likeness. In order to fulfill our destiny, we had to have been created in just that way.

How do we know when we have fulfilled such destiny? We might not ever know with complete certainty in our lifetime. The purpose of our lives is not to complete ourselves; rather, it is to make this world more complete—to provide Shalom, peace, and wholeness—so that the future remains bright for those yet to come. Each of us plays a unique and equally important role in the world's continuing creative process. As we continue to grow and evolve in a spiritual way, so, too, do we enhance the evolution of the spirit of our world.

Learning Acceptance of Life's Givens

Accepting such an important role in the process of God's ongoing worldly creation, we must begin to recognize that all things are possible. However, given that each of us embodies certain skills and abilities, be they physical, intellectual, or spiritual, we must also recognize that each one of us may not be at all capable of accomplishing all things. We can certainly be die-hard faithful God-worshipers, but let's be realistic—we each have our limitations.

Some of us are given height and strength; others are given exceptional compassion and artistic talents. Some of us are blessed with five senses and bodies considered to be anatomically complete; others have learned to use their bodies to the greatest potential possible given any variety of physically abnormality. All people are capable of giving and receiving according to their own capacities.

So often, though, we fail to live up to the potentials each of us have. Often, as a result of getting comfortable with the pattern of life that we have adopted, we see no need to broaden our talents, to hone our skills, or to attempt something new. Perhaps it isn't so much the rut we've created for ourselves but rather a certain fear of the attempt. Making substantive life changes can be frightening, and for some it can be overwhelming. Changing who we are or what we do too quickly leads to an unfortunate misunderstanding of our abilities. When we try to become someone we are not, when we try to achieve a sudden mastery of a task that should take years, when we try to work in a manner that is inconsistent with our common mode, we only set ourselves up for the inevitable disappointment that comes with failing to meet the challenge of these outlandish goals.

When we try to improve our lives, slowly, over time, then we begin to understand our own potential through a process of internalizing the greatness that can be achieved by the task itself.

But in trying to improve our lives, there exists another difficulty. Recognizing that we have to take chances in making such life-changing steps, we risk defeat and failure. We risk letting ourselves down. The flip side, however, is that we also face the possibility that we might just be able to succeed.

While not necessarily condoning lottery or sweepstakes programs, I happen to recall a great advertising campaign slogan from a few years ago that prodded people, "You can't win if you don't enter." This simple statement speaks volumes on the heart of this very issue. If we are not willing to do for ourselves—by making the attempt—we can not possibly expect our goals to be reached. Just by taking the first step toward the attempt is a success. Recognizing that there is more that we can do is a win. There is only so long that our "charm and good looks" are going to move us along in life. Eventually we all must rely on the real talents with which we are blessed.

But each one of us has potentials yet unrealized. Each one of us is capable of more than we have yet accomplished. We know that when push comes to shove and our backs are against the proverbial wall, we usually come through with only a few minor cuts and bruises. And as we have all heard before, "What does not kill us will only makes us stronger." Not to be taken literally, to be sure, this commentary suggests that we learn from our mistakes. We must learn that the first mistake each of us makes is in failing to take the chance at all.

Take the first step toward something new. Explore a talent someone might have once mentioned that they saw in you. Maybe you enjoy cooking and singing, but let's face it—you aren't going to have your own television show on the Food Network or stand in the spotlight on Broadway. Or maybe you will! How will you know until you make the attempt? Do it for yourself first. Then bring your talents to the world.

LEARNING TO BE A PART OF THE WHOLE

We have all heard the famous cliché, "There is no *I* in T-E-A-M." I wonder, though, how many are familiar with the follow-up cliché, "But there is *M-E.*" The first cliché must have been created by someone deeply committed to selflessness, someone who believed that working together was far more important than working alone. Recognizing the value of the efforts of all involved is better than suggesting that the effort of a single individual made all the difference. The second cliché, however, offers us insight into those who see the world as their own playground, where no one else is allowed to play but them. It is helpful for us to first recognize which statement best reflects our own life and then consider which statement characterizes those with whom we associate.

Some of the greatest musical talents of our time possess amazing gifts. They shine in the spotlight as we listen to their hearts and their souls, their visions, and their emotions pour out through their instruments and their voices. We are moved by their spirit. We are touched by their grace. How much more so, then, are we embraced by those feelings when their solo talents are accompanied by the majesty of an orchestra? Accompanied by trumpet and trombone, piano, and percussion, the elegance of the ensemble gives us a complementary sound of perfection in motion.

So, too, do we each bring to our friends, families, businesses, organizations, and every other group or place with which we associate something uniquely special—as a gift—which enhances the orchestra of our lives. Those who believe they can do things better on their own are missing out on a tremendously wonderful world of possibilities, and the world is missing out on sharing the talents of those individuals as well.

We each have a measure to give, and we each have a measure to gain. Taking the skills we each have and putting them together with the skills of those around us helps to make the whole something better than the individual parts. As partners, we can excel to much greater heights. As partners with God, we can reach greater, never-before reachable potential. When we begin to act as if the world really does depend on us, we truly begin to serve God.

The prophet Jeremiah teaches us a wonderful lesson about sharing our personal gifts with the world. He admonishes us, "Let not the wise glory in their wisdom, nor the strong in their strength, nor the rich in their riches. But let them glory in their understanding and knowledge of God." (Jeremiah 9:23–24)

In essence, what Jeremiah is sharing with us is the feeling that we each must undoubtedly remember that the gifts we have are gifts that must be shared. It is God who has given us these talents, yet it is we who must hone them and share them with others. We are not a people of selfish spirits. At the base of the Statue of Liberty we find the famous words, "Give me your tired, your poor, your huddled masses yearning to breathe free, the wretched refuse of your teeming shore, send these, the homeless, tempest-tost to me, I lift my lamp beside the golden door." Written by Emma Lazarus, this poem, "The New Colossus," speaks to all people the important message of inclusion, of inviting *all* to share in the gifts of the *one,* that together we become a larger *one*. We are more complete when we share what we have.

We learn this from the very earliest days of our lives. Whether it is toys, talents, or time, we learn the value of giving up something of great worth. The value, though, is only realized when it is shared. Nothing kept for ourselves is worth anything.

When we share, when we give our light to illuminate the path of another, we open ourselves to the glory of God. Then we truly shine as a partner with God and with our world.

Chapter Response by Pastor Grimbol

I once read a wonderful book by Erich Fromm titled *You Shall Be as Gods*. The premise of the book was obvious. Fromm reminded his readers that it was the call of God for us to behave as gods. What did Fromm mean? He means that we are God's crowning creation; that we are to think of ourselves as capable of miraculous things; that we were given dominion over this earth, due to God's confidence in our capacities. In a nutshell, the book makes the point that to be created in the image of God is truly a magnificent thing. To have this image imprinted upon our soul challenges us to take seriously our lives, talents, gifts, longings, and callings. It also makes the powerful point that it is in being, and not doing, that we best express our God-likeness.

I heard this same sentiment in this chapter by Rabbi Astrachan. His advocacy for us to think of ourselves as the center of the universe is made not as encouragement to arrogance or conceit, but as a declaration of our purpose in the eyes of the God who created us. Jeff gives clarity to the notion of being as a god, when he states, "We are endowed with the power to command our destiny and to provide blessings to others."

The Christian faith has long struggled with this notion. Christianity tends to encourage its followers to walk humbly with their God, and often such humility is thought of as *acting* lowly or being meek. Unfortunately, we Christians often think of humility in self-deprecating terms. Frequently we have been encouraged from the pulpit to dwell upon our sinful nature and to neglect our God-likeness. I recall as an adolescent thinking of my catechism experience as an endurance test of shame. I certainly never heard the idea of behaving as a god.

At my own confirmation I remember trying to look unworthy. Isn't that funny? Isn't that sad? How the hell do you look unworthy?

I truly thought that the goal of the Christian faith was to appear as if you knew that you didn't deserve one ounce of God's love or respect but were happy to get it anyway. Ugh! What a nightmarish theology. "You shall be as gods" would have been thought to be pure heresy by my catechism teachers. They spent so much time tearing us down that there was little room for God to build us back up.

Why me? If you see yourself as a worthless sinner, the answer is that you deserve whatever you get and that you should never expect anything better. If you see yourself as a god, the answer is that you must share God's pain and anguish and still believe that the best is yet to come. The difference in perspective is as wide as a canyon.

I think that Jeff would agree with me that one of the toughest aspects of faith is to claim both its power and its powerlessness.

This is the true paradoxical nature of faith. Faith begins with the radical acknowledgment that we are powerless, that God holds all the power, that we are in fact nothing without God. Our power to behave as gods stems directly from making this claim. Once we admit we are powerless, we are free to claim our true god-like powers and God is free to work within us and through us. Jesus makes it clear that we find our very lives in losing them. Once we know we are not God, we are free to become as gods—little "g," but with big "G" impact.

I find far too many Christians who claim to have found Jesus behaving as if they have no power. The fact that we lay claim to a faith in Jesus as the Christ does not transfer all power to Jesus; it is Jesus' power that is supposed to transform us.

Faith in Jesus is a dependency, but it is not an addiction. We know we need Jesus, but we also know that Jesus has granted us the courage and conviction to act in his name. To function as if you can't move without first asking Jesus' permission is no more than faith as an addiction. A healthy yet dependent faith is one that functions freely and often independently.

Why Is There Evil?

Rabbi Jeffrey R. Astrachan

I recently had the opportunity to teach a course for Jewish adults on Long Island. During one of my early sessions, I focused my lecture on the concept of God and the role God plays in our lives and in the general workaday world. I introduced a variety of commonly held theologies and their implications. Among these is the widely accepted notion that God may be likened to a toy maker (the analogy may come in a variety of forms, but the concept is the same) who created a wonderful mechanism of masterful quality. The potential for what this mechanism could do was seemingly without limits.

Having completed his work with meticulous skill, the toy maker wound the mechanism and sat back to watch as the possibilities began to take shape, each part of the mechanism functioning in its own way, each part working in concert with the other parts to effect a variety of results. The mechanism had been designed to operate freely and wholly independent of the toy maker so that the parts would interact in potentially unpredictable ways, thereby producing potentially unpredictable results.

In the case of our world, the toy maker is God. Masterfully and skillfully creating this wonderful mechanism we call Earth, God finished, wound it up, and sat back to watch. Of course, this concept of God is not without its great difficulties. Paraphrasing the thoughts of one of my students, this sounds like God saw the world merely as an experiment and each one of us as mere guinea pigs. It certainly gives us great insight into the term "rat race." With this concept of God's creative process, it does, however, explain much about the question of evil. If we were created and then simply set in motion by this Unmoved Mover (i.e., God), then the same unpredictable results might be expected.

A more acceptable concept of God, however, involves various responsibilities that were given to us in order to help facilitate God's ongoing creative process. As I mentioned earlier, creation should not be viewed as a one-time, finite event in history (regardless of our belief in theories of creation or evolution). The greatest of our rabbinic sages were of one mind in understanding that human beings have been endowed with not only the potential, but the obligation as well, to assist in the perfection of our world. In Hebrew the concept is called *Tikkun Olam*. This *mitzvah* (one of the 613 commandments handed down through tradition) ordains humanity to the task of repairing the errant ways of misguided actions or events.

But the fact of the matter is that most scholars also ascribe to the belief that humanity was created by God with free will. That is, the understanding that we have been instilled, from birth (or before), with all the potential of our being and now must actualize that potential in relationship to the world around us. God has given us life; now we must use this life to do God's will. The choices we make each day are not being guided by God's hand. Mistakes are not being governed by God's eternal might. Accidents are not caused or prevented at God's whim.

In this chapter we will explore some avenues toward understanding the evil that exists in our world. Implications of decisions we make, anger and rage in others, damage we do to others or have had done to us, people who truly may not have the capacity to tell right from wrong, and others who just don't seem to understand the role they play in protecting the interests of dependent souls in their care—here we will examine why some people do what they do and who is really to blame.

GOD CREATED THE SNAKE IN THE GARDEN

"Now the serpent was more subtle than any beast of the field which the Lord God had made. And he said to the woman, Has God said, you shall not eat of every tree of the garden? And the woman said to the serpent, We may eat of the fruit of the trees of the garden; But of the fruit of the tree which is in the midst of the garden, God has said, you shall not eat of it, nor shall you touch it, lest you die. And the serpent said to the woman, surely you shall not die; For God knows that in the day you eat of it, then your eyes shall be opened, and you shall be as gods, knowing good and evil. And when the woman saw that the tree was good for food, and that it was pleasant to the eyes, and a tree to be desired to make one wise, she took of its fruit, and ate, and gave also to her husband with her; and he ate. And the eyes of them both were opened, and they knew that they were naked; and they sewed fig leaves together, and made themselves aprons."

—Genesis 3:1–7

This Biblical passage has occupied the attention of scholars throughout the ages. This text begs the question of blame and responsibility for all of the world's problems. Some blame the snake. Others blame the woman we call "Eve." Still others blame God directly. Judaism holds fast to the notion that none are punished for the actions of others. In Deuteronomy 24:16 we find "The fathers shall not be put to death for the children, nor shall the children be put to death for the fathers; every man shall be put to death for his own sin."

As human beings, we are faced with the issue of blame and where to place it. Far too often tragic events enter our lives that jar us from peace and serenity. Our country is hardly removed from the initial feelings following the horrible attacks on our way of life on September 11, 2001. Each day following we have been faced with the unsettling notion that there are those in our world hell-bent on destroying us, our freedoms, our security, our peace of mind, and our underlying feeling of control. We could label these people as *evil,* to be sure. But where does *evil* come from?

Our tradition secures our faith that evil does not come from God. Although there are Biblical passages in which God seems to act in vengeful or painful ways, the concept of God is one of eternal justice. We know from Abraham's argument with God regarding the destruction of the wicked cities of Sodom and Gemmorah (Genesis 18) that God is asked, "Should not the judge of all the earth deal justly?" And we learn, in the end, that the righteous ones whom Abraham had hoped to find in order to spare the cities' fate were not to be found. We must maintain a faith in a God who was, is, and always will be eternally fair and just, even in cases where justice seems absent. Our history is filled with such examples.

However, the evil that we experience in our world is caused by people *in* our world. In accepting a concept of free will granted to all people, we may not be selective. We cannot say that only the people who act in good ways are eligible for this gift, and the people who act out against others must be restricted to play by a distinct set of rules only for them in order to protect us. But by accepting this notion we condemn ourselves to the probability, like the toy maker's mechanism, of living in a God-created world where anything, both good as well as evil, is possible.

This notion, then, creates its own theological challenges for us. If we believe in a world in which all people are endowed with free will and can, therefore, act out in ways unpredictable, do we not also relegate our understanding of God to a being who does *not* have infinite power? The answer to this dilemma is that by allowing us to consider a God who may not be omnipotent, we allow ourselves to grow with God. Still others reject this notion, given that if we stop growing so, then, does God stop growing. If humanity ceases to be, so, then, does God cease to be.

So here's the rub: If we accept as true the story of the Garden of Eden (rather than just accepting the message of the story), we find ourselves entangled in a kind of chicken-and-egg conundrum. Let us be content to accept that the world and everything on it, over it, and within it was created by God and that because we are given the opportunity to make choices, we must also be prepared to live with the choices made by others—both good and bad. God may have created the snake, but as God's partners we are equally responsible for how it crawls.

Some Folks Are Volcanoes (Oppressed and Enraged)

Pent-up anger and frustration often go to the heart of how many of us react to situations we are confronted with. When we fail to communicate effectively or when others fail to hear our message because of their own inability to communicate, we each can become time bombs waiting to explode. While we would certainly like to think of ourselves as fully capable to express our likes and dislikes, our needs and wants, our feelings and opinions, the fact of the matter is that all too often we run into people who couldn't care less about something that is important to us.

How many of us have sat in leadership positions or management or customer service vocations when we have had the opportunity to share an idea we considered to be valid and of significant merit only to have that idea glossed over or outright "poo-poo'd" by others in the group? Once is not so horrible. Certainly everyone has had an idea cast aside. But what if your ideas were consistently overlooked? What if every time you started to say something, the eyes in the room began to roll, the pencils began to tap, the watches on wrists were glanced at? It would not take long, for most of us, to realize that there was a greater problem to consider.

Our feelings would be hurt. Our pride would be shaken. Our desire to continue to give input and be heard would dissipate—we might even be insulted, angry, or incensed at our callous treatment by those we considered our peers. We might be part of a team, but there's only so many times a player can be benched before realizing the team is working without him. Who needs this? Not any of us, that's for sure!

On a less personal level, let's consider various religious or ethnic groups. At some point in the history of every group of people, a time has come when they were put down, kicked out, beaten up, denied rights, shunned, defeated, conquered, or overcome by another group of people. It has happened to every group of people on the face of the earth—granted we can come to certain agreement on an ordered listing of the severity of such oppression against various groups over time. We can also clearly identify which groups did not survive such oppression and are no longer extant.

As we look back through historical chronicles, we can read detailed analysis of the rise and fall of any one of a number of peoples. For one group to rise to power, another had to fall. As their rule was diminished, another was in line to take control. As nature abhors a vacuum, so does power. It appears to be human nature (studied in an endless variety of research projects) to crave dominion over others. The Bible gives us this understanding from the beginning of Genesis, when God tells us that mankind will have dominion over all of God's works. The problem is that I do not believe that God intended man to dominate man—it only happens this way because of God's gift of free will.

Although it initially sounds great—we can be free to shape our own destiny—we see that with free will comes others' desires to shape our destiny for us. What, generally, is the scapegoat reason for such oppression? Not just power, but religious superiority. "*My* God is better than *your* God!" You can almost hear the childish chanting and cat-calling were it not for the sound of guns and bombs in the way.

More personally, have you ever found yourself so frustrated by all the absurdities in our world that you've just wanted to stand in the street and scream at the top of your lungs? How about this: Go ahead and scream! Do it. Take your frustration, walk to the middle of the street, open your mouth, fill your chest, and bellow at the top of your lungs. It'll feel great—I promise! It may not accomplish anything in the grand scheme of the world, though it might draw the attention of a few neighbors (with varying degrees of concern for both your and their safety), but it sure will make you feel better. Why? Because each of us has an inherent need to be heard. When it seems like no one is open to hearing what we have to get off our chests, we might just need to let it out any way we can in a manner that will allow us to clear our heads and soothe our minds.

Okay, so maybe not all of us are quite ready to make such a verbal statement. There are other ways. Never underestimate the power of writing. Jotting notes, drawing pictures (yes, even adults doodle), writing letters, keeping a diary, composing poetry, writing songs, or painting pictures are all wonderful ways of expressing outrage, concern, or any of the other emotions we might feel depending on the mood we happen to be in. Sometimes we have to be our own therapists, best friend, and confidant. Sometimes when we feel that life is kicking us in the gut, the best thing to do is kick back—but in a less violent way.

When we learn to channel our anger—if only the rest of the world's troublemakers would find a way to channel their anger—we can begin to really make a difference in the world. Before we can affect the world, we must find a positive way to affect ourselves.

Some Folks Are Damaged Goods

Most of us learned from an early age that some people can be mean, others can be insensitive, and still others can be downright cruel. There is, of course, a healthy quantity of people who are patently kind, sensitive, caring, and genuinely good. When I think back to my own days in grade school, I recall that it was, generally, the nice kids who were picked on or harassed by the mean kids. There were those, it appeared, who just had a knack for making other kids feel miserable. They seemed to actually get a thrill out of ruining some other kid's day as they ran to tell their friends of some stunt they pulled or some hurtful statement they made.

I was a good kid, which means, therefore, that I had firsthand experience with the mean kids. As I look back to those days, though, a rather disturbing recollection comes to my mind. No matter what ridiculous things were said or done to me (and now I realize none of it was really all that horrible), I headed back to those same kids day after day, trying to be friends, trying to help them with their work, trying to show them that there were nice ways to play together. In return, they would always show me the same cruel side of life which I eventually came to accept as the way life was to be.

As I got older, I found that there were different kinds of people and that I was much better off finding relationships with people who were more like me, just as other kinds of people forged relationships with people more like them. As we got older, we called them "cliques." As we got even older, we began to call them "social circles." The labels matured, but the fact remains that there were the "good" people and the "mean" people.

Most of us are able to tell the difference fairly readily, but there are those who still, unfortunately, get themselves caught up in the wrong social circles or the wrong cliques—or get emotionally involved with the wrong people. The problem is not so much finding the group—in fact, that's usually the easy part. The problem is recognizing the mistake and then, even more challenging, finding our way out.

As I look back to those early days in grade school, I am not entirely sure what continually possessed me to go back to the same group of kids who teased me. I can only say that possibly I was more interested in the attention I received from them than whether that attention was positive or negative. And I suppose that analysis could be transferred to adult situations of abusive relationships as well.

The fact that one human being could impose his physical, emotional, or sexual will upon another human being without his true consent is frightening. This societal ill is pandemic, knowing no boundary of religion, ethnicity, gender, race, creed, color, orientation, or any other designation. There are abusers among every group of people, and there are those who are abused by them. So often we have no idea who might be one or the other. I know that for some that may sound ridiculous. We boast that we could spot an abuser a mile away. We expect that someone being abused would act in a certain manner. Unfortunately, we do not always know.

I recently found myself speaking with an old friend—someone with whom I had lost contact with for the more than 20 years since I had moved away from the community and only recently returned. We used to be neighbors. Catching up and reminiscing, we talked about all the people we knew on our block. I mentioned somebody, and she told me what she knew about them, where they went to school, when they moved out of the neighborhood, and all kinds of other candid information. I came upon one family's name, and she paused. My friend shared with me that shortly after my family moved from the neighborhood, the wife left the husband and fled the country after putting up with his physical and emotional abuse for years. None of us knew. Looking back at that couple, I *still* couldn't tell. How frightening. How sad.

We share this world with a population consisting of great people who have done great things. But amidst the masses there are those who cause suffering and those who suffer because of them. None deserve such treatment, and none deserve such power. There is no easy solution, however. We cannot simply offer a prayer to God and wake up to a completely renewed life. God does not work that way. We know that each of us has responsibilities to carry out. For some of us, those responsibilities include reaching out to help others. For those who are suffering, those responsibilities include reaching out for help.

Our traditions teach us that we must not stand idly by while our neighbor bleeds. As nothing in the Bible is to be taken literally but rather as a tool toward a better understanding of what God expects from us, we learn from this text that we are obliged to act.

We are obliged to act.

Take that thought all by itself and consider its meaning and its implications for our lives. What can we do if we are unaware of such abusive activity? Likely, nothing at all. What can we do if we suspect? We can ask. We can report. We can condemn. We have been an idle society for too long, and too many people have been irreparably affected by the abuse they have suffered while others blindly watched on. How many of us have heard people arguing or watched people fighting or saw parents hitting children much harder than necessary ... and we did nothing because it was not our business? How many of us have been involved in such an incident and prayed as hard as we knew how that someone would step in to help? We can make a difference in another person's life if we would stop worrying about someone else's business not being our own.

In the Talmud we learn of a wonderful concept called *Pikuach Nefesh,* which can be translated to mean "saving a life." The term, however, is much more figurative than literal. It does not mean, necessarily, that we have to look for someone drowning in the ocean to save. Rather, it can mean reaching out to comfort a broken soul, restoring the faith of one who is hurting, sharing a smile, or mending a heart. This ancient tradition teaches of our obligation to be good people and to renew wholeness to the life of another.

In "Why Me? Now? Here?" I mentioned the correct usage of the Hebrew word *Shalom,* indicating that although generally translated to mean "hello," "good-bye," or "peace," the significance of

Shalom goes far beyond such simplicity to more accurately speak of *completeness* or *wholeness*. Those who suffer from abusers' cruelty are living in a world lacking wholeness. Their lives are incomplete, and their potential is unfulfilled. As we reach out to help, and as they find ways to help themselves, we can begin to extend Shalom to their soul.

SOME FOLKS HEAR VOICES (MENTAL ILLNESS)

None of us is perfect, not in our deeds but in our very constitution. Even the healthiest among us are troubled with some imperfections. For some this might be something as simply overcome as acne or athlete's foot—treated with relative ease, this kind of malady does not make any person a social pariah. These kinds of temporary problems, while describable as a medical condition, certainly do not cause the afflicted to shout out in disgust to God or to question their lot in life. We buy medication, we see a specialist for a few weeks perhaps, we take better care of ourselves, and we're better soon enough. Certainly, conditions that affect our outward appearance can be troubling. For many of us our appearance is of particular importance, but all in name of vanity. When we think of what *could* be, it is remarkable how often our pride clouds our vision.

But what of those for whom a simple rash would be the easiest of life's challenges? What of those who suffer from much more serious ailments—from illnesses of the mind that afflict an individual throughout his life? Mental deficiencies have a profound affect on the families of those with such illnesses. Although great strides are made in research every day, there as yet exists no cure for many of the most common mental health conditions.

We know that medications exist and are in very popular use for a wide variety of mental illnesses, each with varying degrees of success for each person and each situation. We also know that in recent years, great progress has been made to provide mainstreaming opportunities for those with such illnesses. The fact of the matter, though, is that as a general population, we still have a tendency to look with downcast eyes upon those who we do not consider to be *normal* as we commonly use the term. The problem is really that most of us do not recognize the potential of such individuals not only to succeed in their own right but also to positively affect us and our world.

Those faced with the challenge of raising a child with mental illness may have experienced great anger and rage. Despite our upbringing, which might have taught us to love all of God's creation, there is, nonetheless, great bitterness—perhaps, for some, a feeling that God deceived them into believing in the possibility of a perfect world and a perfect child. Sure, we would each cry out as did the prophet Job. Why should we be tested in such a way as to have the burden of a mentally ill child? What have we done to deserve this? But we also learn that every life is a gift and every life is a world unto itself. Having created a new life, we are counted as having created a world.

Within Jewish tradition is a certain movement toward understanding God on a high spiritual level. In *Kabbalah* we are taught that God has placed 36 angels on Earth in the form of human beings. In Hebrew, the number 36 is represented by the words *lamed* (pronounced: *LAH-med*) and *vav* after the alphabetical letters in a peculiar counting system. Therefore, these 36 messengers of God, called *lamed-vavniks,* roam the earth in full view of all of us. They do God's work, they serve as God's liaisons, and they assist God in keeping people just in a world filled with injustice. According to the Jewish legend, these 36 are so righteous and just that their prayers are always answered and they live in such secret that they, themselves, do not know who they are.

We are further taught that we are to act toward all people as though they are one of these lamed-vavniks, not because of any particular reward we might receive (as we are instructed not to act for the sake of any reward), but rather because these lamed-vavniks are holy and righteous and deserve to be treated with such respect. We are never told that these individuals will appear on this earth as perfect human beings; we are told only that God is perfect and that humanity is in the constant pursuit of perfection—of ourselves, of others, and of our world.

Mental illness is not evil. It is not the workings of an angry God. Evil is something that one person brings upon another person through a controlled will and a disturbed soul. Science and medicine teach us that mental illness results from any one of a number of genetic mutations or deficiencies in the birth process. Religion teaches us that whatever the cause, we are obligated to treat each other with kindness. The effect for us all will enable us to continue to repair our imperfect world, to improve the lives of others, and perhaps even to gain a greater understanding of ourselves.

SOME FOLKS THINK THEY ARE GOD (GOD-PLAYING)

Really trying to understand who we are can be a difficult task. In conversation with a class of 15-year-old students, I had the opportunity to address this issue at considerable length. What the students eventually came to realize is that people often express themselves in untrue ways. They hide themselves behind any of a variety of masks that are used to create illusions of appearance, attitude, or condition. In effect, they said that people lie about who they are and what they want. As the discussion progressed, I asked the students to put themselves into categories according to the kind of people with whom they associated. In this small group we found freaks, nerds, jocks, Goths, and a host of others (some of which I had never heard of and couldn't really explain in any great detail).

More important, I believe, was our discussion on the presumed hierarchy of these groups, at least insofar as school is concerned. Although the students attend different schools, there seems to be a universally accepted structure regarding which groups "dominate" other groups; that is, which groups are more or less popular, which groups are more or less annoying or scoffed at, and which groups are more or less controlling or dominant within the system of school life. Strikingly, none of my students seemed at all concerned with whether or not they fit neatly into any one particularly defined group or about any so-called "status" among peers. For them, categorizing life was less important than simply living it.

As we mature through various stages of life, we find ourselves concerned with a variety of issues, not the least of which is where and how we fit in. Whether as children, teens, or adults, we search for ways to make our lives satisfying and fulfilling. For many of us, we are content living a quiet, nonintrusive life, going about our daily tasks and not thinking so much about whose life we might effect or what aspect of civilization we might dominate. Rather, like my students expressed, we just live our life in a way which enables others to go about living theirs.

There are those, however, who seem unfulfilled living such an unassuming life. Some people have an uncontrollable desire to have a commanding or dominating presence over others. There's a popular joke which, I believe, sheds light on this issue:

> "What is the difference between a doctor and God?"
>
> "God doesn't think he's a doctor."

Of course, the joke works with a variety of occupations or groups of people—so no particular slight against doctors is meant. The point here is clear, however—that many people believe that their destiny is to guide, shape, mold, or bring order to the lives of everyone around them. They hang a shingle on their front door, inviting us to seek their wisdom and their counsel. But although most often the advice and treatment that we are given is offered with great skill and compassion, there are those who abuse their authority and the powers granted them by a human board or governing body.

Legally, our lives are in the hands of lawyers; medically, our lives are in the hands of physicians; spiritually, our lives are in the hands of—do I dare say—clergy. Let's face it, those who are in such positions are there because they believe they have someone of great value to share with others.

What we must remember is that both those who are them and those who seek them are just people, doing their jobs (often as vocation, sometimes as avocation, occasionally as both), and trying to improve life and the capacity to live it in peace, health, and purity. We must also remember that although God created each of us in his image, that does not mean that we should try to *be* gods. Rather that we should be as God would expect us to be: to act nobly, peaceably, generously, and with compassion for those in need. If we have a gift to share, let us share it with only the best of intentions. Abuse not the gifts which are ours.

In "Who Is My Neighbor?" I spoke of the great first-century Rabbi Hillel. Among his greatest statements is the following often misquoted maxim, which was spoken to one who questioned Hillel about the most fundamental teachings of God's Law: "Do not do unto others what you do not want to have done unto you, this is the essence—now go, study the rest." We learn much from

Hillel's statement. We are told that Hillel was asked to expound on life's most precious teachings while standing on one foot. Therefore, to him, this was the single most important rule for living. If we learn anything from Jewish traditions, it is the basic premise that we are all created from a single image of God with the same potential qualities and characteristics. Abusing others through an abuse of our own power is nothing more than an abuse of the God-like spirit within us.

Let us learn from Hillel's teaching. Let us regard our role as sacred. Let us continue to learn that we might continue to teach. And let our respect for the rights of others know no bounds.

ALL LIFE IS SACRED

In summary, the problems which exist in our world—problems which we might term "evil," are not creations from God. Whether we are talking about ill-fated walks to the corner store or a mugging in Central Park—or even some as grand-scale as the recent terrorist attacks on our nation—it is important for us to realize that God is not responsible for the actions of those who perpetrate such vial acts.

All life is sacred. It should matter not a person's background, origin or belief. It should matter not a person's abilities or deficiencies. Each one—endowed with God's greatest gift of all: life, along with the gift of free will, must undertake to repair our world through simple acts of kindness. Unlike the suggestion on the popular bumper sticker, I do not believe such acts should be "random." They should be regular and constant. I would argue that evil exists because people fail to open themselves up to understanding the substance of others' lives.

We begin to diminish evil when we begin to increase goodness. It is widely recognized that fewer muscles are needed to smile than to frown. So, too, I believe, it takes less effort to do good than to do evil. If that holds true, then perhaps some people just need to stop working so hard at doing something so mean. Maybe they'll find goodness sneaking out.

Chapter Response by Pastor Grimbol

An essential task of the rabbi is to be a scholar. I applaud Rabbi Astrachan for his scholarship, especially within the context of this chapter. Jeff offers a succinct and solid review of how his Jewish faith speaks to the enormous issue of evil.

Again, I find myself in agreement with most of what Jeff has to say. In fact, in this chapter, my main response would be, "ditto." Both Judaism and Christianity see evil as the free choice of human beings. Our capacity for evil is painful to face. A refusal to face this capacity leads to God-playing and the kind of grandiosity that can only be destructive. Nazi Germany, condoned by a bulk of Christendom, saw itself as a superior race, incapable of making flawed choices. It was this warped spiritual premise that led them to display evil in its most wanton form.

I would concur with Jeff that we may have looked to God after the evil events of September 11, but it was not to ask God "Why?" It was only to ask that our tears roll down God's cheeks. The compassion of God is one both faith traditions share. God grasps our anguish with mercy and renews our faith to fight the evil in our world.

Jeff did an outstanding job of delineating the sources that can turn a human toward evil. The belittling of others. The verbal abuse within families. Being scapegoated, teased, or left on the outside. Sexual abuse and incest. Physical abuse of any kind. The spiritual abuse of shaming a person into submission. The volcanic explosions of stress. Being burned out and up. The mystery of body chemistry and mental illness. Evil has a root system that is vast and hopelessly tangled in human and family relationships.

I loved Jeff's use of the word *shalom* in this regard. The idea of a person living without shalom brings to mind the lack of inner peace that can yield evil. To be without shalom is to be ill at ease, to feel uprooted, foreign, isolated, and utterly alone. This sense of abandonment and isolation leads to a spirituality of despair, and despair easily transforms into evil pursuits.

Despair speaks in the language of "Who cares?" and "Why bother?" This is a language that spells trouble, and that trouble has evil on its mind.

We are like a piece of crystal. Hold us up to the right light and we can reveal a dazzling spectacle of rainbows. Treat us roughly and we can be easily shattered. A shattered soul is capable of evil.

One addition I would to make to Jeff's chronicling of the sources of evil is emptiness. I find so many folks these days feeling spiritually empty, especially the youth with whom I work on a daily basis. This emptiness is expressed as a lack of interest, a sluggishness or lack of energy, excitement, enthusiasm, a cynical attitude, negativity, and as a complete void of hope. Hope is the belief that our lives matter and that the world and we who dwell here are on a spiritual path of improvement. I find many folks believing that things and people are only getting worse. Many youth live like lemmings. When I hear the phrase "They live as if there is no tomorrow!" I can only say, "You got that right."

Emptiness is fertile soil for evil. If one believes he cannot be creative, then the choice to be destructive looms on the horizon. If our youth see the world as racing hopelessly out of control, then what impact does that have on their behavior, let alone their faith? Out of the chaos comes creativity. Emptiness is an absence, even of chaos. Emptiness is the belief that there is nothing new under the sun. If such a belief becomes a lifestyle, it will be a life full of the potential for evil.

Hate is, for me, the one word that still best captures the spirit of evil. It is not a Christian or Jewish term. It is a word that speaks of disrespect and rejection. It is concept coated in the grime of envy and grudge. I cannot think of hatred without feeling the quivering presence of evil. Hatred is infused with evil, unless that which one hates is the evil itself, and even then the potential for evil remains lurking in the shadows. Hate the sin and not the sinner? I have heard that one a million times, but most times I sense that it is the sinner who remains the recipient of much of the wrath.

I appreciate Jeff's commentary on mental illness and God-playing. I found both sections to be of particular importance and help. I was also fascinated by the concept of Kabbalah and intend to learn more about it in the new year—probably from Jeff.

WHY DO WE DIE?

Rabbi Jeffrey R. Astrachan

Most of us who have been with someone in the moments following the tragic death of a loved one have likely heard them cry out, "Why did they have to die?" They extol virtues: "He was such a good person!" They languish: "I didn't have enough time to say good-bye!" And they pine in their grief. Death is hardly understood, although easily explained. Our bodies, we know, are mere vessels for life; the soul that resides within is shielded by the external casing of skeleton and flesh. Jewish tradition teaches that when we die, only the body is laid within the earth. The spirit returns, in purity, to God who gave it to us.

We often hear people rationalize a death, saying "It was time for her to go." I don't believe we can know when it is our time to go—or anyone else's time to go. Our hearts wrench at the thought of an infant dying of SIDS. Our minds go numb when we hear of a child killed by a drunk driver. Time explains nothing. It only gives us an excuse. Until we learn what God's purpose is in taking our loved ones from us at such an early stage of life—or at any stage in a painful and terrible way—we must not assume that God has a purpose—or that the deaths are God-related at all.

In this chapter we will read about the necessity of death despite the pain such loss inflicts upon our own spirit. We lose a loved one, and we are bereft. We are drowned in sorrow, and we are drawn to anger and hate as we struggle to find meaning in something so devoid of meaning. Here we will explore understandings of life in order to make some sense of death. Beyond faith and science, there is no other explanation. New life will come. Existing life will pass on. How long we are each granted the privilege of living is unknown to us. Uncertainty comes to instruct us on the value of enjoying those who are a part of our lives as long as we have them to enjoy.

Death Is the Frame for the Art of Living

Author Gary Mark Gilmore wrote "death is the only inescapable, unavoidable, sure thing. We are sentenced to die the day we're born." A sobering notion for many of us. In essence, life itself is a death-sentence. This is, sadly, how many people evaluate life: The "woe-is-me" crowd who has difficulty appreciating the sunrise and rainbows and understanding that relationships matter and that accomplishments are important.

As an optimist—and as a person whose life's ambition is to help others see that life is a beautiful gift to be cherished at every turn—I can't help but be saddened by thoughts that life is painful and burdensome all the time. Certainly we all have moments, days, extended periods of uncertainty or doubt, trouble, or worry which heap misery and anguish upon us. None of us lives a life of fluff and whimsical merriment. Even the eternal optimists face hardship and sorrow. But as long as we're here, why not enjoy the time we have?

I have a friend who, despite the best efforts of lots of good-hearted people, never is happy. He is, generally, a good, wise, intellectual, loving person. He is available to help others through their own crises. He offers support and advice to troubled souls. But looking at him you would think you were staring at A. A. Milne's Eeyore in human form. I've known this person for 10 years now. In 10 years he has come to the aid of probably hundreds of people suffering from all kinds of emotional difficulties, family tragedies, personal issues, and other matters of the heart, mind, body, and soul. But to meet with him on a friend-to-friend level, I can almost literally see pain and sorrow oozing from his pores. Why? He's never shared, and I never pushed.

Why do I share this with you? Because, quite simply, while I like this person very much and have infinite respect for his wisdom and capacity to give of himself to others, it pains me to see him carry the weight of the world on his shoulders every day of his life. I wonder how many people know someone like this. I wonder how many people there are like this going about their daily tasks from morning until night, suffering and in pain from untold grief.

What can we do? Can we do anything? Most of us realize that although life is finite, it's all we've got. Judaism, in particular, does not focus on what comes next. While hypotheses abound regarding an afterlife, Judaism focuses its attention on the present: to life and living life to its fullest. How do we live? How do we promote the lives of others? What do we do throughout our lives that define our purpose? These are questions that only we can answer for ourselves.

Rather than considering death inevitable, living each day in wait, consider instead that we should live each day as if *tomorrow* will be our last. That is, today we are perfectly healthy, vibrant, active, aware, able, conscious, involved, and a host of other things that we won't be when we are dead. While we are here and while we can freely choose to do or not to do, let us do. None of us had any say about how, when, or why we were conceived and born. Most of us, however, will have a say in how we will die. Of course, disease and discord effect and too often cut short life—but the choice to face our end-of-days with courage, fear, joy, sadness, faith, or emptiness is left for us to make.

True, life is not always easy or pain-free. True, not all of us are healthy. But it is true that we are free to make choices as to how our lives will be fulfilled. Death is inevitable—and undisputed truth. Approaches to death are how we frame our lives. While we are here and while life is pretty good, let us make the best of a great situation and love ourselves and love each other. Let us use our time to teach others how to love life and how to make every second count for something.

In Psalm 90:12 we implore God, "So teach us to number our days that we may attain a heart of wisdom." Let us so live that when our day does arrive we are able to look upon our lives and say that we made a difference to somebody, that our life had a purpose, and that the legacy we leave behind will be cherished by those we leave behind.

Death Enables Us to Cherish Life

Each of us makes a multitude of difficult decisions every day. When we drive, we must carefully consider the choices we make at every intersection and at every turn. When we are engaged in our daily business, our choices may effect the company we work for either directly or indirectly. Deadlines, time schedules, routines, and on and on. But life is full of relatively insignificant choices as well: peach pie or pecan pie? cotton or wool? paper or plastic? Nothing that will necessarily change the course of future history, certainly.

But what if we were faced with the following dilemma: We are given the opportunity to never die. We could always be alive, always be healthy, always share the family and friends we have now. Everybody would be just the same as they are now, forever. We would not be God or even gods. None of us would have any special powers or abilities. We just simply would not age. Our health wouldn't change, and we would exist and do what we do in our regular normal lives from now until the end of time. The only caveat to this scenario, however, is that just as no one would ever die, so, too, no one would ever be born. There would be no new life, no babies, no new learning and experiencing. The course of nature as we understand it would simply come to rest with what presently exists, but no more.

I hope all of you reading this chapter agree with me that although on the surface the idea is certainly intriguing, the ramifications of such a decision would be devastating. What would be the purpose of life if no new life could be created? The fact is that God had a pretty good handle on the concept of life and death from the beginning.

Judaism offers us the maxim that we must do everything possible to prolong life so long as it does not prolong death. That is, there is a clear understanding that all people must die at some time. Ecclesiastes 3 teaches us that there is a time and a purpose to all things, including dying. Yet as the moment of death draws near for a loved one, we know how difficult it is to say good-bye, to turn off a machine, to let go of the life we have cherished. Just the same, we know how overjoyed we become when a new life joins us. When we see arms and legs flailing, hear cries of life echoing from the nursery, and feel the tiny fingers of a newborn instinctively grasp one of our own, we utter, without thinking, the very first prayer-sound: "Ah!" This awakening experience is the dawning of the ultimate reason for death: It is part of the natural course of life. In Psalm 90 we are reminded that "we come and go like grass which, in the morning shoots up renewed and in the evening fades and withers." We enter this world with nothing but potential, and it is up to each one of us to decide whether we leave this world having used all of that potential to make our life something for others to cherish.

DEATH DECLARES WE ARE ALIVE

We know that all that lives must die. We can view our lives as the period of time we are given to express ourselves between the our great "morning" and our great "evening." This "day" is what we would call life—as we awake at birth, we stretch and begin to examine the world around us. In the natural course of a person's life, barring accidents or injuries, we continue to live throughout our fullest day until the twilight hours call us to sleep forever. What we do between the two endpoints of birth and death—or morning and nighttime—create our purpose for living.

There are, however, other forms of death while being alive. We can be fully functioning biological beings—breathing, eating, sleeping, working—yet be dead inside. Our spirit, our purpose, and our soul fails to live as our body lives. We are depressed, without faith, devoid of meaning. We are limp and cold, un-feeling.

We are not alone. To be sure, there are millions of wandering souls on this earth who appear, externally, to be living in every sense, experiencing the world as one would hope and enjoying their time and their task. Internally, however, there is sadness and grief, loneliness and sorrow. They are not really alive; they are just living.

Ezekiel 37 tells of an entire people faced with diminished spirit, whose passion for life had gone and whose faith in God had expired: "The hand of the Lord came upon me. He took me out by the spirit of the Lord and set me down in the valley. It was full of bones. ... And He said to me, 'Prophesy over these bones and say to them: O dry bones, hear the word of the Lord! ... I will cause breath to enter you and you shall live again. ... I will put breath into you, and you shall live again. And you shall know that I am the Lord!'"

The prophet Ezekiel is charged with regenerating an entire people who had fallen on their faith. We are in many ways and at many times much like those people. We are hungry and thirsty for knowledge of God. Our lives are often unfulfilled, and we find ourselves spiritually or emotionally dead. Without a prophet to bring God's word to us, how can we really know that God is with us and that we have reason to be alive?

Family, friends, children, animals, hobbies, sports, work, play— these give us purpose. Poetry, art, creativity, love—these give us expression. Prayer, introspection, passion—these give us hope. When we engage the world around us, we are engaged. When we interact with people, they interact with us. When we communicate with God, our spirits are filled with the presence of God. We do not have to wait for another to pray on our behalf. There need be no intermediary between us and God. This relationship can be created, enhanced, and nurtured all on our own. Prayer can occur anywhere we happen to be. Any space we create in our minds for the purpose of prayer becomes a sanctuary. We can renew the life of our soul by finding a way to reach out to God. But if we just sit and wait, anticipating that God will simply come to us, we may find our valley of dry bones growing larger and our thirst more difficult to quench.

Further, what of our natural death—how do we ensure that our spirit will live on beyond our bodies? The best we can hope for throughout our lives is that when our days on Earth are done, we have succeeded in providing for those we leave behind a legacy of love and justice, of character worthy of emulating, of life worth living. "When we die we carry nothing away, our glory does not accompany us." (Psalm 49) Although we may take nothing away, we certainly have the opportunity to leave plenty behind. Let live so that our glory will remain with those whom we love and that our soul may be bound up on the bond of ever-lasting life here on Earth. (Adapted from 1 Samuel 25:29.)

DEATH REMINDS US WE ARE NOT GOD

When we were children, we learned many important lessons: how to be polite, how to tie our shoes, how to use the bathroom. We learned school work and values. We were taught how to communicate and how to share. But we were also taught many difficult lessons about life as well. For example, our parents may have taught us that "nothing lasts forever," in response to a toy breaking, a friendship dissolving, or a loved one dying. We learned that all things come and go. What is in our lives now may likely not be in our lives in the coming years. This is a painful part of the natural order of our world.

Hopefully, however, we learned as we got older that God, in fact, does exist forever. Our traditions teach us that God was, is, and will forever be. For many of us this concept of God's eternality brings great comfort to our lives. With all the other people in our lives, who are so precious to us, leaving us—as well as our knowledge that at some time we will leave others—we are strengthened through God's constancy.

In Exodus 3, Moses encounters God's presence in the story of the burning bush. After God instructs Moses regarding the Israelites' enslavement in Egypt, Moses calls out to God inquiring of God's name. God responds, "Ehyeh asher Ehyeh." The implication of the Hebrew name suggests that God "Is what God always will be." That is to say, God's presence and existence cannot be qualified by time. Unlike living beings on Earth, God was not born, and God will not die.

There is a certain Jewish theology offered by the great twelfth-century thinker Rabbi Moses ben Maimon (often called Maimonides or *the Rambam* as an acronym for his full name) that suggests that it is easier to describe God by using qualities and characteristics that God is *not,* rather than what God *is.* For example, we can say that God is *not* a person, God is *not* a tree, God is *not* any *thing.* Therefore, we can conclude that none of *us*—while striving to be *like* God—*is* God.

In Jewish liturgy there is a wonderful poetic text often read as a part of our Sabbath worship, which says the following:

> "Who, O God, is like You?
> None is like You. One God alone created all things.

> "Who is like You, O God?
> None is like You. You are spirit, whom we feel but cannot ever see.

> "Are You stone and tree, O God? Are You breeze and sky?
> You are God who made them all: the Creator, not the creation.

> "Who is like God? Who can be compared to God?
> Neither man nor woman, nor any thing on Earth or in the sky. Only God is God."

Our Jewish traditions teach us that although our spirit was given to us by God, the spirit itself is not God. Although God lives within each of us, through our souls, we are not God. Although our souls will live forever and our spirit will return to God when our days have ended, God exists for all time and we do not. Accepting that we are not God, Maimonides goes further to suggest that "to know more about what God is not, is itself a very significant increase in positive knowledge." (Jacobs, *A Jewish Theology*)

In order to fully accept the notion that only God is God, there must be an appreciation for the theology of God and the notion that one cannot be more than one. That is, we are human, not God—and God is God, not human. Additionally, we must accept that although we can approach knowledge of God, we can never reach full understanding of God. The concept of what God *is* is vastly overwhelming for even the most well-considered theologian or religious philosopher. We have enough trouble in our lives trying to figure out who *we* are, let alone trying to come to know God on any intimate plane. Fifteenth-century Jewish theologian Joseph Albo commented on another theological point that God is, in fact, unknowable; purporting further that "If I knew God, I would be God."

The text of Exodus must work for us, then, as well. "I am that which I will always be." And what each of us will always be is human brought to life by the scientific processes involved in procreation in the ongoing events of our interactive relationship with the original unmoved mover we call God.

DEATH LIFTS UP THE ONGOING MYSTERY OF LIFE

There are those who believe that an entire volume is necessary, yet still not enough, to address the issue of what happens after we die. Without wanting to sound haughty, I believe that I can concretely summarize all the books ever written on the subject in three simple words: "*We don't know*." I am sorry if I have just put a lot of authors out of work and a lot of theologians out of business, but the fact remains that we have absolutely no earthly clue about what happens to anything after it leaves this existence. Is this merely one plane of existence? Is there a heaven and a hell and some middle-ground place in between? Do we have to pray for another's soul to help them reach their "deserved" space in some eternal resting place? We don't know.

But what we *believe* happens to us after we die is something entirely of a different matter. Certainly there are not enough trees to provide us with the paper and enough chemicals to provide us with the ink in use to satisfy the needs and wants of all of us in such matters. Theologies and philosophies abound that attempt to discover God's plan for us after we leave this world of living humanly. Where does our spirit go when we die? Jewish tradition tells us that it returns, pure, to God. But where is that place? What does God do with it? Is it reused in another body? Are we reincarnated? Or does that soul just go on top of the pile of souls somewhere in the back of God's bedroom closet?

Sure I'm being facetious. Why? Because we still don't have any answers—only suggestions. Theology doesn't give us answers, only ideas. Let me share with you, however, a very wonderful and powerful possibility to explain what might actually be the answer to this all-consuming question.

There is a wonderful parable of a woman pregnant with twins. Inside her womb the twins grow and develop. As they reside together, they begin to communicate and come to discuss their theories of what their lives are all about. For them, they exist in a world that is dark and wet, a world in which their every need is met by various tubes and fluids. They lack nothing and are cared for in every way. Life, for them, is good. The darkness doesn't matter, as they have no concept of light. The wetness doesn't matter, as they have no concept of being dry. Their lives are as they are, and they have each other to share space and time. They promise each other that they will be together forever and that one could not go on without the other. They are inseparable ... until one day.

After existing in their soothing world for all their days, things suddenly begin to change. Their world begins to churn. Their home begins to shift this way and that. The brothers hold hands as they fear what might be happening to them. A short time passes and one of the brothers begins to loosen his grip on the other as he begins to disappear from sight. For but a moment the remaining twin sees a bright light yet hears only loud noises and sharp, piercing cries. He fears that his brother has left him only to pass on to a horrible world of chaos and pain. Struggling to keep from passing to the same fate of his brother, he tries to grab on to anything he can. But he, too, finds he cannot stop what is eventual. He, too, passes through to the other side—to life, to love, to be with his brother once again.

It is a very beautiful and moving story whose origin, at least to me, is unknown. The message, however, is expressly contained in the words. These twins feared that what was on the other side was only pain and misery, and so the two developed a fear of that world. Thinking that the womb was all there was to enjoy, they did not want to leave it. So, too, with us. We have no idea what truly awaits us after this life. There is no "official" belief. There is, however, "popular" belief that serves us well.

The rabbis have, throughout the generations, been careful in their prediction of what occurs in the hereafter, only going so far as to say that something must exist beyond the reality of this life that we know. But Judaism, as a faith, has never stressed another world beyond our own with any great attention. We certainly have a variety of terms for places believed to be the resting ground of the spirit after death. We have adopted various concepts of God's treatment of souls based on how lives were lived out on Earth. But we, as a general principle, place our attention in matters of life, itself, rather than on death.

Because there are no certainties about death and, more specifically, what happens to us after we die, Judaism as a religion has focused on the importance of what we do with our lives while we are alive. Do we live to the fullest potential of our being? Do we make a difference in the lives of others? Have we improved our own Earth? Have we worked to preserve the goodness that exists, and have we worked harder to eradicate the wickedness that exists? Did we raise a family? Were we a good friend? Did we treat others with kindness? In essence, the rabbis teach us, can we account for our lives and have we been responsible with the soul given to us at birth? We need to ask ourselves—in our terms—how large the cleaning bill will be for our souls when they get to their final resting place.

CHAPTER RESPONSE BY PASTOR GRIMBOL

It was spiritually impossible to read this chapter without referring to my own struggles with the loss of my wife, Christine.

Her tragic death from complications following surgery has forced me to deal with death on most intimate terms. Though I found Jeff's reflections to be comforting and easy to digest, I was also keenly aware that this is one question that not only has no real answers, but for which our human tendency is to spit out most answers rather than swallow.

There were, however, many places where I was in full agreement with Rabbi Astrachan:

- ✦ Every day we are living, we are also dying.
- ✦ Death is a given.
- ✦ Refusal to face death leads to a life on the run—exhausting and deadly dull.
- ✦ Death is the frame that surrounds our painting of life.

- Death does enable us to cherish life.
- The idea of endless life may be intriguing, but it is also frightening as literal hell.
- We can be dead before we are dead.
- Many of us lead deadening lives.
- We need to be conscious of the legacy we will leave.
- Death reminds us to celebrate being alive.
- Death reminds us that we are not God.
- Death remains the ultimate mystery of life.

I also absolutely agree with Jeff that we *do not know* what happens to us after we die. Any suggestion otherwise is a leap of faith. Though I may respect such a leap, I will not offer it up as proof or even evidence. It is simply what I or someone believes to be true. If I knew for certain what happens after we die, I would not call it faith, I would call it fact.

Where I differ with Rabbi Astrachan is again more a matter of focus than on the substance of belief. I share with Jeff the belief that God alone is eternal. Though Christianity is deeply invested in the belief of the resurrection of Jesus Christ to eternal life, a belief I do hold, I find that this belief has led to some glaring misinterpretations of the meaning of eternal life.

I find nothing in the Christian Scripture that makes the case for resurrection as endless time or immortality. I find in the events of Easter a conviction that at death we come home to God. I do not hear of Bill Grimbol being Bill Grimbol eternally, surrounded by friends and family and fans and doing only that which I love in places I enjoy. I cannot think of heaven in earthly terms. I reject the notion of heaven as life without the "bad parts." I hear of no definitive description of heaven other than as the experience of the peace which passes all understanding—which is good enough for me.

The danger of making heaven the hope of faith is that it makes the end the hope, and the battle to get in, a raging arena of judgment. I see heaven as the guarantee of my faith in Jesus Christ. I believe steadfastly in the reality of eternal life. I also claim that I have no control over who gets in or what it will be like when I arrive. In fact, even using words like *arrive* seems silly. Heaven is for me so utterly beyond my reason, so fully mystery, that faith alone can grasp its meaning.

I believe that Jesus would share the Jewish focus on what we do on Earth as being of greatest importance. During Jesus' lifetime he remained fixed on building the Kingdom of God on this earth.

He spent little time addressing the matters of life beyond the grave, other than to assure us that we need have no fear, for we would be home with God. The Lord's Prayer makes it clear that our spiritual focus is to bring heaven to Earth. Sadly, the way many Christians describe heaven is nothing more than dragging Earth to heaven. I believe that Jesus understood the dramatic difference.

PART 6

THE HOW QUESTIONS

How questions are questions of empowerment. While we are certainly still inquiring about the many myriad events in our lives, we can, through "how" questions, learn effective ways of approaching and successfully grappling with them. Whereas questions of who, what, where, when, and why are all great questions, they are, nonetheless, passive—that is, they remove the responsibility from us and shift it away to another more remote source. How questions empower *us* to do something for ourselves.

How questions are problem-solving questions. They are analytical questions that tell it like it is. If you want something done, here's how to do it .... If you don't like something, here's how to change it .... How questions tell us to go out there and make a difference. They instruct us in ways of correcting problems in our lives. They don't just hold our hands and console us. Rather, they get behind us and push us to act.

In my opinion this is the best way to conclude our book. Having learned that we all have common issues present in our lives, it is now time to go out and do something to make a change, to exchange passivity for activism, to take responsibility for our own actions, and to make a real difference. This is the final step in the process of becoming who we are meant to be.

How Do I Make Friends?

Rabbi Jeffrey R. Astrachan

In life there are very few options left completely up to us. We do not choose our family. We are born into a family. Many of us choose a career for ourselves but then are given a variety of required tasks by the very nature of the business we are in. Your boss, your directors, your investors, your customers—to a certain degree *they* determine the course of your day and remove from you the autonomy to make choices about what you believe is important.

With friends we have choices all our own. No one tells us who our friends have to be or how we have to interact with them or even how long we have to be friends with them. If we do not like how one of our friends is behaving or responding to our needs, we can dissolve the friendship and seek a new one. As we grow and mature, our desires for friendships change. Perhaps the people who have been our friends are not growing in the same way we are, necessitating a change in association. In this chapter we will explore the wonderful power that friendship gives to our lives.

Here we will develop a sense of the importance of maintaining friendships, the joy of having them at all, how we have to work to keep them, and what a real friend is. There are differences between acquaintances and friends. We all have individuals and groups with which we associate or affiliate, but that does not necessarily make them our friends. A friend is a person who gives us some emotional and, yes, perhaps even spiritual, fulfillment. They move us in positive ways as we move them. This chapter will give us the opportunity to find out how we must evaluate ourselves in order to help us choose our friends wisely.

IF YOU WANT FRIENDS ... BE ONE

There would not be enough time or room to include in this chapter all of the criteria that we might use to determine what a true friend is because for each one of us that criteria would, most likely, be different. Each of us has different needs, desires, and goals for a relationship. Some of us want a friend to share similar interests or values. Others want a friend who offers a completely different set of interests or values—one who is the opposite of ourselves—that they might make our lives more "interesting."

But regardless of the specifics, I believe we might all come to a consensus that a friend is someone whom we trust, respect, admire, and care about. I admit that what one may call *trust* another may call "able to get away with something and know that person will cover for me." One whom we *respect* might be for another a person who does dangerous things and doesn't shy away from a challenge. A person whom we *admire* might be for some an individual who stands up vocally for an unjust cause another supports. Who is to say what brings people together— commonalties or curious differences?

I cannot be judgmental here. Whatever you call a "friend" is up to you. I have discussed in previous chapters the idea that people are endowed with free will and can, therefore, make certain decisions for themselves which may, very well, adversely effect other people or society in general. Despite this, when two or more people get together and share a special bond, they can consider themselves "friends," regardless of their will or desire.

In order for friendship to happen in the first place another person must give us some reason to believe that such personally desirable qualities are inherent to that individual. There must be some expression or display that allows us to experience some of what we are hoping our friend will be and what they might add to our lives.

According to the *Random House College Dictionary* (1979), a friend is described in numerous ways. A friend may be a person attached to another by feelings of affection or personal regard. But a friend may also be considered one who is a supporter or an ally. These are great definitions that we might consider when we are looking for someone to be our friend. But what about standing on the opposite side of the friendship coin? What qualities or characteristics are there in *us* that make *us* open to being a friend for someone else?

We all know people who we just cannot imagine what anyone would see in them to want to be their friend. They are taxing, dull, and pessimistic. They are draining and depressing. Or perhaps we know people who are arrogant and haughty. Or bigots. Maybe we know people who are all-consuming, either of themselves or of work or of any one of a million things. In short, they bug us! And we cannot stand to be around them. At best, we offer cordial niceties but try hard to go no farther than that.

That wouldn't be *us* in someone *else's* eyes, would it? Could we possibly be someone that another person might see and think, "Friends with *them*? You have *got* to be kidding!" We almost always look at ourselves as the perfect person to be with. After all, we share qualities and characteristics that we like. We dress the way we like. We do, act, and say the things we like. Of course, not *everybody* likes themselves (see "Who Is My Enemy?"), but in general we don't mind being seen in public with "me." On the other hand, can we say, with any degree of certainty, that we are the kind of person who others would want to be friends with? Do we behave in a fashion that others would not find offensive or distasteful? Are we polite? Are we concerned with others more than we are about ourselves? Do we return phone calls and write return mail? Do we expect others to always do for *us* and reach out to *us* and call *us* and sacrifice their wants and desires for *us?* If so, perhaps we are not the kind of person who so readily attracts others for friendship.

Friendship is a mutual relationship. None of us likes to be taken advantage of, yet we might do it to others without giving it a second thought.

My son is, as I have mentioned before, three years old. About two months ago he walked up to me in our living room, sat down on the couch holding a book, stared up at me, and said, very proud of himself, "Daddy, you are my best friend." Despite the fact that I wanted to burst out in emotional tears, I held back the lump in my throat, leaned over, kissed him gently on the top of his head, and told him that he was *my* best friend. I asked him if Mommy could be his best friend, too. He said no, got up from the couch, went over to his sister, and continued playing. The whole scene took about 30 seconds but will forever replay in my mind (I hope) as one of the highlights of my life as a daddy.

I hope that some day when my children are older, my son and daughter will still feel comfortable to sit next to me and tell me that I am still their friend. Then I will know that I have continued to act toward them the way that I would expect them to act toward others. Each of us should make this one of our greatest goals in life: Be nice to people, and be the kind of person with whom you would want to be friends.

Friendship Is a Presence and a Present

There are few greater gifts in life than the gift of friendship. Companions to travel with us down life's pathways help us learn, encourage us to enjoy our days, support us in our moments of weakness, and share our accomplishments with us. And we reciprocate. We all have friends. To be in a friendship, however, all aspects must be mutual. We must be fully present in a relationship for a friendship to develop.

A great Jewish philosopher of recent history, Martin Buber (1875–1965, Vienna), is probably most well known for his concept of relationships according to a construct he called *I and Thou*. In his discourse his premise relies on our interaction with people (and with God) on two very distinct levels. On one level, which he calls "I-It," we interact with others in a way that is nonpersonal; we do not fully engage others and do not fully participate in whatever the relationship might be. We cannot "connect" with any person or with God when we approach relationships in this way. In the "I-It" we approach all relationships with both people and with God as though they were mere objects. We share nothing of ourselves—of our soul—with the other person.

In a relationship that Buber would characterize as "I-Thou" we move to a higher plane of relating to another person and to God. Here we are not only fully present in the moment, but we are also willing to engage that person in a way that expresses our inner self—the spirit that is who we are. In such a relationship—in such a friendship—both parties are equally part of the "I" in that the relationship has come to a point where each is as important as the other. There is, for the two people, no distinction between the two; they have become one in their interaction.

Yes, this is a difficult concept; even more, it is difficult to explain here in only two paragraphs. But the message is an important one when we consider the friendship we want to maintain or build. If we only view our relationship as a one-sided investment where we are more concerned with the *expectations* of the other person rather than the possibility that the two people can interact as a single unit, spiritually, then we lose a very important part of what a friendship can be. This is not to say that such a friendship can or should exist with every person we meet. Although, according to Buber, it is possible and is something to which we all ought to aspire. Given this, let us at least strive to approach the friendships we already have with an enhanced sense of relating, that we move our friendships from the level of "I-It" to "I-Thou."

If "I" goes out to look for a relationship by looking for an object, then "I" will never find that which "I" seeks. (See Buber's *I and Thou.*)

Friendship Is a Good Laugh and a Good Cry

From the earliest moments of a budding friendship the spark between two people who recognize something wonderful in each other forges a bond of such strength that no time, distance, or travail can separate the pair. Buber does a great job of providing for us a very philosophical definition of friendship, which I eluded to earlier. But for those of us who are just average folks looking for someone to call a friend, we might not be so interested in becoming laden with philosophy. Most of us just want someone who understands what life is about, that pain exists, that we want to have fun when we can, that our finances are tight, and that our lives are filled with the same mess as the next guy's. We want a friend who doesn't mind getting out of bed at 2 in the morning because we need to get something off our chest or because we need to talk about the date we just got home from. We need someone whose shoulder is always available to lean on or cry on—or to put an arm around for a friendly embrace.

As those who have been so fortunate to maintain such a friendship will attest, it is these very experiences that fortify the bond between them. Allowing others into our lives to enjoy our happiness and to console us in our suffering are, for many of us, the only expectations of friendship. We place no demands on the other party; it is when we allow others to come into our lives that we begin to create this special human covenant.

"Covenant" is a very special word. Throughout the entirety of the Hebrew Bible the word is used 282 times. In the Torah, the word appears 81 times. Of those 81, every instance, without exception, refers to the special bond—the relationship or agreement—between the people and God. Of the remaining 201 occasions where the word appears, nearly every instance (with fewer than 5 exceptions) makes the same reference. So here I use the word with great care, as to toss it about would diminish its significance. Therefore, with the highest level of understanding the responsibilities that come with the term, I dare say the truest of friendships enters close to a covenantal relationship.

As we share with God our most intimate thoughts, our hidden secrets, and our most intense visions, so do we allow ourselves to share with our closest friends. With friends we let down our guard. We open ourselves up for criticism. We invite opinions that may very well be in contradiction to our own. With friends we allow masks to be removed and hair to be let down. The beauty of a friendship is the understanding that no harm will come from doing so.

While we were sitting quietly at home, our telephone rang. My wife answered it, said hello, listened quietly for a moment, then burst into tears. A moment later she was laughing. Yet another moment passed and the two emotional outbursts blended into a majestic cry of "I'm so excited! I can't believe you're pregnant!"

A very dear friend of ours, after trying to become pregnant for many months, had called my wife to share this fantastic news. Aside from her husband and her parents, my wife was the only one she had called to tell because she had literally just learned of the pregnancy and wouldn't share the news with anyone else for several months. My wife and this woman are two of the luckiest people I have ever met in my entire life. The bond they share, going back nearly 15 years, is as close to a covenantal relationship as I can truly imagine.

Not an event goes by in either of their lives that isn't shared with immediacy. In fact, as I recall, I'm pretty sure my wife's friend was the first call after I proposed over six years ago. I suspect we all know someone who has such a relationship, though we, ourselves, may not be so fortunate as to have one ourselves; and that's okay. Most of us go through our entire lives with lots of good friends, a few great friends, but no single friend who we would unabashedly share every minute detail of our lives. That kind of friendship comes very rarely and is a treasured gift; one to which not all of us are privileged.

I believe that we are far better off understanding the friendships that we have made and in which we find ourselves, evaluating how strong those friendships are, and then carefully striving to attain a level of closeness based on whatever factors are important to us. Before sharing such intimacies with another human being, we must safeguard our emotions. But we must also be careful not to hold our cards so tightly to our chest that we lose sight of the possibility that our best and most cherished friend just might be right in front of us.

FRIENDSHIP IS FORGIVENESS

I once was speaking with a student of mine about the value of relationships. We talked about the advantages and disadvantages of having good friends. He shared with me his belief that the best thing was that if he did something "wrong," he never had to say "I'm sorry." I was very surprised by his statement. In fact, as we continued to discuss his position, he asserted, basically, that if someone was really your friend, you could just about get away with anything and everything and your "friend" would brush it off; he said they would just *understand* and, his words, "keep being your friend."

Very carefully I attempted to explain that—in my view—one of the greatest advantages of friendship was that when you said you were sorry, you knew that your friend would still be there. The fact is that when we assume we can get away with anything just because that person is someone we call our friend, we eventually wear out our welcome. Instead of considering the advantages, we *take* advantage. Who needs that?

The same argument may be to blame for a multitude of marital difficulties and eventual divorces. Too many of us forget that the greatest obligations—including keeping a family together—come when we want to hold on to something of value in our lives. Relationships—friendships—demand our attention and our respect. When we fail to give that, at the very least, we cannot expect a friendship to be sustained by anything else.

Can we look back on failed relationships and qualify the loss as a result of our taking advantage of someone else's good nature? Have you ever walked away from a relationship because someone was taking advantage of *your* good nature? We have all been disillusioned by those we thought to be our friends, only to find that we were simply a convenience for someone else's misuse.

Being friends *means* accepting responsibility and saying, "I'm sorry" *because* the friendship means something special to you. It is only when we care nothing for another person that we give no thought to making amends. Friendship depends on the honesty of getting hurt and making up. It means accepting the faults of those we have befriended and respecting their unique qualities that brought them into our lives.

Friends give us the opportunity to try and to fail, to search and to come up empty, to fall and to pick ourselves up. Friends are the ones who, when we *do* fall, are right there to help shake the dust off, clean up the mess, and keep pressing on despite our failings. Friendship is the ultimate honesty. We should certainly feel an obligation to do whatever we must to maintain something as precious as that.

FRIENDSHIP IS TENUOUS

I remember that I made some pretty close friends in the years I spent in high school. I was in the school band. It was a great group of 50 or so kids under the direction of the amazing "Mr. D." Everyone called him that, and I suspect that each year there was a freshman or two who honestly didn't figure out his full name for a week. Anyway, Mr. D. was the great friendship-maker. He had a knack of getting everyone in the band to like each other through mutual respect and genuine concern for each others' musical abilities. From the first days of my involvement in "the band" I knew that I had just entered into a massive *friends frenzy*. Everyone was great. Even the seniors were nice to the freshmen—go figure!

By the time my own senior year rolled around, I had made a lot of good friends. We had parties, we got together at each other's houses, we went to the movies—always with different people, because that's how Mr. D. taught us. Everyone ran in everyone else's circles. I suppose now that I look back on those years it was kind of surreal, but at the time no one knew any different, and we just enjoyed it while it lasted. The funny thing was, we always thought it would last forever. At the end of my senior year, as is commonly the case, we all gathered in one place for the milestone ritual of signing yearbooks. I still have mine. Let me paraphrase for you some of the thoughts expressed in my book:

> "It's been great knowing you. Keep in touch. [phone number given]"

> "It's been a cool two years. Keep in touch."

> "It's been real fun. I hope we stay in touch."

> "It's been a really fun year. Hope to see you in the future."

> "Good luck in college. I'll be waiting for those visits. I'll miss ya'."

Every one of the comments in my book is followed by the name of a person I couldn't tell you one thing about now if they were standing in line bagging my groceries! I am also fairly confident that if I actually picked up the telephone right now and dialed any one of the nearly three dozen phone numbers included with these notes that not one person would have the faintest clue what to say to me after all these years.

In considering what to write in this chapter I came to this story immediately. We all have similar stories of friendships we thought would last forever. Very few of us ever see our high school friends again. Of course, many people still live in the same place they did when they went to high school, so they might occasionally run into someone they knew "way back when." But rarely do those relationships carry forward much past graduation. The same is true throughout the course of our lives.

When we leave a company where we may have worked for many years, we leave the same way we left high school: with wishes for a good future and with a lot of "keep in touch" sentiments that are shot from the hip and never really meant. People we hung out with by the water cooler day after day, shared a lunch table with, helped with a project or two—people we thought of highly and regarded as our friends—we never see again.

The reason is simple: We don't work at the relationship. When we fail to exert ourselves, the friendships are doomed to disintegrate. They cannot simply *exist* in their own vacuum, waiting for us whenever we feel like coming around again. By the same token, we don't need to be strung along by someone else who just *expects* that we will be there for them when they come around to us. It is important that we realize the responsibility that comes with a friendship lies within both parties. It must be mutual.

If we forget that we have a responsibility to give to a friendship what we hope to get from it, we might as well throw in the towel now and wish our friends a good life as we send them on their way. Like everything else that exists, a friendship must be tended to with great care.

When we treat a friendship with the attention it deserves, miles and years can separate friends without deconstructing the bond that exists between them. But when the relationship is neglected, it cannot help but deteriorate into nothingness.

In the Bible we read of God's presentation of a gourd to Jonah. Jonah is thrilled to receive this wonderful gift—he is, in fact, in awe of its beauty. But he doesn't tend to the gourd, so it dries up and fades away. Jonah, we know, becomes angry and distressed at having lost that which he loved so. And God responds to Jonah that the gourd went away because Jonah did not do anything to care for its well-being. So we learn of friendships.

By the way, if anyone reading this thinks they know me—and, perhaps, thinks they went to school with me—I graduated from Cranston High School West in Rhode Island in 1986. I was the tall kid who played the trombone in the band uniform that was always two inches too short. If you think you know me, give me a call. I'm sure I wrote my phone number in your yearbook!

CHAPTER RESPONSE BY PASTOR GRIMBOL

My review of this chapter will be short, sweet, and very much to the point. I have little to add to Rabbi Astrachan's words and much to commend. We are basically on the same page in regards to friendship, and our faiths share a common belief in the central importance of friendship to life.

I appreciate where Jeff placed stress in this chapter:

✦ On the importance of being a friend in order to find one.

✦ On the importance of mutuality in friendship.

✦ In his depiction of Buber's "I-Thou" relationship as one of integrity and intimacy, a true swapping of souls.

✦ In reminding us that friendship is a presence that grounds both souls in the amazing present.

✦ In acknowledging that true friends share life's peaks and valleys, laughter and tears.

✦ On the importance of covenant in building strong friendships.

- ✦ On the central importance of forgiveness in sustaining a friendship.
- ✦ That even the best of friendships is fragile.

As a Christian, I find in Jesus a powerful example of the importance of friendships, as he did not choose to minister alone. He chose 12, not just to be his followers, but to be his friends. In sharing his ministry, Jesus offers a poignant symbol of the human need to share our lives with our friends.

HOW DO I MAKE PEACE?

Rabbi Jeffrey R. Astrachan

As a rabbi, I have the opportunity to encounter a great many people who are struggling with life's slings and arrows of misfortune. For any of a variety of reasons, they are bereft of happiness and contentedness. Work. Marriage. Kids. Bills. Who knows? I might encounter people with very serious concerns such as the trauma so many of us felt (and continue to feel) following the September 11 attacks on our country. I hear stories of children waking with nightmares, of adults fearful of spouses traveling to work on the subway, of teens needing to call home from school just to make sure everyone they know is okay.

Or perhaps the issues may not be so worldly or as traumatic but are nonetheless concerning. I have met with couples who are unhappy that their child has decided not to go to college—or has not selected the college of their parents' choosing. I have met with kids who suddenly feel that God is not important to them and so they do not feel the need to continue with their formal religious school studies.

So often the problems I encounter within family dynamics have at least something to do with the fact that people are not communicating. No one wants to talk to anyone else who is actually involved so they come to me—usually after the issues have been festering for such a long time that contending with the issues now is a greater challenge than needed to be. I typically find pain, anger, distrust, and, often, apathy. These feeling grow like a fungus, needing very little to spread from something so small and relatively insignificant to something huge and boundless.

In this chapter I will present some very real, practical issues of personal interaction and finding a way to live in some harmonious fashion. We may not be able to salvage all relationships all the time, but at the very least we can establish the groundwork in order to find a middle ground, which we hope, may eventually lead to peace.

ADMITTING YOU ARE AT WAR

I know a man who is kind and gentle. He has a good job, a lovely wife, and a dog. He has nice hobbies and is involved in a popular community civic organization. He is a great asset to his community. And he hasn't spoken with his daughter in nearly eight years. I had, at one time, talked with him about this at considerable length. Apparently there was some family reunion that his daughter chose not to attend in favor of another event she had planned with friends. From that moment he declared that she was no longer a welcome part of his family until such time as she would call to apologize.

Ouch! Pride is a painful defense. Few of us are immune to the controlling power of pride, that feeling that if we rose up to our higher selves, we might actually see that there is another side to an issue, but if we do that, we might also find ourselves humiliated or embarrassed. "How can we back away from a firm decision that we made?" we ask ourselves. "How would we look to everyone we know?" In the meantime, how many of us are in similar situations?

I had lunch with a man who told me that because of some bizarre business issue, his relationship with his sister was put on hold for nearly 10 years. Ten years because of a business decision! I pressed him a little to disclose more about the issue that actually sparked the separation, and the sad part is, he could only remember scant few of the details. He kept saying things like, "Well, it was something like ...." and "I think she might have said something along the lines of .... " The fact of the matter was that he actually could not recall what specifically set the two of them off on their separate ways. In the meantime, a parent had died, and he didn't go to the funeral because he didn't want to run into his sister there. Can you imagine? A feud of unspecific origin could actually keep siblings from coming to a parent's funeral!

When I asked if he had made any recent contact with his sister, he sharply replied that it wasn't really a big thing anymore. They just don't talk to each other. He had no sense that his blame in this mess was equal to that of his sister's. Nothing I said was going to convince him of that.

Here lies the problem for many of us. It is not easy to accept fault or blame. It may be even more difficult to accept our personal failure in maintaining a relationship. Perhaps the stories in this chapter sound similar to an event in your own life. Perhaps we have parents we haven't called in months—or longer. Is our marriage crumbling before our very eyes because we refuse to accept the blame or the responsibility for something we did? Coming to terms with who we are and what role we have played in these scenarios is the first important step toward negotiating a peace with someone else.

But unlike the man who hasn't talked to his sister in so many years, we must start by accepting the fact that there is a problem—that we have something to fix in the first place. For a large majority of us that, in itself, is problematic. Our pride gets in the way of doing the right thing. Instead of picking up the telephone, we put down our fist. Instead of driving to their home, we drive home a futile point. If we ever hope to resolve differences and restore broken families and torn relationships, we must take proactive steps toward that goal. Here are just a few suggestions:

- ✦ Send a note in the mail giving a simple update of what has been going on in your life; make the tone of the note moderate and unpresuming.

- ✦ Follow up your note by picking up the telephone. A call is very personal and allows the other party to hear a genuine tone.

- ✦ If they are local, invite them for a quiet cup of coffee at a neutral location; meeting at one of your homes can be perceived as a "home-field advantage."

- ✦ If you do meet, leave the big issues alone for now. You both know that the issues are still there; they do not need to be resolved right now. Simply try to have a peaceful moment without rehashing painful memories. Save it for another meeting.

However you choose to do it, do it. Stop waiting for it to be someone else's turn to pick up the phone. Stop making excuses, and reprioritize family as your ultimate obligation. Make the effort, and hopefully reap the rewards. Family is too important to keep at bay. Draw them as close as you possibly can and love them with an open heart and an open mind. Admit your own failings and accept each other's faults. Everyone has some; it's what makes us unique.

PEACE IS NOT AN ABSENCE

Avoidance is a terrific defense mechanism, especially if you really don't want to accomplish anything. Otherwise, perhaps the time has come to reconsider that avoiding people does absolutely nothing to solve problems. Whoever said "Absence makes the heart grow fonder" failed to include the caveat that there must be some fondness there to begin with. Those who simply say "Good riddance" fail to see that perhaps by casting off that offending person, they have lost an important part of their lives.

How we treat the people in our lives is extremely important. Just as we cannot re-gather the dandelion seeds we blow to the wind, so, too, our words, once spoken, can never be recalled. People, however, can change their ways and re-gather their feelings. In Hebrew we call this process of spiritual turning *t'shuvah*. On one level, t'shuvah is a shift in our behavior or a new assessment of personal strengths and weaknesses. At its deepest level, however, t'shuvah refers to a complete overhaul of priorities. Brad Artson, in his *It's a Mitzvah,* writes the following:

> "The universe poses these questions: 'What are you?' 'What is your worth?' We articulate an answer in the deeds that constitute our lives. Living itself is the response—either a response of smug indifference or one of involvement and compassion.

> "When we put ourselves at the center of everything, it is impossible not to judge everything else by its usefulness for our own purposes. ... Such a stance reduces the universe to the standards applied to choosing among models of vacuum cleaners.

> "In a world that mistakes things for goals and status for worth, t'shuvah corrects our vision and makes us whole."

Artson is saying that when we allow another human being to leave us because of some dispute of which we were an active part, we have failed ourselves by putting our own personal agenda first, forgetting that we are responsible for the entire partnership. T'shuvah is possible at all times, for all people. Artson goes on to say that we all "have the ability to recognize our own wrongdoing, to resolve not to repeat that transgression and to rectify the wrong to those who were hurt by the error."

If we have pushed another away or have failed to strive to get them to return with diligence and sincerity, admitting where we may have been wrong, then we have not made t'shuvah. We have not returned.

Each year on Rosh HaShanah, the Jewish New Year, Jews listen to the wailing sound of the *shofar,* or ram's horn. Tradition teaches that the shofar is sounded for many reasons: a call to war, an invitation to a celebration, announcement of a death, or any myriad other events. The shofar, however, has come to symbolize at its highest level a stirring of our souls to act: for forgiveness, for introspection, for spiritual awakening. Today its sound calls us to wrestle with our own tendency toward self-centeredness. If we successfully reach inward to find the goodness in our soul, we must come to recognize that living without the love of a hurt friend or family member is the greatest stumbling block toward finding t'shuvah.

Our tradition also teaches us that although God stands ready to forgive and does, in fact, forgive for all our sins committed against God, only a person whom we have wronged can offer forgiveness for something we may have done to them. Forgiveness, we know, can only be offered after we have made the initial effort to apologize—to admit that we have missed the mark. Only when we lift ourselves up to the level of considered repentance, can we open our lives to accept the gift of family and friendship and to the peace of involved presence rather than a wasted absence. Peace comes from fulfillment, not from the removal of everything outside of ourselves.

PEACE IS A PRESENCE AND A WAY OF BEING

How we find peace is an individual process. My mother, for example, recently discovered the wonderfully relaxing techniques of yoga. I never previously considered my mother to be the kind of person who would enjoy such a spiritual exercise—I have always known her to be a relatively spiritual person, and I know that she regularly exercises (Jane Fonda videos, step aerobics, etc.), but I never imagined her putting the two together. In thinking more about the idea of yoga, I can see how one might use it or other similar relaxation techniques to help bring about an inner peace and create a spiritual wholeness that might not be otherwise possible.

In order to be healthy, we must, I suppose, consider that health goes beyond the anatomical, biological, and physiological processes of a person and extends into the inner psyche as well. We must care for the soul as we care for the symbiotic processes that keep our physical bodies at their peak. Perhaps, however, we are not into yoga. Maybe we need something that does not require such physical flexibility. Here are some possibilities, each accompanied by a challenge, which I believe may help each of us find real peace of mind without having to stand on our heads.

BEING HONEST AND TRUE

The soul within each of us remains the closest connection many of us regularly maintain with God. Judaism teaches that the soul is pure at birth as well as at death. Between those two events, however, lies a vast array of possibilities for testing the constitution of the "self" that is who we are. If we live our lives being unfaithful to our own soul, we cannot expect to find peace. Rather, we must learn to trust in the internal senses that God has given us: conscience, heart, mind, and maybe even a little "gut" (which many call "intuition"). When we learn to trust ourselves, we begin to bring peace back into our lives.

We cannot find truth until we are true. We cannot expect from others that which we do not expect from ourselves. We cannot hope for peace until we strive for peace. Turning to the Psalms, we find that we must "seek peace and pursue it." (Psalm 34:15) Midrashic commentary (ancient rabbinic writings which seek to confront practical issues through spiritual means) teaches us that the Torah does not obligate us to pursue God's commandments, rather only to fulfill them at their proper time and at their appropriate occasion. Peace, however, must be sought at all times; at home and away from home, we are obligated to seek peace and pursue it. (Numbers Rabbah 19:27)

Living to improve the health of our own soul can be easier than you might imagine. Here is a challenge:

Spend one month conscientiously recording your day's spiritual events in a diary. This is not the time to jot down every moment of your day or how you felt when you saw that good-looking man or woman looking at you in the grocery store—unless that event helped you define a spiritual moment for yourself. As you are engaged in this exercise of the soul, try reading from the Book of Psalms. Gradually cultivate your personal favorites. Some find particular comfort in Psalms 19, 20, 86, 91, 121, and 130, each of which deal with thoughts of turning to God and God's turning to you. After one month of diligent writing, go back and read your entries. What have you learned from yourself? Conclude this portion of your journal with a personal statement of how your awareness of your inner spirit has helped you grow to be a better person.

BEING SLOW AND SIMPLE

Taking each day as its own reward is a great way to appreciate the peace that exists in all that is. God made such awesome miracles in creating our universe and has turned it over to a people who fail to notice. So many time-honored clichés have come to our present generation that remind us of the beauty of nature ... of people ... of the gifts we have been given by our most basic interactions with everything around us.

Near the end of this past summer, I had the amazing experience of standing in my front yard with my two children. I had just come home from work, and Abby and Steven, my three-year-old twins, were watching me bring my things in from the car. It was about 7:30 P.M. My daughter was watching me intently, offering to help carry anything she could—she loves helping her daddy. All of sudden I heard a scream—really more of a squeal, then a little cry—from my son. I could see the look of fear on his face as he gazed at what appeared to be absolutely nothing. Then my eyes focused on a very slow-moving, almost hovering, pair of black wings that suddenly lit up in green all aglow. I knelt down near my son, reached out my hand, and brought the firefly toward him. He took a step back, sat on my knee, and watched as the firefly lifted from my hand and flew off with another green glow. My son laughed and screamed again. Only this time he shouted with it, "Again, daddy! Do it again!"

I hadn't noticed a firefly in years. I mean, sure I saw them. They're hard to miss. But I haven't taken the time to really stop and see them the way my children saw them this summer. I saw them again, for the first time. As I was catching fireflies for my kids, my wife, Shelley, ran into the house and found a small Tupperware jar with a lid. For 15 minutes we caught fireflies and watched them glow like mini flashlights. When we had finished, my kids helped me open the lid and we watched as, one by one, the fireflies flew off into the evening sky, each flittering with its own green glow. I told my children the fireflies were doing that to say good-bye and to thank them for playing. My children started waving and shouting, "Good-bye, firefly. Thanks for playing with me."

That night my children helped me realize that so much of what surrounds me is lost to me. The grandeur of the nature in our own front yard is lost to us all. Children are great at reminding us of this, but we can do it all on our own just the same. Here is a challenge:

Go outside. (So what if it's raining or cold—get a jacket and open an umbrella! Stop making excuses!) Take a deep breath. Look around. Don't go back inside until you have counted 10 bits of nature that you can experience with any one of your senses. Do the same thing the next day—but no repeating. Try this for 10 days. Think of it as a prescription from your doctor. Here's the label on the bottle:

> Indulge the senses with nature
> Find 10 kinds of nature once a day for 10 days
> Refills: As needed
> Expiration: None
> Warning: Impossible to overdose

BEING A WINNER AND A LOSER

Peace comes to those who accept that with joy comes sorrow; with love comes loss; with gain comes setback. Life has to give us the opportunity to challenge ourselves and to fail along the way. Using failure as motivation to excel the next time can lead to a tremendous sense of accomplishment as well as to personal and spiritual growth. When we improve because of failure, we have won. Booker T. Washington—one of the foremost black educators of the late nineteenth and early twentieth centuries—said that "Character is the sum of all we struggle against." What I believe he meant by this was that we each become who we are as a result of the experiences we have each faced. No two people face the same adversity; therefore, no two people can be the same. We build ourselves up by not being brought down.

But only when we revel in our gains, do we lose sight of what is most important. Remember the journey that is our life. The one who dies with the most toys doesn't win. They only fail to give generously enough to those less fortunate. When we finally find the balance, then we find peace.

As long as we have the power to relieve human suffering, we have an obligation to do so. Feeding the hungry is one of the simplest and most important ways of helping others who are in need. I challenge you to call your local Red Cross and get a list of shelters that provide meals to the homeless or those who just need some extra assistance. Make an appointment to visit the facility. (Most are more than happy to show the community the good work they are doing.) Before hanging up, find out what the most pressing tangible need is (towels, soap, pillows, etc.) and buy whatever you can reasonably afford. Take it with you when you go, but deliver it in a quietly respectful way to someone in charge of the facility. Here is a second challenge: Ask if you can sit with one of the residents and listen to his story. It won't kill you to sit for 30 minutes (or longer!) to hear what life has dealt to another human being.

I wrote earlier in "How Do I Make Friends?" that friendship is tenuous. People living in shelters are living examples of how tenuous life can be as well. Learn from them. Help someone in the process.

CEASE-FIRES AND CALLING A TRUCE

With so many things to do, places to go, meetings to attend, people to call, appointments to schedule, and errands to run, who has time to think about anything important? We hardly take time to consider our life let alone acknowledge the fact that we are alive. But we have to! If we do not take the time to consider the reasons for our running around in circles, we may never find a way to stop. The Torah teaches of a prescribed period of time, created, by God, which ensures that people are given the time necessary to slow down, regroup, spend time with family, enhance soulful lives, and rekindle weary spirits. On the final day of creation, God made this special time of rest. God knew that human beings were and still are an imperfect part of creation. We need to strive toward perfection.

Most religious faiths maintain a certain period of time set aside specifically for the purpose of restoring the self. How many of us take advantage of that time; how many of us heed the commandment to do no labor on the Sabbath? Many argue that such a practice is impractical in our modern age. Life presents us with too many challenges, work-related pressures, family obligations, and on and on. The problem here is that we create much of the pressures on our own. A great many extremely successful people have managed to blend family, business, and faith seamlessly, finding the time to find the time.

In order to begin that process, we must consider what values are most important to us. Chief among them may be health. Without our health our bodies may not be capable of fulfilling the tasks in life God would expect of us—or that we might expect of ourselves. Or perhaps the most important is a kind heart. With a kind heart, we might be more likely to reach out to tend to the needs of others.

Perhaps what we really need to find is *hope*. When we have hope, we have possibility. We have a chance. Hope opens our hearts and our minds to what can be: rekindled relationships, renewed friendships, regained vision. For Jews the Sabbath brings peace. It provides us with the opportunity to spend quality time with family, not thinking about work or school, for the purpose of bringing everyone that matters in our world closer together by closing off the rest of the world for just a short while. One Jewish tradition maintains that on the Sabbath Jews receive an extra soul. This Sabbath soul stays with us throughout the day and helps us feel a greater spiritual connection with what is most important in our lives. When the Sabbath leaves us so, too, does that extra soul, returning to God for another week. We hope to have gained by the experience and grown stronger and closer to those we love.

It is, of course, a tradition—part of the faith of our religion. It doesn't work for everyone, though, because not everyone chooses to allow it to happen for them. So they continue to go about their regular routine on the Sabbath, not even thinking for a moment that the day is any different than any other day. So the stress continues, the pressure continues, the noise continues, the tensions that always existed have no chance to be relieved. It is no wonder, then, that for many the problem of overcoming the feuds in our lives seems futile.

When will the feuding end? It will end when one of those involved in the war finally decides that there is a better way;

peace will never come by waiting for the other person to give in or tire out. Make the call, write the letter, send the e-mail, make a friendly gesture, do an unexpected kindness, smile—and mean it when you do. Make peace with yourself and then reach out to make peace with others.

CHAPTER RESPONSE BY PASTOR GRIMBOL

As in the previous chapter, I find myself in fundamental agreement with Rabbi Astrachan. I found this chapter clear, thoughtful, and of obvious spiritual benefit.

I share his concern for the inability of folks to know they are at war. The wars are often silent, or passive aggressive, or waged in symbolic battles for power. Frequently the weapon of war is silence. The wars of addiction are still battled as matters of will power. The battle of depression and mental illness continue to be hidden as signs of weakness and vulnerability. The wars of marriages are covered over by new purchases or the achievements of the children. The wars of grief or anxiety are waged alone and in hiding. There can be no peace in an unnamed or unclaimed war.

I also agree with Jeff that peace is not about the elimination of the enemy, but rather finding a way to embrace the enemy. "Good riddance" has nothing to do with peace-making. The lion does not devour the lamb. The asp does not bite the child. Peace is not an absence but a presence. Peace is the presence of acceptance, the experience of grace.

The Hebrew concept of t'shuvah, the spiritual process of turning or transformation, speaks beautifully to the continual potential for peace-making. Jeff makes it clear that "T'shuvah is possible at all times, for all people." Peace-making is predicated on the belief that we can change, we can forgive and heal, our hearts can be made tender, and our minds opened. I was also struck by how the Jewish holy days consistently call people to do the hard work of peace-making.

For me as a Christian, however, I truly turn to Jesus for an example of peace-making. It is to his message and ministry that I look for the how-to's of peace-making. From the life of Jesus I have learned ...

+ That I must be at peace with myself and my neighbor.

+ That I must forgive as often and as much as is required to being peace.

+ That I must welcome the outcast to my table and home.

+ That I must love my enemies.

+ That I must turn the other cheek.

+ That I must live at peace with all.

+ That I will reap what I sow.

+ That peace of mind is rooted in the grace of God.

+ That to be at war with others is be at war with God.

+ That a soul or spirit at war cannot love or show mercy, and thereby cannot serve God.

+ That if I fail to have the spiritual strength to forgive, but am truly willing to turn the matter over to Christ, he will accomplish the making of peace for me—in this matter Christianity breaks with Judaism.

+ Peace is seeing the world through Christ's eyes.

+ Peace is speaking the words we believe Christ would choose to be spoken.

+ Peace is to live in conformity with Christ's will.

- The making of peace is rooted in respect, honesty, commitment, prayer, and open and consistent communication.

For the Christian, Christ is the Prince of Peace. Christ came to Earth to heal the wounds of wars. Jesus calls the world to an eternal cease-fire. It is in Jesus that we find the wish and the will to make peace. Peace is always in search of makers. Jesus leads this quest.

I do not see Jesus as the best peace-maker. Matters of faith defy such foolish rankings. I simply contend that, for me, I find in Jesus the single greatest source of inspiration to make peace.

I also believe, however, that much of what Jesus taught on peace-making, as well as how he lived, was fueled by his close identification with the Hebrew prophets. The prophetic heritage saturates much of Jesus' peace-making ministry.

HOW DO I BE FRUITFUL?

Rabbi Jeffrey R. Astrachan

The whole of the Bible is a wonderful gift to humanity. Regardless of your belief in the authority and authorship of the text, the words speak of many beautiful lessons that help guide our moral pathways through life. Was there a Garden of Eden? Were there really two people called Adam and Eve? Likely not. Can we learn, nonetheless, from the story of Adam and Eve in the Garden of Eden? Absolutely. In fact, the Garden story is one of the most popular tools for the purpose of teaching about God, responsibility, personal accountability, and so much more.

In Genesis 1:28 God issues the first commandment directed specifically toward the objects of his creation. God says, "Be fertile and increase" (another translations: "Be fruitful and multiply"). Even before Eve is brought into the Garden (Genesis 2:18), God establishes a directive to procreate; that is, to continue God's creative efforts, instinctively, in order to bring about new life.

On its most basic level we understand this commandment as an instruction for human beings, animals, and all of nature to procreate for the simple purpose of procreation. People engage in the biological process of sexual intercourse (or, today, more scientific methods are often applied as necessary) so that we can bring new life into our world. But underneath and beyond this interpretation lies a much deeper and more engaging understanding of the commandment.

In this final chapter we will explore the ways in which our obligation to be fertile and increase is fulfilled daily. Through various forms of giving—talents, resources, possessions, mind, heart, and soul—we give to God's powerful creative works an even greater purpose.

Giving of My Possessions

It is no big secret that most of us have more unnecessary stuff than we really need. We are suckers to advertisements and come-ons. We live for the next big sale at the mall. We tear through the Sunday circulars to see what we *have to have* that week. I'm not really so much of a retail shopper. Instead, I love a good yard sale. I can't pass them up. If you are planning a yard sale, I hope you will call me so I can see if it fits into my weekend schedule. I love to impulse-shop from other people's discarded treasures. You never know when you might need an extra fondue pot or a mother-of-pearl back-scratcher. (Oh, I wish I had one of those right now! If you've got one, I might just take it off your hands.)

But here's the problem: Most of us forget, or at least don't think about it often enough, that there are people living in our own communities who have as close to *nothing* as one could only begin to imagine. In the immediate aftermath of the September 11 attacks, I spoke with dozens of people who either lost their jobs, had to lay people off, or had their own businesses suffer massive financial setbacks as an effect of either directly or indirectly related issues. I met with a man recently who found himself involved in this mess because his shipping company—which has been in his family for 15 years—suddenly saw a 70 percent drop in business. Money had become, to say the least, very tight, and his concern was for his family.

He mentioned to me that immediately after the bombing he went to the special job fair that had been set up by the City of New York powers-that-be. Along with an estimated 30,000 others, he waited in lines to meet with perspective hiring officers of various companies doing their part to help. He, like so many, needed help. Fortunately, he was hired by a very good company and is well on his way to recouping some of his lost finances and his damaged pride. But not so for thousands of others who have suddenly found themselves in a situation they never imagined: jobless, homeless, and destitute.

We never know if it might happen to us. We hope it does not. We pray that it will not. But we have no idea—especially in light of the age of concern in which we live—what tragedies might befall us. So we must prepare ourselves and learn lessons. Even if it has not happened to us, we must learn from the experiences of others, and we must be prepared to help in any way we can.

A great twelfth-century Jewish philosopher and thinker, Rabbi Moses ben Maimon developed a system of giving which has come to be called the *Eight Degrees of Charity*. According to what many consider to be his greatest work, the *Mishne Torah*—an authoritative compendium of Jewish law codes—Maimonides wrote:

> "There are eight degrees of charity, each one superior to the next. A person reaching the highest degree is the one who upholds the hand of [another] reduced to poverty by handing that person a gift or loan, or by entering into a partnership with [them], or by finding [them] work in order to strengthen that person's hand, so that [they] will have no need to beg from others."
>
> —*Mishne Torah*, 10:7–15

These are Maimonides's eight steps:

1. (the best) Giving a loan or getting a job so that one who is in need will not need charity any longer
2. The giver does not know who he is giving to and the poor person does not know who he is getting from (example: using an intermediary organization such as the Red Cross)

3. The giver knows who he gave to, but the recipient does not know who he is getting from (and may receive pity from the giver)

4. The giver does not know the recipient, but the recipient knows the giver (and therefore may feel an indebtedness to the giver)

5. Giving directly to one in need before being asked to give

6. Giving after being asked, but giving happily

7. Giving, but not giving generously

8. Giving sourly, sadly (however, even this kind of giving is adequate fulfillment of the commandment to give)

In Hebrew the word *tzedakah* is commonly used to refer to "charity," although tzedakah means much more. A better translation might be "justice" or "righteousness" and relates to a passage in the Book of Deuteronomy that reads, "Justice, justice shall you pursue." (Deuteronomy 16:20) We are told that a righteous person is called a *tzadik*. It is a *mitzvah*, a commandment, to perform acts of tzedakah.

When we give of ourselves in order to bring about positive change in another human being, we have fulfilled God's command to be fertile and increase. We all have much to give regardless of our own personal financial situations. Even the poorest among us has something to give, even if it happens to be something other than money.

GIVING OF MY TALENTS

In our synagogue's religious school—like nearly every other religious school—each week we collect pocket change from our students (on a voluntary basis), which we then donate as a collective pool to worthy causes throughout the year. This ongoing tzedakah project teaches children how easy it is to do good in our world with only a few coins each week.

But we also try to instill in the minds of the children in our care that tzedakah goes far beyond this exercise. We teach them that we can do wonders toward effecting positive change in other human beings without ever having to pull out our wallets or write a check or do anything at all that has to do with money. Here two stories that illustrate what I mean.

As I mentioned earlier in this book I have the privilege of overseeing the bar mitzvah program within my synagogue. Our cantor trains the students, teaches them the necessary prayers, instructs them on the importance of this milestone event in their lives, and gives them some insight into who they are as individuals. The children come away from their experience with the cantor, better people through this process of growth and maturing.

As a religious institution we put many demands on our bar mitzvah students. Chief among these responsibilities is the obligation to learn and conduct a Sabbath morning worship service in its entirety. This is no small task and takes each student many years to master the Hebrew necessary to reach this goal. In addition, we require each student to commit to a special *mitzvah project,* which involves their effort, combining talent and time, to make a difference in the life of another person.

The students are given great latitude in what this project can be. Recently I was working with one particular young lady whose bat mitzvah was approaching, and she shared with me what she had elected to do for her special project. She chose to go to a cancer center for children to play with the kids there, to read to them, and to share a part of her day with them. At first she told me that she was really just doing this because it was a requirement of our program. Her mother was somehow involved in this cancer center so she made arrangements for her daughter to go in to fulfill this obligation. In speaking with this young lady, I discovered that her life had forever been changed by this experience. This 13-year-old girl had discovered a part of herself that she never knew was there. A heightened awareness was beginning to develop despite her efforts to keep the time spent at the center as merely the fulfillment of a required task.

After completing her mitzvah project, I know she made plans to dedicate additional time to the children at the cancer center and expects to have regular contact there following her bat mitzvah.

What she discovered is what so many of us can discover about ourselves: that we have so much to give of ourselves *and* so much to gain in the process.

My second story involves two strangers—both to me and to each other. The scene is an airplane, the time is completely unimportant. The story is true. I was seated comfortably for takeoff when I first noticed the two people sitting across the aisle from me. Because I love people-watching, I took a few extra lingering seconds to take in the scene: an older woman and a younger man, each traveling alone. She had the blue flimsy "blanket" the stewardess gave her wrapped around her shoulders, and her eyes were already closed. He was sitting tall, staring into his laptop computer, typing the last few words of whatever was so important before he would have to put it away for takeoff. The two did not speak or acknowledge the other's presence.

For the first half-hour of the flight, the armrest between the two strangers seemed to separate them by miles. She tried to start a conversation. He avoided it with one-word responses. She took the hint quickly and went back to her solitude. Shortly thereafter the flight attendants came through the cabin distributing the long-awaited soft drinks and bags of peanuts. Each stranger partook of the feast. Moments later the most wonderful thing happened: contact.

As the bag of peanuts was placed on the tray in front of the woman, her hands, trembling from what I suspected was Parkinson's Disease, emerged from under the blanket. She reached forward to take the bag, but as she did, the young man leaned toward the grandmotherly woman and offered his assistance. She accepted with a smile, and two engaged in a conversation that lasted the remainder of the flight. I could not help but watch the two, no longer strangers. Buber would have characterized their interaction as a clear "I-Thou" event. They were each engaged by the other, sharing what became an obviously soul-filled moment in their lives. This was likely not a lasting friendship, but that was not their goal. It was, however, a wonderful experience of giving, each to the other. It was much more than the opening of a bag of nuts. It was the opening of two hearts. Had she declined the snack, the two may have never spoken a word.

GIVING OF MY MIND

This chapter is all about giving of ourselves to others. There is so much that we can give that to enumerate the possibilities would fill volumes and then only begin to scratch the surface of a truly comprehensive list. Each of us has different things to share at different times and with different people.

> What have I learned?
> What do I know?
> What have I got to teach?
> Keep me from false humility and self-doubt.

> Let me teach what I can, and if anyone, young or old,
> gleans something from my life and thought,
> I will have been a true teacher.
>
> —Author unknown

The fact is, when we teach something to another human being we engage them in a unique way. We enhance their spirit, and we raise their soul to a greater level of understanding of the world in which we live. When we use the knowledge we have amassed through our own interaction with other people at some point in our past, we have carried on a great tradition of giving. As knowledge is power, so is the gift with which we all have been blessed by God to share with others those thoughts that have been created and categorized in our minds.

There is no one alive who has nothing to teach. And nothing survives if no one continues to teach about it. In the Book of Deuteronomy we read, "You shall teach them diligently to your children." (Deuteronomy 6:7) This Biblical passage, part of the regular daily liturgy of a Jewish worship service, specifically instructs one generation to share all they know with the next generation, and so on in an endless cycle of learning. We are, in essence, commanded by God to teach.

The survival of a people is dependent upon the instruction of a knowledgeable generation upon an ignorant one. The fact is, depending on the information, we all fall into both of those categories. We must learn in order to teach. Therefore, we must never shut ourselves off from the possibility that someone *else* might have something important to share with us. Learning is, therefore, as important as teaching. We would be wise to do both.

According to Rabbi Brad Artson, in *It's a Mitzvah,* "learning is that process by which we incorporate new experiences into the way we understand the world, our place in it and ourselves." In order to actualize what Rabbi Artson is suggesting, I would like to propose a few challenges, as I did in the previous chapter. Here, though, the challenges are more self-fulfilling while allowing you to interact with others. They will enable you to learn how to teach and learn how to learn while keeping focused on the beauty of nature and the power of God's blessings.

STEP ONE: FIND A TEACHER

This person can be anyone at all. They need not be a scholar or an expert in a particular academic field. A friend will do nicely as long as they are willing.

STEP TWO: FIND A SUBJECT

I suggest, for the purposes of lifting the spirit, that you consider beginning with Psalm 1:1, but any text or topic will certainly do just fine. Remember, this is a process whose means is more important than its end. Study and learn for the sake of the task, and you will enhance your life in ways you never expected.

STEP THREE: FIND THE TIME

Set aside a regular, fixed time each week to sit with your teacher and your text. Find a quiet place and engage each other with the text for whatever period of time you have agreed to do so. Start slowly—30 minutes.

STEP FOUR: READ A REGULAR PASSAGE

Pick one passage, beside the one that you know you are going to study together, and read that one passage every single day. But do not just read it so that you can memorize the words to the point where they mean nothing. Just the opposite: Read the words so the meaning becomes clear. Perhaps you might consider something like the Ten Commandments or Genesis 1—the story of Creation. Read it and find something new each time you do. Wrestle with the text a little and learn something new.

STEP FIVE: TEACH SOMEONE ELSE

Every time you learn something new, do not hoard the information. This is not an exercise in storing useless knowledge. Rather, this is about enhancing the lives of others by sharing with them whatever you know. The adage of "learn something new every day" is valuable. When we fail to learn something new, we die a little—a piece of our soul withers and our potential is reduced. Given that we have few enough days on Earth, consider how important each day really is, and do not squander the opportunities that are before us.

Teaching and learning creates a bridge that spans the generations of history from the earliest days until this very moment. Teach as often as possible and learn as often as possible. It is what sustains us.

GIVING OF MY HEART AND SOUL

"Hear, O Israel! The Lord is our God, the Lord is one. You shall love the Lord your God with all your heart and with all your soul and with all your might. Set these words which I command you upon your heart. Teach them faithfully to your children. Speak of them in your home and on your way, when you lie down and when you rise up. Bind them as a sign upon your hand and let them be a symbol before your eyes. Inscribe them on the doorposts of your house and upon your gates."

—Deuteronomy 6:4

This Biblical command comes to describe the importance of passing traditions from one generation to the next. Of even greater importance, however, is the lesson that we must do so with a sense of the greater obligation to love God. When we are connected—in whatever way we feel right doing so—we find strength, peace, contentment, and wholeness. We become complete, and our resolve is strengthened.

Our faith traditions teach us much about the value of giving, and I have already explored some avenues for doing so. None of the preceding sections of this chapter are worth anything, however, if the heart and the soul of the individual is not fully engaged in the process. When we act without compassion, without love, without joy—without spirit—we are simply going through motions in search of reward. The reward is a feeling that comes only when we know what we have done has been for the right reason. Each of us has so much to give.

Material things quickly come and go, with few lasting results. Love, attention to what is really important, and a trusting and generous spirit can enter people's lives and stay there for a very long time. When we truly reach inside ourselves and give what is most precious to another person, we have given a gift above rubies, above all wealth.

CHAPTER RESPONSE BY PASTOR GRIMBOL

"Be fruitful and multiply." This is a commandment that Christians and Jews share. We both affirm and acknowledge that God calls us to share in the glorious process of Creation. We are challenged to be co-creators. We are heralded as those who will have dominion over all Creation. We are given remarkable freedom and great responsibility.

What does it mean to be fruitful? I would venture to say that Rabbi Astrachan and I would find our answers to be either identical or having much in common. We certainly share the same focus:

- ✦ Fruitfulness means sharing.

- ✦ Fruitfulness means serving others.

- ✦ Fruitfulness may mean sacrificing on behalf of others.

- ✦ Fruitfulness means charity, and charity necessitates justice.

- ✦ We cannot be fruitful if there are those who must go without.

- ✦ We cannot be fruitful if there are social or economic structures that favor some over others.

- ✦ Fruitfulness in a context of injustice is nothing more than greed and gluttony.

- ✦ In the Jewish faith, a fruitful life is one of mitzvah; for the Christian, it is one of stewardship.

- ✦ Fruitfulness means to be generative, which is to care about what we create.

- ✦ We live in a culture that does not seem to care about what it creates.

- ✦ The good life in America has little to do with goodness.

- ✦ It is hard for our Jewish and Christian children to value goodness in a world addicted to accumulation.

Both Judaism and Christianity call their followers to live lives of goodness. Goodness is crafted from the materials of giving and sacrificing on behalf of others. A fruitful life is one spent giving it away. In Paul's letter to the Romans, Christians are asked to become living sacrifices. I believe that to be a living sacrifice is what Jeff calls a tzadik, a person who pursues justice. In both cases, the result is a life of mitzvah or discipleship.

It is the concept of justice, however, which, to me, is the strongest bond between the Christian and Jewish faiths. We both celebrate equality, diversity, and the responsibility of the haves to care for the have-nots. We both seek to preach good news to the poor.

We both recognize love and mercy as life's juiciest and choicest fruits. We both see life on Earth as the arena where faith must be actualized. We both recognize that the values of the world are not those of God. We both call our followers to travel a road less traveled.

I personally believe that our respective roads will one day converge in the heart of God.

INDEX

R

S

soul
  existence of self, 4-6
  giving of your heart and soul, 280-281
  nefesh, 11
  spirit (ruach), 11
  spirituality, enough, 120-121
  stories, defining truth, 71-73
  strangers, existence of others, 23-24
  suffering yields joy, Christ's concept
    of enough, 131-132

T

t'shuvah, 259
talents, giving of your (fruitfulness),
  274-277
tenuousness, friendships, 250-253
timing (making good choices), 94-95
  all in good time, 97-100
tolerance, 25
trace left by truth, 74-75
tragedies that challenge your beliefs,
  purpose of existence, 49-51
trickle-down theory (enough), 121-124
truces, making peace, 266-268
truth, 65-66
  faith, 73-74
  making peace, 261-263
  mystery, 70-71
  silence, 67-68
  stories, 71-73
  trace left by truth, 74-75
  viewing beauty, 69
  what truth is not, 65
tzadik, 274
tzedakah, 274

U–V

uniqueness, existence of self, 9-11
unquestioned blessings, "why me?"
  questions, 190-193

vaye'chu-lu, 194

W

weakness yields glory, Jesus' concept of
  enough, 130-131
"what" questions
  what is my purpose?, 77
    being creative, 83-85
    being holy, 85-87
    being human, 78-81
    being perfect, 87-88
    being real, 82-83
    being yourself, 81-82
    individuality, 77-78
  what is the point?, 47-48
    finding meaning, 48-49
    learning, 56-58
    learning how to die, 59-61
    life is the point, 51-53
    living fully, 53-56
    loving, 58-59
    tragedies that challenge beliefs, 49-51
  what is truth?, 65-66
    faith, 73-74
    mystery, 70-71
    silence, 67-68
    stories, 71-73
    trace left by truth, 74-75
    viewing beauty, 69
    what truth is not, 65
"when" questions
  when is enough, enough?, 119
    addiction, 124-127
    Jesus' concept of enough, 127-133
    spirituality, 120-121
    trickle-down theory, 121-124
  when is the right time?, 93
    all in good time, 97-100
    Christian church seasons, 98-99
    life choices, 93-97
  when will it end?, 105-107
    bittersweet endings, 115-116
    dead ends, 112-115
    good endings, 117
    living with loose ends, 107-110

Y–Z